Federalism and Education: Ongoing Challenges and Policy Strategies in Ten Countries

A Volume in:
Research in Educational Policy:
Local, National, and Global Perspectives

Series Editor

Kenneth K. Wong

Research in Educational Policy: Local, National, and Global Perspectives

Series Editor

Kenneth K. Wong
Brown University

Educational Opportunity in Rural Contexts: The Politics of Place (2015)
Sheneka M. Williams & Ain A. Grooms

Charting Reform, Achieving Equity in a Diverse Nation (2013)
Gail L. Sunderman

Partnering for Progress: Boston University, the Chelsea Public Schools, and Twenty Years of Urban Education Reform (2009)
Cara Stillings Candal

Cross-National Information and Communication Technology Policies and Practices in Education (Revised Second Edition) (2009)
Tjeerd Plomp, Ronald E. Anderson, Nancy Law, & Andreas Quale

The Testing Gap: Scientific Trials of Test-Driven School Accountability Systems for Excellence and Equity (2007)
Jaekyung Lee

System-Wide Efforts to Improve Student Achievement (2006)
Kenneth K. Wong & Stacey Rutledge

Cross-national Information and Communication: Technology Policy and Practices in Education (2003)
Tjeerd Plomp, Ronald E. Anderson, Nancy Law, & Andreas Quale

Improving Results for Children and Families: Linking Collaborative Services with School Reform Efforts (2001)
Margaret C. Wang & William Lowe Boyd

Federalism and Education: Ongoing Challenges and Policy Strategies in Ten Countries

Edited by
Kenneth K. Wong
Felix Knüpling
Mario Kölling
Diana Chebenova

IAP
INFORMATION AGE PUBLISHING, INC.
Charlotte, NC • www.infoagepub.com

Library of Congress Cataloging-In-Publication Data

The CIP data for this book can be found on the Library of Congress website (loc.gov).

Paperback: 978-1-64113-172-8
Hardcover: 978-1-64113-173-5
E-book: 978-1-64113-174-2

Forum of Federations
The Global Network on Federalism and Devolved Governance

fundación
Manuel Giménez Abad
de Estudios Parlamentarios y del Estado Autonómico

The Forum of Federations, the global network on federalism, supports better governance through learning among federal experts and practitioners. Active on six continents and supported by nine federal countries, it manages programs in established and emerging federations and publishes scholarly and educational materials.

Printed in the United States of America

CONTENTS

CHAPTER 1

FEDERALISM AND EDUCATION

Cross-National Lessons on Governance, Standards, and Accountability for the 21st Century[1]

Kenneth K. Wong, Felix Knüpling, Mario Kölling, and Diana Chebenova

INTRODUCTION

Federalism matters. Federalism is formally institutionalized in approximately 25 countries, encompassing about 40 percent of the world's population. Federalism is a system of government that divides power and functions between the central authority and its decentralized units. The distribution of power and functions is framed by a nation's constitutional framework. Federalism allows for a certain degree of fiscal autonomy at the subnational level and supports electoral independence at the regional and local levels. The constitutional framework places constraints on the exercise of centralized power in education.

[1] The co-editors acknowledge the generous support of the Forum of Federations in Ottawa, Canada, and Fundación Manuel Giménez Abad in Zaragoza, Spain for this project. The co-editors appreciate the helpful comments from several reviewers of the chapters as well as the excellent research assistance from Asher Lehrer-Small at Brown University.

Federalism and Education: Ongoing Challenges and Policy Strategies in Ten Countries, pages 1–18.

To be sure, political and policy tension puts ongoing pressure on federalism. In the U.S., the arrival of the Donald Trump administration has created new intergovernmental conflict. Many states and cities have declared their status as sanctuaries in defiance of federal enforcement of immigration policy. State and local leaders have indicated their commitment to the Paris Accord on meeting the international standards to temper global warming, despite President Trump's withdrawal from the agreement. When a federal commission of electoral practices requested individual voting data, states categorically refused to submit the information. Across the Atlantic Ocean, Brexit has generated new uncertainties regarding the structure of the United Kingdom, as the Scottish public pushes for independence. In Spain, the government of Catalonia promoted a referendum to gain voters' support for provincial independence. But a move for provincial independence requires constitutional action by a two-thirds vote in the Spanish parliament. In other words, federalism continues to evolve.

Federalism has played a central role in charting educational progress in many countries. With an evolving balance between centralization and decentralization, federalism is designed to promote accountability standards without tempering regional and local preferences. Federalism facilitates negotiations both vertically between the central authority and local entities as well as horizontally among diverse interests. Innovative educational practices are often validated by a few local entities prior to scaling up to the national level. Because of the division of revenue sources between central authority and decentralized entities, federalism encourages a certain degree of fiscal competition at the local and regional level. In contrast to the unitary system, federalism values local and regional control of public education (Tucker, 2011). Locally elected entities govern local school systems. In other words, decentralized control places substantial constraints on the exercise of centralized power. According to some analysts, decentralization is found to have contributed to student achievement. Blöchliger, Egert, and Fredriksen (2013, p. 6) showed that a 10% increase in measures of "decentralization" is associated with a 4-point increase in the results in the Program for International Student Assessment (PISA) for 15-year-old students.

To be sure, the division of responsibilities varies from one federal system to another. The balance of centralization and decentralization also varies across institutional and policy domains, such as the legislative framework for education, drafting of curricula, benchmarking for accountability, accreditation, teacher training, and administrative responsibilities at the primary, secondary, and tertiary levels. Further, decentralization enables regional variation in policy and practice. Innovative practices at the local level can be scaled up to the national level.

Financing of education is particularly important in federal countries due to discrepancies in regional wealth, and thus discrepancies in available resources for education between jurisdictions. For this reason, many countries include federal equalization and transfer schemes as part of the financial framework of their education system (Cameron & Hofferbert, 1974). Consequently, researchers have paid attention to how different federal countries address the division of authority, quality of services, and efficiency in the use of resources (Lauglo, 1995; Manna & McGuinn, 2013).

Canada, Italy, the United States, and the United Kingdom, for example, have developed funding transfer schemes as part of their education system. In Australia, 2012 legislation promotes needs-based funding, providing supplemental funding for students with disabilities, students from lower socio-economic backgrounds, and students of indigenous background. Finally, federalism allows for policy stakeholders to revisit the appropriate balance of power between layers of government. In Australia, for example, the national government and states are revisiting the funding arrangement to support parental choice. In the United States, Congress has replaced the No Child Left Behind Act (2001) with the Every Student Succeeds Act (2015), granting more authority to the states in measuring progress and ensuring quality.

Given these critical issues in federalism and education, the Forum of Federations, Ottawa, Canada, in collaboration the Fundación Manuel Giménez Abad in Zaragoza, Spain, has organized a Program on *Federalism and Education: Governance, Standards, and Innovation for the 21st Century*. The Program on Federalism and Education aims to examine how countries with federal systems of government design, govern, finance, and assure quality in their educational systems spanning from early childhood to secondary school graduation. Particular attention is given to functional division between governmental layers of the federal system as well as mechanisms of intergovernmental cooperation both vertically and horizontally. The Forum aims to draw out comparative lessons and experiences in an area of great importance to not only federal countries but also countries that are emerging toward a federal system.

The Federalism and Education Program hosted a 2-day invitational conference in Zaragoza, Spain in April 2016, when researchers, governmental officials, and other policy stakeholders engaged in extensive exchanges on education governance and policy issues. Researchers presented their research papers on federalism and education in Australia, Austria, Belgium, Canada, Germany, Italy, Spain, Switzerland, United Kingdom, and the United States. The following ten chapters are the revised version of the conference presentations.

To facilitate our common understanding of federal-state arrangements across the ten countries, Table 1.1 provides the official names of the countries and the subnational entities that employ shared governance in their education systems.

The 10 case studies examine several key issues:

- On education governance, what types of authorities and power reside with the national government? What types of authorities and power remain at the regional or local level? What is the relative balance of power between the national and subnational government in education? Is the trend moving toward greater centralization?

TABLE 1.1 Official Terms, Countries and Subnational Entities.

Country	Federal/Central Government	State/Subnational Entities with Statutory Autonomy
Commonwealth of Australia	Federal Commonwealth	6 States and 2 Territories
Republic of Austria	Federal Government	9 States (Länder)
Kingdom of Belgium	Federal Government	3 Regions (Flemish, Walloon, Brussels) and 3 Communities (Flemish Speaking, French Speaking, and German Speaking)
Canada	Federal Government	10 Provinces
Federal Republic of Germany	Federal Government	16 Federal States (Länder)
Italian Republic	Government of the Republic	20 Regions
Kingdom of Spain	Government of Spain	17 Autonomous Communities and 2 Autonomous Cities
Switzerland	Swiss Confederation	26 Cantons
United Kingdom of Great Britain and Northern Ireland	Government of the United Kingdom	Greater London Authority, Northern Ireland Executive, Scottish Government, and Welsch Government
United States of America	Federal Government	50 States, 1 Federal District, and 5 Self Governing Territories

- On education finance, how are the funding responsibilities in elementary and secondary education distributed among the different levels of government? How does fiscal federalism work in education? What is the intergovernmental trend in education funding?
- On academic standards and quality assurance, which levels of government exercise the control? Is this an area of shared responsibility among levels of government? Is the trend moving toward nationalization?
- On performance-based accountability, how does the case-study country perform in PISA and country-specific assessments on core subject matters in the benchmarking age groups and/or grades? What are some of the key factors in explaining these outcomes? What are areas that need greater policy attention in promoting better academic outcomes?
- As the school-age population becomes growingly diverse, how does the country's education system address the changing needs? Are there effective policies and practices in this area?
- What are key areas of current policy debate in the case study country? For example, is teacher development policy a concern? Does the system create sufficient incentives for innovation? Are learning technologies integrated to teaching practices? Has the system been effective in improving lower performing schools and students (Mourshed, Chijioke, & Barber, 2010)?

- What are key lessons on functional division among layers of government from the case study that may be shared with other systems?
- What role will federalism play in promoting educational quality and progress in the 21st century?

In the following sections, we highlight some of the key lessons learned from the 10 federal systems as well as synthesize the current literature on federalism and education.

KEY LESSONS

Federalism Exists in Countries of Different Population Size

Federalism prevails in countries with different population size, as suggested in Table 1.2. The smaller federal systems include Austria, Belgium, and Switzerland. These countries have between 1.2 million to 2.4 million students at the pre-primary, primary, and secondary levels. Further, Australia, Canada, Italy, and Spain each have a student population approximately between 5 million and 9 million. Finally, larger federal systems include Germany (12.4 million students), the United Kingdom (12.4 million), and the United States (57.2 million).

Education Involves Shared Responsibilities Between Layers of Government

Federalism has played a key role in shaping the division of responsibilities in education between levels of government. With an evolving balance between centralization and decentralization, federalism is designed to promote quality-based

TABLE 1.2 Student Population in Pre-Primary, Primary, and Secondary Public Schools, 2012.

Country	Pre-Primary	Primary	Secondary	Total
Australia	334,387	2,127,730	2,384,025	4,846,142
Austria	239,904	327,246	697,388	1,264,538
Belgium	456,989	764,137	1,206,574	2,427,700
Canada	536,812	2,182,843	2,734,631	5,454,286
Germany	2,207,123	2,890,468	7,289,386	12,386,977
Italy	1,686,095	2,860,957	4,594,302	9,141,354
Spain	1,465,571	2,934,648	3,296,359	7,696,578
Switzerland	149,660	483,466	606,162	1,239,288
United Kingdom	1,258,174	4,622,158	6,496,973	12,377,305
United States	8,721,127	24,417,652	24,095,460	57,234,239

Source: World Bank Databank, http://databank.worldbank.org/data/reports.aspx?source=Education%20Statistics&preview=off

accountability standards without sacrificing the involvement of local governmental. In Spain, the implementation and inspection of education quality standards involve all levels of the government. While the Belgian national government establishes the quality assurance standards, each of the three language-based Communities assumes primary responsibility in monitoring educational progress and quality. In Switzerland, while Cantons and communes assume the primary responsibilities of compulsory and upper-secondary education, these entities collaborate with the Confederation to produce an education report on educational quality and progress every four years. In Germany, quality assurance standards are decided by the Standing Conference of the Ministers of Education and Cultural Affairs of the *Länder* (Germany's states). Because of its control over admissions to higher education institutions, the German federal government exercises its general influence on educational accountability. In Austria, schools are governed by recently adopted federal standards on German, English, and mathematics.

Federalism also creates incentives for horizontal cooperation. Horizontal federalism is gaining prominence as seen by both the quality and quantity of subnational collaboration efforts. Interstate or interprovincial exchange and transfer of human capital, financial resources, and professional knowledge is growing. In Switzerland, for example, the transfer of education funding among the 27 Cantons has increased by several times in recent years. And across the 13 provinces and territories in Canada, the Council for Ministers of Education in Canada (CMEC) supervises the Pan-Canadian Assessment Program (PCAP), which is conducted in both English and French. The PCAP aims to "complement existing jurisdictional assessments with comparative Canada-wide data on achievement levels attained by Grade 8-Secondary II students across the country" (CMEC, n.d., p. 1)

The Canadian version of federalism is particularly illuminating. The Canadian system allows the provinces and territories to maintain high levels of autonomy from the federal government, yet they themselves are highly centralized with parallel governance structures in the area of education. Some analysts use the notion of deconcentration to describe this high degree of state control in education. The Canadian system ensures common standards and comparable funding, which makes it easy to transfer insights and effective practices across systems. But despite provinces and territories having high levels of autonomy, Canada maintains high levels of geographic equality (although the northern territories do lag behind in achievement). This comes largely because transfer payments are distributed to areas with higher costs of operation on an unconditional basis. The Canadian federal government, like its U.S. counterpart, uses its redistributive function to address regional disparities.

Some of the particularly promising Canadian practices include a model of Outcomes Based Learning, employed by all provinces and territories, in which decision makers specify specific learning targets, but teachers then decide how the materials should be instructed. This minimizes tracking and heightens teacher autonomy. Another practice comes from the province of Quebec and lies at the structural level where students attend a two-year program after 11th grade that can prepare them for university, for technical colleges, or for the workforce. There is no rift with the other provinces and territories because students from Quebec who go on to university only attend university for three years rather than the traditional four. Finally, the testing and assessment methods used in Canada are also important to highlight. Mandatory low-stakes testing is common to provide information on what instruction areas need attention and improvement. The results of these tests constitute a small to medium-sized percentage of students' grades and do not impact school funding. Additionally, all students aged 13 and up participate in the Pan-Canadian Assessment Program at the beginning of the school year as a means for common testing measures across provinces and territories. It is run by CMEC in association with Statistics Canada.

These practices have led to strong student achievement. On the 2015 international PISA exams, Canada's student scores ranked second in reading, seventh in science, and tenth in math. Canadian scores were notable for their particularly high levels of consistency across provinces and territories, despite their autonomy from the federal government. While Canada has some work to do to improve educational opportunities for indigenous peoples and in the northern territories, its federal system of governance functions effectively and will provide the means for making those improvements through increased unconditional funds and greater autonomy for the territories—changes that have already yielded improvements in recent years.

Further, Switzerland illuminates the dynamic interplay between vertical and horizontal relationship among governmental entities. Though Switzerland prides itself on providing strong public services, in 2000, the country tested significantly below expectations on the first international PISA examinations. This shock spurred changes in the education system ranging from more targeted reforms such as language training for disadvantaged groups (including students with migrant backgrounds) to larger attempts at harmonizing curriculum across Cantons (the Swiss version of states). As a result, scores improved in the ensuing years, especially in reading and science where Switzerland had tested particularly poorly in 2000. Data suggest that programs targeted at specific groups were particularly effective: the percentage of students with weak reading competency declined by five percent (from 18% to 13%) between the years 2000 and 2012.

Despite these improvements, there is controversy over the role of the Swiss Confederation in education. Cantonal sovereignty is one of the most cherished rights in Switzerland, and thus, movements towards standardization have been strongly resisted in many Cantons. To avoid the federal government taking on an expansive role in the Swiss education system, many Cantons have formed agreements for inter-cantonal cooperation through mutually supporting teachers' colleges, setting up systems for transfer payments from wealthier Cantons to financially strapped Cantons, and other strategies. But despite these strategies, the Confederation plays a rather active role in determining which subjects receive the most attention through monitoring learning objectives in the subjects of language, math, and science. Following a similar pattern as the U.S. did after its increases in standardized testing, Cantons have tended to skew their resources away from history, geography, religion, music, and sports because those subjects are not tested or monitored. Such changes disturb many Swiss citizens who believe the classic humanistic curriculum provided the proper balance. However, given international pressures, it seems that further vertical coordination will be all but inevitable.

Institutional Reconfiguration Takes Time

In countries with a history of strong central authority, the process of de-centralizing power in education takes several decades. A good example is Spain, where the post-Franco dictatorship has been replaced by a gradual transition toward regional autonomy. The historic Autonomous Communities where co-official languages are maintained, namely, Catalonia, Basque Country, and Galicia assumed the competences in education (non-university education) at the beginning of the eighties. Autonomy in education was granted to the remaining 14 Autonomous Communities between the early 1990s and 2000. In other words, the Spanish experience suggests a multi-phase in the transition from centralization to decentralization.

Similarly, Austria faces the challenge of finding the proper balance between its central authority and the states. A formerly centralized structure rooted in the Austro-Hungarian Empire, Australian federalism tries to move toward a hybrid with greater state autonomy. However, states' policy preferences are often overshadowed by larger federal objectives, with laws limiting local school control to influencing only 15% of instructional hours or to only elective courses (in the case of vocational education). Nonetheless, centralization is found to foster successful pre-school activities, foreign language classes in elementary schools, and various remedial programs.

As a formerly centralized state, Italy has been moving towards distributing governance powers to localities; however, the transition has been mixed with the central state maintaining control of key policy areas such as the setting of general rules, the recruitment of personnel, and the distribution of finances. The Ministry of Education, University, and Research (MUIR) creates framework laws, which set guidelines that individual schools must follow in the creation of their POFs (Educational Offer Plans). Though the POFs must comply with MUIR standards, they also act as a mechanism of local control: the plans are created by a teachers' council at each individual school and allow for some wiggle room for the council to shape the plan to the specific needs of the region (such as using flexible schedules or including personalized courses). But despite such apparent local control, the central state's control over education finance restricts the regions' power to truly cater education to their own needs. Based on 2007 figures, the central state pays for about 82% of the total national education budget. And despite a promise to function based on the *subsidiarity principle* in which local entities dictate and run most school administration, in practice, the *parallelism principle* has proved dominant in which those that have legislative competence actually deliver the services in education. Thus, because of the central state's dominant role in school funding, it maintains a strong role in school administration.

Constitutional and Legislative Framework at Different Governmental Levels Plays a Key Role

Federal systems do not always highlight education as a national responsibility. In the United States, Canada, Germany, and Switzerland, education is explicitly reserved in the domain of state government. State or provincial constitutions in these countries provide more details on the government's responsibilities and their citizens' right to education.

At the same time, several federal systems rely on the national constitution and national legislation to specify the power and function of the shared responsibility between the national and the subnational jurisdictions. In Spain, the 2013 Organic Act on Education Standards expands the Constitution by providing clarifications on the distribution of powers between the Central Government and the Autonomous Communities. The Spanish Constitutional Court arbitrates policy disagreements between layers of the federal system.

To improve the structure of the Italian school system, the legislature passed the Good School Reform in 2015. In its planning, it was open to public consultation online, and the main results are an empowering of school principals to give teachers merit-based pay bonuses and to hire qualified local teachers from pre-approved MUIR lists. The 2015 reform also allows schools to seek voluntary tax donations (which would likely widen the gap between affluent public schools and poorer public schools) and gives tax breaks to families enrolling their children in private schools. These measures reflect an effort to get rid of the centralized requirements on local schools, yet they may widen inequity in the process.

Competencies in Education across Levels are in Flux

In federal systems, education involves competencies at both the national and the subnational levels. However, the distribution of those competencies varies case by case. Austria, for example, exhibits higher levels of centralization through maintaining national standards and assessment, while Switzerland and the U.S. are, on balance, more decentralized, granting stronger autonomy at the subnational level. Over the last 150 years, the 26 cantonal school systems have continued to harmonize their competencies and autonomy with the Confederation. Between 2007 and 2016, for example, 7 cantons rejected the national education framework, suggesting substantial cantonal power.

Further, the distribution of competencies is in flux. In Italy, for example, the 2015 national legislation on Great School Reform is in favour of re-centralization by empowering the national Ministry of Education, University and Research

(MUIR) to establish uniform learning standards, criteria on certificates and diplomas, and the definition on the scope of school autonomy.

In contrast to Italy, Belgium provides an example in which education policy-making power is non-centralized, yet a history of centralized control has placed limits in the development of local policies. Belgium has two simultaneous sub-state levels of government: there are three Communities (which group Belgians culturally and linguistically into a French, Flemish and German Community) and also three Regions (which group Belgians geographically into Wallonia, Flanders and Brussels) and in 1995, the question of language of instruction in school drove education policy to become a competence of the Communities (rather than a federal competence). However, funding still comes primarily through block grants from the federal government, so Communities are somewhat limited in their financial power. The Flemish Community augments the money coming from the government and organizes itself in a decentralized manner in which religious schools are included as recipients of public funds. The French Community remains much more centralized and does not add to the sum of money that comes from the federal level. As a result, they are constantly strained financially, and OECD testing has found results in the French Community to be significantly lower than in the Flemish Community.

Innovation is an Ongoing Process

Education policy priorities have continued to be shaped by regional and local needs, which reflect the changing demographic and cultural characteristics of the local communities and their school age populations. Further, as a laboratory of diverse practices, federalism enables governmental and non-governmental organizations at all levels of government to experiment with innovative ideas (Council on Foreign Relations, 2012). For example, states in the U.S. have played an active role in launching charter schools and urban districts have embarked on the diverse service providers' model that enters into contracts with both non-profit and for-profit organizations. Non-governmental organizations, such as the Bill and Melinda Gates Foundation, are promoting the integration of technology in teaching and learning and developing new tools for professional development.

In the devolved system of United Kingdom, England and Northern Ireland are expanding their school choice initiatives, including free schools in England that are similar to charter schools in the U.S. In contrast, Scotland and Wales are dominated by principles of democratic socialism, where standardization remains in place to support their substantial number of low-income students. Interestingly, Wales moved away from publishing the annual Transparent Public Rankings (TPR) of school performance following devolution as a symbol of its divergence from central policy. However, Wales reinstituted TPR in 2010 when PISA showed declining test scores, especially in the lowest-performing schools.

In Australia, private schools are included in state and Commonwealth funding schemes. States spend about a third of their budgets on private schools and the Commonwealth allocates a majority of its funding to private schools. The result of this funding is that private schools receive, on average, about 85% as much government funding as do public schools. This support for private schools represents Australia's efforts to promote school choice, yet these private institutions retain the right to charge tuition and select their student bodies. As a result, far fewer percentages of students from disadvantaged backgrounds end up in the private school system. However, when public and private schools serving similar student populations are compared, public schools often outperform private ones. With so many surprising and almost contradictory realities, the Australian education system can be deemed highly complex.

Further, Italy has five regions that have special statutes granting them policy discretion. These regions have linguistic minorities that require instruction in languages other than Italian. Consequently, these regions have produced innovations in multi-lingual schooling (in Ladin, for example, they have achieved remarkable success in teaching students three or more languages) and areas such as vocational education (as is the case in South Tyrol, where their system is held up as a best practice). In supporting such innovation, Italy will have to figure out how to maintain a level of equity from region to region.

Fiscal Federalism Fosters Institutional Commitment and Stability

The percentage of GDP allocated to primary and secondary education remains quite stable across the ten countries. In 2013, on average, OECD countries allocated 3.4% of the GDP to primary and secondary education. To be sure, there are variations across countries. As indicated in Table 1.3, the 10 case-study countries allocate between 2.7% and 4.3% of the GDP to primary and secondary education. These percentages are higher if tertiary and higher education are included. For example, Switzerland allocates about 6% of its GDP and Canada allocates about 6.7% of the GDP to all educational purposes. Further, per pupil spending in secondary education is higher than per pupil spending in primary education, with variations among the 10 countries, ranging from Switzerland's $18,994 per pupil in secondary education to Spain's $8,520. Overall, when compared with the OECD average, three case-study countries show a lower per pupil spending in primary education and two case-study countries have a lower per pupil spending in secondary education.

Education Funding is a Shared Responsibility

In federal systems, primary and secondary education spending is a shared responsibility. The joint financial contribution from the national and the subnational government enables different levels of the government to negotiate for their priorities.

TABLE 1.3 Public Spending on Primary and Secondary Education 2013, in Percent GDP and 2013 USD per Pupil.

Country	Percent GDP	Primary Per Pupil in USD	Secondary Per Pupil in USD
Australia	3.4	$8,289	$10,932
Austria	3.2	$10,780	$15,024
Belgium	4.3	$9,957	$12,763
Canada	3.2*	$9,130	$12,086
Germany	2.9	$8,103	$11,106
Italy	2.9	$8,392	$9,023
Spain	2.7	$6,956	$8,520
Switzerland	3.5	$15,930	$18,994
United Kingdom	4.1	$10,669	$12,200
United States	3.3	$10,959	$12,740
OECD Average	3.4	$8,477	$9,911

Sources: *OECD, Education at a Glance (OECD Paris), Table B1.1, "Annual Expenditure Per Student by Educational Institutions for All Services (2013)." OECD Data.* Retrieved from https://data.oecd.org/eduresource/public-spending-on-education.htm#indicator-chart. OECD (2017) Public Spending on Education (Indicator). doi:10.1787/f99b45d0-en (Accessed on 09 August 2017).
Note: 2012 data.

In Spain, the Central Government provides about 15% of the education spending and the Autonomous Communities provide about 85%. In the U.S., the federal government provides about 10% and the state and local communities make up the remaining 90% of education spending.

In Switzerland, the federal government provides about 10% of the education spending, while the Cantons provide 63% and the municipalities 27%. Among the 26 Cantons, education expenditures range from 2.4% to 7.8% of the GDP. Interestingly, there is a growth in horizontal transfers of funding between Cantons due to inter-cantonal collaboration in education.

In Australia, while states retain authority over primary and secondary education, the Commonwealth (Australia's central government) is taking on increasing power in the name of standardization. Increasing amounts of tied grants, earmarked grants that come from the federal government for specific purposes, have allowed the Commonwealth to exercise greater control over funding decisions of states and localities. At the same time, internal reviews such as the *Gonski Review* of 2010 have concluded that the states are in the most advantageous position to carry out school funding and policy decisions, leading to ongoing dispute over the federal role.

Education is a Key Policy Instrument to Address Regional and Socio-economic Disparity

Federalism, while recognizing regional and local autonomy, involves some degree of allocating resources to equalize the fiscal disparity among local communities. Canada, Italy, the United States, and the United Kingdom, for example, have developed funding transfer schemes as part of their education system. In Australia, 2012 legislation promotes needs-based funding, providing supplemental funding for students with disabilities, students from lower socio-economic backgrounds, and the indigenous populations. In Canada and the United States, special appropriations are directed at Natives or Aboriginal peoples given their unique challenges. The Canadian federal government maintains several allocation streams, including the Canada Health Transfer, the Canada Social Transfer, the Territorial Formula Financing, and equalization grant. Finally, federalism allows for policy stakeholders to revisit the appropriate balance of power between layers of government. In the United States, the Congress has recently replaced the 15-year No Child Left Behind Act (NCLB) by granting more authority to the states in measuring progress and ensuring quality in the 2015 Every Student Succeeds Act (ESSA).

With the decentralization of their education system as a measure imposed by the allied powers after the end of WWII, many elements of the German system seem contradictory. Germany is caught in the middle of assuring the constitutionally guaranteed cultural sovereignty to their states and at the same time moving towards harmonizing their curriculum and system to minimize disparities. As it stands, some Länder have far better education systems than others. Top states spent an average of over 5,000 euros per pupil between 2005 and 2012 while poorer states could only invest 1,500 per pupil over that time span. These disparities are reinforced by the fact that wealthier districts can offer teachers higher salaries and better benefits, thus causing instructional quality in poorer areas to suffer. In efforts to fix such problems, Germany employs a method of power-sharing known as cooperative federalism. This means that the Länder and the federal government share responsibility in legislating and administrating basic functions such as teacher hiring and curricular development. However, cooperative federalism has led to difficulties in supporting the 1.1 million immigrants who entered the country in 2015–16 as well as students with special needs because although these populations obviously require greater resources, the ambiguous balance between the federal and state government has led to inefficient services. Programs run and funded more fully from the federal level such as pre-school expansions have been hailed as clear successes. In short, public demand for accountability, benchmarks, and standards seem to call for a stronger unitary structure, which threatens the cultural sovereignty of the Länder.

The Australian system offers a complex picture of the role of education in addressing different types of disparities. Student outcomes differ along geographic lines (78% of young Australians from urban areas gain year 12 qualifications whereas for those in remote areas, only 43% of students gain such qualifications), socio-economic status (30 percentage point gap between the top and bottom quartile for achievement of year 12 qualifications), and Indigeneity (32 percentage point gap between non-Indigenous and Indigenous students). These gaps occur despite the fact that states spend a comparable amount of school funding per pupil.

Achievement gaps for specific student populations notwithstanding, Australia's school system has narrowed the gap for several groups. For one, Australia has ensured schooling opportunities for a very diverse population. More than half of all Australians were either born overseas or have a parent who was born overseas, and contrary to Germany or Austria, Australia has been highly successful with students of migrant backgrounds from non-English speaking countries. A higher percentage of this population completes tertiary education than non-migrants. This may in part be because of state and commonwealth policies including free translation services in schools and fully-paid English language learning tuition at many worksites. Additionally, some states have found success despite overall trends of stagnation or decline on international exams. Queensland, for example, made improvements through investing in preschool education and adding an extra year of primary school.

Regulatory Oversight Occurs at the State or Regional Level

A decentralized system relies on the capacity at the state or regional level to monitor and ensure schooling quality and success. At issue is regional and local utilization of resources to pursue educational goals. In Canada, for example, the 13 provinces and territories closely regulate their districts and schools to ensure the local implementation of the common curriculum, comparable levels of funding, and the professional quality of the instructional staff across the province and territory. In the United States, the 2015 legislation on the Every Student Succeeds Act has weakened direct federal intervention. Instead, states are now given the primary responsibility in developing their accountability policy to oversee school performance, even though the legislation preserves the federal role on civil rights issue.

The evolution of Belgium's School Inspectorate offers an alternative form of accountability to the strategy of relying on high-stakes standardized testing as employed in the United States. Before federalization, the Inspector was responsible for making sure state standards were achieved in schools and did so primarily through site visits and administrative evaluation. Since federalization, the Flemish Community has given much of this responsibility to the schools themselves, who simply have to clear their inspection strategies with the Central Inspector. In the French Community, however, inspection remains centralized.

Federal Systems Support Substantial School-level Autonomy

Federal systems seem to facilitate school level autonomy. This project examines the extent to which school principals are granted responsibilities in teacher hiring/firing and school budgeting, based on the 2012 PISA survey. As indicated in Table 1.4, an overwhelming percentage of school principals in 7 countries indicated that they hold the responsibility of hiring teachers. However, a lower percentage of the school principals reported that they have the responsibility to fire teachers. Finally, on budgetary decisions within the school building, only Italy showed fewer than 50% of the school principals having this responsibility.

Disparities in Student Academic Success Persist across Countries and Regions within Countries

When comparing the PISA mean scale scores in reading mathematics, and science between 2000 and 2015, the 10 countries show mixed results. As indicated in Table 1.5, in reading, 2 countries show improvement. In mathematics, 3 countries show improvement. In science, 5 countries improve in the mean scores.

There is further variation in student performance across regions within individual countries. For example, in Spain, academic outcomes vary across the 17 Autonomous Communities. Graduation rates in compulsory secondary education range from 63.1% to 85.4%. The percentage of low-performing students with PISA 2013 reading skills below level 2 ranges from 10% to 30%. The percentage of low-performing students with PISA 2013 math skills below level 2 ranges from 14% to 33%. Similarly, in the United States, about one-third of all 50 states

TABLE 1.4 Responsibilities Granted to the School Principal on Teaching Hiring and Firing and on School Budgetary Matters, as reported in the principal 2012 PISA survey (numbers are the percentages of principals reported having the particular responsibility).

Country	Teacher Hiring (A)	Teacher Firing (B)	Difference A – B	Within-School Budget
Australia	82	55	*27*	93
Austria	48	25	*23*	89
Belgium	82	73	*9*	77
Canada	84	37	*47*	91
Germany	63	22	*41*	73
Italy	12	16	*–4*	43
Spain	31	30	*1*	52
Switzerland	88	70	*18*	81
United Kingdom	98	85	*13*	99
United States	94	87	*7*	72

TABLE 1.5 OECD PISA Mean Scale Scores on Reading, Mathematics, and Science, comparing 2000 and 2015.

Country	Reading 2000/2015	Mathematics 2000/2015	Science 2000/2015
Australia	528/503	533/494	528/510
Austria	492/485	503/497	505/495
Belgium	507/499	520/507	496/502
Canada	534/527	533/516	529/528
Germany	484/509	490/506	487/509
Italy	488/485	457/490	478/481
Spain	493/496	476/486	491/493
Switzerland	494/492	529/521	496/506
United Kingdom	523/498	529/492	532/509
United States	504/497	493/470	500/496

perform well above the PISA OECD average scores, while about one-third of the states are underperforming.

Austria provides an example of the multifaceted challenge of educational inequality in the context of federalism. While the federal government controls the vocational track, the Länder maintain the general education track. The former is disproportionately represented by students with lower SES background and maintains a low rate of educational upward mobility. At the same time, PISA results show a substantial gender gap in math and science. These challenges will require ongoing attention of federal and subnational policy makers.

ONGOING CHALLENGES AND PROMISING STRATEGIES IN EDUCATION

The 10 case studies suggest a number of trade-offs in federalism and they also offer promising strategies to manage some of the ongoing challenges in education. First, federalism, while providing incentives for subnational engagement, may create uncertainty on service quality. Autonomous entities tend to pursue their own priorities in education. Under these circumstances, families who move across regions and communities are likely to experience different educational standards. The case studies suggest several strategies in ensuring service quality across regions within a country. Austria, Australia, Italy, and the United States, among others, are developing statutory clarity on meeting standards on equal schooling opportunities. Federal transfers and earmarked grants tend to create fiscal incentives for states and localities to ensure service quality in exchange for additional funds.

Second, federalism may undermine national priority. Consultation and deliberation among regional entities often necessitate policy compromise and tend to slow down reform implementation. Germany, Switzerland, Canada, and other countries have invested in horizontal cooperation with the aim of achieving specific national goals. The central government also relies on regional and local entities to use national grants to support the learning needs of students with disadvantaged backgrounds.

Third, federalism tends to allow for duplication of administration and management at the subnational level. Consolidation of smaller, autonomous regional units may generate cost savings through capitalizing on economies of scale. States and local communities are making efforts to coordinate the use of school buildings and other facilities for cost savings.

Fourth, states and local communities need ongoing data collection to inform their policy and practice. Subnational entities can benefit from a coordinated data collection strategy across the country. Comparable measures of academic progress enable schools and communities to validate their efforts to ensure student success for all. With comparable data across regions and various student populations, Australia and Canada have sharpened their focus on achievement gaps among citizens of First Nations, and Austria has redoubled its efforts to narrow the gender gap in science and math. Italy requires local schools to implement three sets of accountability systems: INVALSI (testing for student outcomes), INDIRE (evaluating internal school development), and the Ministry Inspectorate (evaluating schools and principals).

Finally, federalism offers a strong, diverse leadership pipeline. When state and local leaders show good results, they can anchor their regional success in policy development at the national level. Federalism remains a unique structure to allow for experimentation, validation, and scaling up of education programs.

CONCLUSION

Federalism is well-suited for countries with diversity of people, culture, and governing practices. In the 10 countries that are examined by this volume, federalism has fostered institutional commitment and stability to pursue educational goals. Federalism offers an institutional foundation for a multifaceted system of accountability. While subnational entities focus their accountability to serve regional and local needs, the central government can lead in setting learning standards, ensuring equal educational opportunities for all students, and holding educators and leaders accountability. Federalism also enables national and regional policy makers to develop specific instruments to address contemporary challenges of achievement gap, fiscal disparity, and innovation. Overall, the education sector is generally well-served by the system of federalism in the 10 countries.

REFERENCES

Blöchliger, H., Egert, B., & Fredriksen, K. B. (2013). *Fiscal federalism and its impact on economic activity, public investment and the performance of education systems.*

OECD economics department working papers, No. 1051. OECD: 2013. Retrieved from http://dx.doi.org/10.1787/5k4695840w7b-en.

Cameron, D. R., & Hofferbert, R. I. (1974). The impact of federalism on education finance: A comparative analysis. *European Journal of Political Research 2*, 225–258.

Council on Foreign Relations. (2012). *U.S. Education Reform and National Security.* Washington, DC: Brookings Institution Press. Retrieved from http://www.cfr.org/united-states/us-education-reform-national-security/p27618

Manna, P., & McGuinn, P. (Eds.). (2013). *Education Governance for the Twenty-First Century.* Washington, DC: Brookings Institutional Press.

Mourshed, M., Chijioke, C., & Barber, M. (2010). *How the World's Most Improved School Systems Keep Getting Better.* London, UK: McKinsey & Co.

Lauglo, J. (1995). Forms of decentralisation and their implications for education. *Comparative Education, 31*(1), 5–30.

Tucker, M. (Ed.). (2011). *Surpassing Shanghai: An Agenda for American Education Built on the World's Leading Systems.* Cambridge, MA: Harvard Education Press.

CHAPTER 2

SCHOOLING POLICY IN AUSTRALIA

Concurrent, Complex, and Contested

Bronwyn Hinz

INTRODUCTION

Schooling in Australia is traditionally and constitutionally a responsibility of the States.[1] But increasing Commonwealth government involvement, especially since the 1970s, has resulted in a distribution of roles and responsibilities best described as concurrent, complex and contested. This applies not only to the roles and responsibilities of different levels of government but also to the roles and effects of Australia's public and private school sectors. Australia performs relatively well in international tests and has an increasing proportion of students completing secondary school. However, despite a marginal increase in government spending (in real terms) per student in recent decades, and a range of major policy initiatives at

[1] Throughout this chapter, the term States refers to Australia's state and territory governments, and the Commonwealth government will be used to refer to the federal government. Australia has six states (Victoria, New South Wales, Queensland, South Australia, Western Australia and Tasmania) and two territories (the Northern Territory, and the Australian Capital Territory).

Federalism and Education: Ongoing Challenges and Policy Strategies in Ten Countries, pages 19–42.

State and Commonwealth levels, the academic performance of school students as measured by national and international standardised tests has been flat or falling, and the gaps between educational outcomes for the most and least advantaged Australian school students has widened.[2]

The last decade has been a period of particularly rapid change and uneven moves towards greater national consistency in an effort to minimise this fragmentation and to raise educational performance, equity and accountability. Since 2007, Australia has introduced new national standards and testing, a national curriculum, new national agencies and intergovernmental funding reforms. Some of these initiatives have been the product of genuine intergovernmental collaboration. Others have been pursued unilaterally. But the terms centralism or convergence do not adequately describe the dynamism and shifts over time in Australian schooling policy, because concurrent with these moves towards the centre, there has been continued innovation and divergence among States, where most administrative power over schooling still resides.

This chapter begins with a presentation of the constitutional, fiscal and intergovernmental background. Next it considers the functional distribution of responsibilities, and performance outcomes on academic and equity measures. The concluding section synthesises these analyses and relates them to current policy debates and reform attempts, musing on the future of this highly dynamic and politically-charged policy sphere.

CONSTITUTIONAL, FISCAL AND INTERGOVERNMENTAL BACKGROUND[3]

The Constitution of the Commonwealth of Australia, under which Britain's six Australian colonies federated on 1 January 1901, made no provision for education in the Commonwealth's delimiting list of enumerated powers (s.51), leaving the matter within the realm of the States' 'residual' powers under s. 107. This coordinate model sits in tension with multiple constitutional provisions for concurrency. (For example, s.109, which states that if State and Commonwealth laws are in conflict, supremacy is to be given to the Commonwealth legislation, and s.90 under which the Commonwealth parliament may "grant financial assistance to any State on such terms and conditions as the Parliament thinks fit," even for spending in a "State" sphere of responsibility). These provisions for concurrency have been of preeminent importance in education, (among other policy areas). Conditional grants—known officially in Australia as Specific Purpose Payments (SPPs) and informally as 'tied grants'—were first used to expand the Common-

[2] Similar equity and excellence issues are also present in early childhood and higher education, which, like schooling, are characterised by concurrency, centripetal forces, complexity, and contestation.

[3] Parts of the first version of this background section were written by Alan Fenna, who was a co-author of the paper on which this book chapter was based, but who withdrew from the book project due to a number of other responsibilities.

wealth's effective area of jurisdiction in the 1920s. They then slowly increased their role in the post-war period, becoming a major and established force across a wide range of policy domains from the early 1970s onwards. In no other federation do conditional grants have such an explicit and emphatic constitutional licence. Furthermore, the power s.96 gives the Commonwealth has been amplified by the extraordinarily high degree of vertical fiscal imbalance (VFI) in Australian federalism resulting from the Commonwealth's successful move in the 1940s to assume full control over personal and corporate income tax (Fenna, 2008).

Since the early 1970s, the States have been dependent on the Commonwealth for roughly half their revenue, and of that, roughly half has come in the form of tied grants, with the exact balance changing each year. Consequently, this dependence of the States on Commonwealth largesse to fulfil their constitutional responsibilities and provide essential services to their citizens (hospitals, transport, policing, schooling and so on) has created great scope for the use of the spending power by the Commonwealth to influence or attempt to influence State policy. This has been particularly prevalent in education, which has been a top issue for voters in State and federal elections.

FROM COORDINATE TO CONCURRENT EDUCATION POLICY

For the first half of the twentieth century, the Commonwealth played a negligible role in education. A turning point came in the mid 1940s with the creation of a Commonwealth Department of Education in 1945 and the social services amendment to the Constitution (s. 51 xxxiiA) in 1946, which gave the Commonwealth Parliament power to make laws for "the provision," *inter alia*, of "benefits to students," thereby authorising Commonwealth funding of education. This saw the Commonwealth's role in tertiary education increase markedly. However, its role in compulsory schooling remained tiny and mostly ad hoc until the election of the Whitlam Labor government in 1972.

Prime Minister Whitlam was determined to use the Commonwealth's financial resources and Constitutional supremacy to reform education across Australia, launching a vast number of funding and program initiatives in schooling via tied grants (Whitlam, 1985).[4] Most significant was the debut of general, recurrent supplementary funding to all schools—public and private—based on an estimate of their relative needs. This funding program, and most funding programs subsequently, was driven primarily by equity goals (increasing funding to all schools up to a 'community standard' in effort to increase equality of opportunity for all students) and secondarily by economic goals (better educated student populations become a more productive workforce in the future). The Whitlam government's school policy had the added benefit of major electoral appeal to voters, including the sizeable proportion of Catholic voters (historically connected to the Labor

[4] In addition, the Whitlam government assumed full responsibility for funding and overseeing university education.

Party) who tended to enrol their children in Catholic schools, which are not part of any public schooling system in Australia.

Every subsequent Commonwealth government has increased its policy and funding involvement in schooling in absolute and relative terms. This involvement has been characterized by strong unilateralism, but with periods or incidences of effective intergovernmental collaboration and partnerships (Hinz, 2016). It has also been pursued through tied grants, Commonwealth legislation, intergovernmental agreements and institutions towards the dual goals of equity and economic development.

An intergovernmental framework for collaboration in education has existed since the Australian Education Council was established in 1936. Initially comprised of State education ministers, it later included the Commonwealth minister as an observer and then as a full member. In 1993, this became the Ministerial Council of Education, Employment, Training and Youth Affairs (MCEETYA), and became answerable to Australia's newly-formed first ministers' meeting, the Council of Australia Governments (COAG).[5] While previously this had been a 'roundtable' of education ministers, its formalization as a ministerial council increased Commonwealth influence significantly. But productive reform still depended on an alignment of the interests of the participating ministers and their governments, and subsequently, the Council's productive output has waxed and waned as power dynamics and political agendas have shifted (Hinz, 2010; Jones, 2008).

Since the 1990s, the Commonwealth has used (or attempted to use) its spending power to draw the States into a more consistent, performance-focused schooling framework. It is important to note here that much of the groundwork had already been laid by the States, who remain the drivers of policy innovation in Australian schooling policy. At various points when Commonwealth governments attached far more prescriptive and punitive conditions to tied grants for schooling, their fiscal coercion provoked significant State opposition and their unilateral conditions were abandoned or modified (Hinz, 2016). On the whole, though, the push for a nationally-consistent policy and funding framework resonated with the Australian public and has been pursued by both sides of politics (conservative Coalition, and Labor), especially, but not only, at the Commonwealth level.

INTERGOVERNMENTAL REFORM, CONSOLIDATION, AND REMAINING ISSUES

A persistent and pervasive dissatisfaction with the growing overlap and 'micromanaging' aspects of tied grants in education and other State spheres of responsibility over the course of the twentieth century led to an overhaul of the whole system of specific purpose payments by the Rudd (Labor) Commonwealth gov-

[5] The Ministerial Council's name has changed several times since then and is now again called the Education Council.

ernment in 2008. Under the 2008 Intergovernmental Agreement on Federal Financial Relations and the related National Education Agreement, nearly 100 heavily prescriptive Commonwealth tied grants were replaced with six block grants to the States. Schooling was a policy sphere that received particular attention in these reforms, due to growing awareness that Commonwealth intervention via tied grants in this domain were limited in effectiveness or even counter-effective. This in turn was due largely to the fact that the Commonwealth neither ran schools nor managed school systems (Commonwealth Department of Education, Employment and Workplace Relations, 2011; Ramamurthy 2012; Watson 1998). Under these agreements, Commonwealth roles were rationalised and States had significant policy autonomy returned to them in deciding how they delivered services and responded to policy challenges. Policy outcomes and assessment measures were determined collaboratively through the Education Council, and mapped out in intergovernmental agreements.

While this is still broadly the system in place, it has been severely eroded by the Abbott (Coalition, Commonwealth) government's unilateral abolition of the COAG Reform Council (the intergovernmental agency under the auspices of COAG that assessed progress in education and other policy areas against the collaboratively determined goals and outcomes) and a reversion to type. Commonwealth ministers and departments have continued to use their financial advantage from Australia's high degree of vertical fiscal imbalance to initiate ad hoc and generally short-term interventions in areas of State jurisdiction through tied grants, which have multiplied in number and complexity since 2009, or through bilateral agreements such as the 2012 National Education Reform Agreement discussed later.

The other major development in the institutional and intergovernmental school policy landscape has been the creation of the Australian Curriculum, Assessment and Reporting Authority (ACARA) in 2008. ACARA administers new national accountability and consistency measures including the Australian Curriculum, a national standardised-testing regime for literacy and numeracy in grades 3, 5, 7 and 9 (NAPLAN); *MySchool* a national, publicly-accessible website reporting each Australian school's revenue from State, Commonwealth and private sources, their performance on these standardised tests, their socio-economic and demographic profiles, and a range of other information. ACARA is an independent statutory agency jointly owned and funded by the States and the Commonwealth, taking directions from them all and reporting back to them through the Education Council (of education ministers). However, research and statements from ministers and government officials suggest that the Commonwealth government's influence tends to predominate, that State curriculum authorities sometimes compete over *announceables* and that ACARA has become a powerful actor in its own right, leading to diverse responses from the States and their curriculum authorities, such as curriculum diversification in Victoria (Savage, 2016).

TABLE 2.1 Phases in Australian Schooling Federalism

	Phase 1: Coordinate (1901 Federation–1973)	**Phase 1: Growing Commonwealth Presence (1973–2007)**	**Phase 3: Concurrent, Complex, and Contested Responsibilities. National, State, and Cmth Policy and Accountability Frameworks 2007–ongoing)**
Constitutional responsibility for school education	State (but constitutional provisions for Cmth involvement)	State (with increasing Cmth involvement via tied grants and later also through intergovernmental councils and agreements)	State (with Cmth involvement through tied grants, intergovernmental councils, agencies, and agreements)
Primary funding sources for schools	Public schools: States Private schools: Private	• Public schools: States, with supplementary funding from Cmth • Private schools: private in 1973, private or Cmth by 2007, with supplementary funding from States	• Public schools: States, with supplementary funding from Cmth • Private schools: Cmth or private with supplementary funding from States
Key federal and intergovernmental action(s) or legislation	N/A But (untied) horizontal fiscal equalization grants help States fund their public education systems.	• 1974 Debut of recurrent Cmth funding for all schools on equity basis via tied grants, legislation and bilateral agreements. • Sharp increase in conditions and accountability components in Cmth grants, and increase in % Cmth flowing to private schools through Cmth Howard goverment's "Choice and Equity" policy and related school funding reforms from 1999.	• *National Education Agreenent 2008* (intergovernmental agreement returning significant policy autonomy to states to pursue intergovernmental-determined goals, conditions on grants reduced) • 2008 ACARA established under Cmth legislation, but funded by and reporting to all govs via council of education ministers

		• Influence of intergovernmental council of education ministers, and number and strength of intergovernmental agreements on schooling, waxes, and wanes • National Reports on Schooling (to council of education ministers) introduced to provide comparisons on spending and outcomes against (intergovernmentally-determined) national goals for schooling	• 2008 Introduction of national testing program NAPLAN, administered by ACARA. • 2012 Australian (national) Curriculum endorsed by council of Cmth and State education ministers, administered by ACARA • *2013 Australian Education Act* sets nationally-consistent school funding approach to accompany Comth National Plan for School Improvement and bilateral funding agreements with States
Federal fiscal and regulatory strategies	N/A	• Conditions in tied grants, Cmth ministerial directives allowed in Cmth legislation relating to schools funding. • Annual National Reports on Schooling.	• Conditions in tied grants, ministerial directives allowed in Cmth legislation relatiung to schools funding. • Annual Natrional Reports on Schoooling. • ACARA data, including national testing resultes

THE STRUCTURE OF AUSTRALIA'S SCHOOL SYSTEMS

Australia doesn't have a unified, national school system. Nor does it have local government or school district governance. Instead, it has a collection of state-based, publicly-funded systems of public schools and mostly state-based systems of private schools.[6] This setup is the product of growing Commonwealth involvement, shifting community preferences and past historical settlements.

The structure of schooling is fairly consistent across Australia. In most States and Territories, schooling is divided into seven years of primary school (Kindergarten—also referred to as Preparation or Foundation depending on which state one lines—to Grade 6) followed by six years of secondary school (Years 7 to 12) culminating in a high school completion certificate administered by State education departments. Preschool education is not part of the Australian school system, although in some states, such as Western Australia, it is often located on school sites. The age at which students begin school varies between states, but most children start when they are around five years old, and finish Year 12 when they are 17 or 18 years old.

Schooling is strongly oriented towards university entrance, which is wholly or mostly determined by nationally-comparable aggregate scores from Year 12 subject exams and assessments. Consequently, almost all secondary schools are comprehensive schools and students undertake generalist academic programs, with the ability to choose many or all of their own subjects in the later years of secondary school.[7] There are very few technical schools. However, approximately a quarter of 15–19 year olds undertake lower-level Vocational and Educational Training (VET) courses through a secondary school or a registered training provider as part of, or instead of, secondary schooling (Lamb et al., 2015; National Centre for Vocational Education Research, 2016). Across Australia there are a growing number of vocational learning opportunities, including some specialist upper secondary schools with a focus on technical and applied learning and sometimes also providing direct pathways into tertiary courses in these domains.

Australia has almost 3.8 million students enrolled in 9,404 schools, and the combination of a high birth rate and a high immigration intake means the student population grows each year. Almost sixty-six per cent of students are enrolled in public schools (also known as government schools or state schools), with the remainder in Australia's large and slowly growing private school system (Australian Bureau of Statistics, ABS, 2017). This private system includes Catholic systemic schools (about two-thirds of the total) and *independent* schools belonging to much smaller systems (e.g. Lutheran or Montessori) or to no system at all. Unlike most

[6] Most private schools are in state-based systems, with a central authority, such as the Victorian Catholic Education Commission, distributing funding and providing some administrative, leadership and coordination and other functions. However, some other school authorities run schools in multiple states.

[7] Only the state of Victoria offers a vocationally-oriented school diploma, the Victoria's Certificate of Applied Learning.

other countries, Australia's private schools receive generous government funding (often equivalent to the funding received per student in public schools enrolling children from similar neighborhoods) while also maintaining the right to charge tuition fees (which range from a few hundred dollars a year to tens of thousands of dollars a year) and the capacity to choose which students they enrol, often based on the student's academic ability or religion. Students in Catholic schools receive on average about 83 per cent of the government funding received by a student in a public school, and almost half of the recurrent funding received by independent schools is from government (National Catholic Education Commission, NCEC, 2016; Independent Schools Council of Australia, ISCA, 2016).

While public, Catholic and Independent schools each cater to a mix of social, economic and cultural backgrounds (Buckingham & Jha, 2016), students from disadvantaged backgrounds are overwhelmingly and increasingly concentrated in public schools—which cannot charge tuition fees and must enrol all those within their 'enrolment zone' who apply.[8] In 2010, the year with the best available comparative data, 88 per cent of Indigenous students were enrolled in public schools, as were approximately 78 per cent of students with a disability, 68 per cent of students from non-English speaking backgrounds, and 80 per cent of students from the lowest socio-economic (SES) quartile (CDEEWR, 2011, p. 10). More recent data indicates that these concentrations have increased since then (Connors & McMorrow, 2015). Since the early 1970s—when private school began receiving recurrent funding from the Commonwealth government—until 2016, the proportion of Australian school students enrolled in private schools steadily increased by an average of 0.4 per cent per year.[9] This enrolment growth was partially driven by a perception that private schools obtain superior results, such as higher average scores in Year 12 exams and higher proportions of students going to university. But when the socio-economic background of enrolled students is taken into account, private schools do not perform better on cognitive or non-cognitive outcomes than public schools (Nghiem et al., 2015). In fact, publicly available data from the *MySchool* website confirms that across Australia, many public schools outperform private schools enrolling similar students in both raw scores and in terms of student growth.

[8] Although public schools are forbidden from charging tuition fees, they can and do charge parents levies for classroom materials such as books, for some excursions and extra-curricular activities (such as music lessons) and strongly encourage families to pay *voluntary* donations for building and grounds maintenance. Almost all public school students have uniforms, which is an additional cost borne by families (Victorian Auditor General, 2015).

[9] There was no increase in the proportion of students enrolled in private schools in 2015 and 2016. It is too early to say whether this is the end of a decades-long trend, or reversal of that trend, or a temporary stability of enrolment shares.

GOVERNMENT ROLES AND RESPONSIBILITIES IN AUSTRALIAN SCHOOLING

Constitutionally and in most practical aspects, schools remain the responsibility of the States. The States and Territories maintain regulatory and accountability frameworks for all schools, administer their own high school completion certificates, maintain their own teacher registration boards, assessment and curriculum authorities, and design their own school curricula—although the Australian Curriculum is the framework for these and is often takes the place of state designs. Importantly, the States deliver and manage public school education. The States also continue to provide 72 per cent of recurrent general funding for schools in Australia, allocated overwhelmingly to public school systems, which is where educational need is most concentrated (ABS, 2017). The States' school funding is raised centrally by State treasuries and allocated to schools by State education departments. There is no local financing of public schools (e.g. by school districts), but public schools are allowed to charge small fees for uniforms, some school supplies, some-extra-curricular activities, and are also encouraged to undertake fundraising activities.

Each State uses a different funding allocation model to distribute funding to their schools, although each of these models take school size, location and a school's relative need into account, using formulas that consider the proportions of socio-economically disadvantaged students, disabled students and students from language background other than English. The States also provide some funding to private schools, though at a much lower rate than that to public schools. A robust horizontal fiscal equalization program (paid to State treasury departments for them to distribute among State services and priorities as they see fit) enables

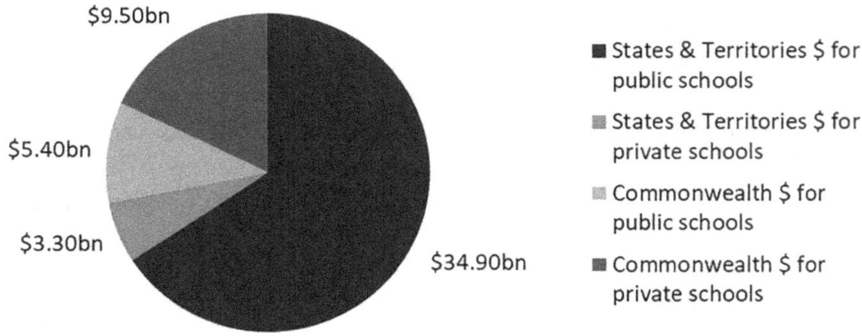

FIGURE 2.1. Recurrent Government Expenditure on Schooling. Organized by level of government and school sector in billions of Australian dollars. Total A$53 billion. Figure is author's own creation using data is from SCRGS 2017.

all States to provide schooling systems of broadly comparable quality, even if in practice there is significant variation in the performance of the States. The degree of State education department involvement varies widely amongst jurisdictions. Public schools in Victoria have essentially been self-managing within a state-wide curriculum and accountability framework since the mid 1990s, including the power to hire and promote teaching staff and offer additional curricula. In contrast, New South Wales has had a highly centralised system but is moving towards giving schools greater autonomy.

Responsibility for public schools in each State, and for schooling more broadly, rests with the State education minister, who is a member of the elected government of that State and a member of the cabinet (which gathers the important ministers into a collective decision-making institution for each government). Each Minister for Education is supported by the education department in their state and a team of advisers from their personal office.

The Commonwealth's involvement in most core aspects of schooling—including funding, programs, regulation, performance accountability and curriculum—has grown exponentially since the 1970s, overseen by Commonwealth Ministers for Education and a Commonwealth department of education. This has occurred mostly through tied grants, but also through intergovernmental institutions such as the Education Council and ACARA. The overlap in government roles and responsibilities in schooling is greater than in any other current federation and greater than any time in Australian history. Yet, despite introduction of national testing, national curriculums, a nationally-consistent school funding formula, and national agreements on roles, responsibilities, goals and outcomes, both levels of government continue to make the majority of school funding and policy decisions unilaterally (Hinz, 2010, 2016).

Of all these policy areas, funding is the most contested. Like the States, the Commonwealth funds both public and private schools (via tied grants *to* and *through* the States). But unlike the States, it directs 64 per cent of its funding to private schools (ABS, 2017). This is based on the argument that all Australian school students are entitled to government funding regardless of where they are enrolled because their parents pay taxes. Because States are constitutionally responsible for public schools and direct most of their funding to their public school systems, the Commonwealth has a special responsibility for private schools. There is also a widely-held belief—especially among conservative (the Liberal Party–National Party Coalition) governments—that school choice is both a means to system improvement and a virtue in itself (Hinz, 2016; Kemp, 1990; Pyne, 2014). Consequently, between 1973 and 2011, Commonwealth funding for private schools increased by a factor of almost 16, compared to a factor of 9 for public schools, well above the increase in private schools' enrolment share over the same period, from 22 to 35 per cent (Connors & McMorrow, 2015). This trend has continued even after the equity reforms introduced by the Labor government between 2007 and 2013. Between 2009 and 2014, combined State and Commonwealth funding to private schools rose at twice the rate of that to public schools, and many high-fee private schools in wealthy suburbs received greater funding increases than nearby public schools, or public schools further away serving poorer communities (Bita, 2015; Knott, 2016). Even in 2015, private school funding continued to grow at a faster rate than funding to public schools (Steering Committee for the Report on Government Services, SCRGS, 2017). So while recurrent Commonwealth funding was initiated to improve educational and racial equities in Australia's schools, it has, over time, contributed to increasing inequities.

Australia's States spend a similar amount per pupil each year in their public school systems, a situation enabled by horizontal fiscal equalization payments (untied grants) made by the Commonwealth to State treasuries. These untied intergovernmental grants are allocated using a complex and contested formula that considers not only State revenue, but also the cost of providing these services given rurality and relative levels of disadvantage in each State so as to enable each jurisdiction to provide a similar level of services to their residents. In this way, Australia is similar to Canada and unlike the United States; states with greater relative levels of disadvantage and a greater proportion of remote students spend more on average, per pupil, than the states which are relatively more prosperous and with populations that are geographically condensed. State expenditure per full time equivalent student includes central administration costs, regional office costs, and the cost of agencies. Services and programs that are to available private schools as well as public schools include high school completion exams, curriculum agencies and state-wide anti-bullying programs.

When all State, Commonwealth and private expenditure is combined, Australia spends US$8,239 per primary school student, which is slightly below the OECD average (of US$8,477/OECD) and spends above the OECD average each year on secondary school students US$10,932 (Organization for Economic Cooperation and Development, OECD, 2016, p. 192). Australian families contribute much more towards schooling than in other countries, mostly due to the high proportion of students that attend private schools charging tuition fees.

Modest rises in government spending on schooling have not translated into better academic performance by Australian students.[10] Over the last fifteen years, educational inequalities have grown and academic performance has fallen or failed to improve. These two worrying trends have prompted a spate of State, Commonwealth and intergovernmental initiatives to enhance performance and accountability. Results of these government initiatives have been mixed and generally disappointing, in part due to an unproductive overlap of government roles and responsibilities (with some State and Commonwealth policies frequently at cross-purposes), funding that is still not adequately targeted to where educational

[10] Much of growth in government funding for schools in Australia is due to the increasing numbers of students. In real terms, government funding for schools has increased 14 per cent over the past ten years, but half of this increase is due to increases in teacher salaries, which increased broadly in line with average salary increases in Australia.

needs are greatest, and a focus, especially at the Commonwealth level, on policies that are electorally popular but unable to be well-implemented by a level of government that doesn't run school systems. These measures will now be discussed.

PERFORMANCE AND ACCOUNTABILITY TOOLS IN AUSTRALIAN SCHOOLING

The States remain responsible for academic standards and quality assurance in their public schools, and for broader regulatory compliance, safety and standards for all schools within their borders, including private schools. However, the most influential tools of assessment are now national and international: the National Assessment Program for Literacy and Numeracy (an annual, standardised, assessment of literacy and numeracy for students in years 3, 5, 7 and 9); PISA (Programme for International Student Assessment) and TIMSS (Trends in International Mathematics Science Study).

Other performance and accountability indicators include levels of student and teacher absenteeism, student attrition rates, the proportion of students who complete Year 12 and gain a Higher School Certificate or equivalent diploma by the age of 19, and the proportion of 24 year olds that are fully engaged in work or study at 24 years of age. For each of these measures, the performance of different groups—girls and boys, Indigenous and non-Indigenous, rural, regional and metropolitan, English speaking background or not—is recorded. The reason for recording this information is to better understand the strengths and weaknesses of different policy and funding settings in Australia and to track progress towards closing equity gaps, especially for Indigenous versus non-Indigenous Australians. Nationally comparable data published in annual national reports on schooling as well as other national reports published by independent government agencies are used to inform policy reform and analysis. However, this data, especially its timeliness and level of detail, could be significantly improved.[11]

Each State and Territory has its own additional performance and accountability measures for their public schools. For instance, Victoria has 140 indicators measuring everything from aspects of student wellbeing to the number of occupational health and safety claims made at individual schools. Performance is measured at a student level, classroom level, school level and regional level, and also for different equity groups, such as low SES background and Indigenous students. Victorian schools that fall below certain thresholds are externally assessed and then receive tailored support from the State education department, including mentoring from other schools, to improve.

Enrolment changes among schools—whether the schooling is losing or gaining students—is also considered an accountability mechanism and an indicator of whether a school is succeeding or failing. However, a major study of all public

[11] There is a lag of several years and it performance data usually aggregated to state level, masking the successes or failures of smaller programs at a school or local region level.

and private schools in south-east Queensland found that a school's performance on the national tests, including improving or deteriorating results, was not correlated with any increase or decrease in their enrolment figures (Jensen et al., 2013).

Together, these national and international indicators are used to monitor progress towards the *Melbourne Declaration of Educational Goals for Young Australians*, national goals agreed to by all of Australia's education ministers in December 2008 as the foundation and framework for school policy and funding decisions. These goals are:

- Goal 1: Australian schooling promotes equity and excellence.
- Goal 2: All young Australians become: successful learners; confident and creative individuals; and active and informed citizens.

The text of the Melbourne Declaration emphasises that "achieving these educational goals is the collective responsibility of governments, school sectors and individual schools, as well as parents and caregivers, young Australians, families, other education and training providers, business and the broader community" (MCEETYA, 2008).

ACADEMIC AND EQUITY OUTCOMES OF AUSTRALIA'S SCHOOLING

Despite record-high spending by Australian governments—and families—on schooling, Australia now has the fifth largest resource gap in the OECD between advantaged and disadvantaged schools. This inequity is reflected in academic performance and post-school outcomes both overall and when data are disaggregated for various groups.

Australia's scores are above or well-above above OECD averages on all PISA measures. However, since 2000, Australia's performance in PISA has declined in both relative and absolute terms. It has slipped from 4th to 12th place in OECD's PISA rankings for reading literacy, from 11th to 20th in mathematics, and from 8th to 10th in science.[12] Australia has fewer high performers and more low performers than it did previously, and the correlation between poor performance and attending a disadvantaged school is strengthening. The achievement gap between students in the highest socio-economic quartile and lowest quartile is about three years ,Thomson et al., 2017). Similar patterns are evident in Australian students' results in other international tests such as Trends in International Mathematics and Science Study (TIMSS) (Thomson et al., 2016).

Results from Australia's annual national assessment program on literacy and numeracy (NAPLAN) for all school students in Years 3, 5, 7 and 9 are similarly lacklustre. Between 2008—when this national test replaced separate State tests—

[12] The average scores for Australian students in PISA 2015 were 503 for reading literacy (compared to OECD average of 493); 510 for scientific literacy (compared to OECD average of 493) and 494 for mathematical literacy (compared to OECD average of 490).

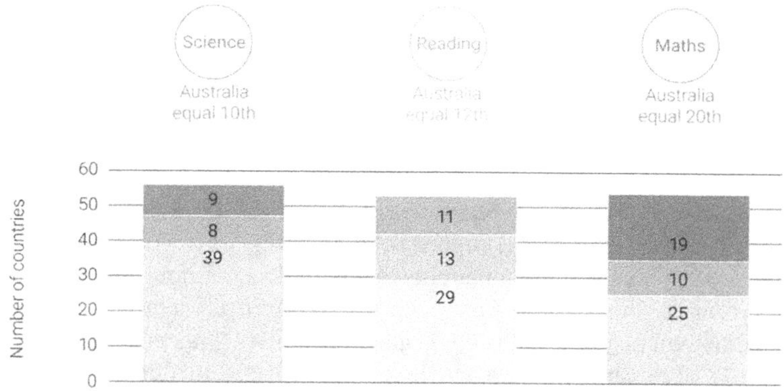

FIGURE 2.2. Australian PISA Results Compared to the World. Figure reproduced with permission from Thomson et al., 2017.

and 2016 there was no overall, significant or consistent, improvement in student performance across Australia. While some States (such as Victoria) continuously outperformed others; some subject areas have improved for some year levels; and some States have improved (notably Queensland, which introduced an additional year of primary school and also invested in preschool education after seeing their initially woeful performance comparative to other States in 2008), overall results have been characterised by stagnation (Australian Curriculum Assessment

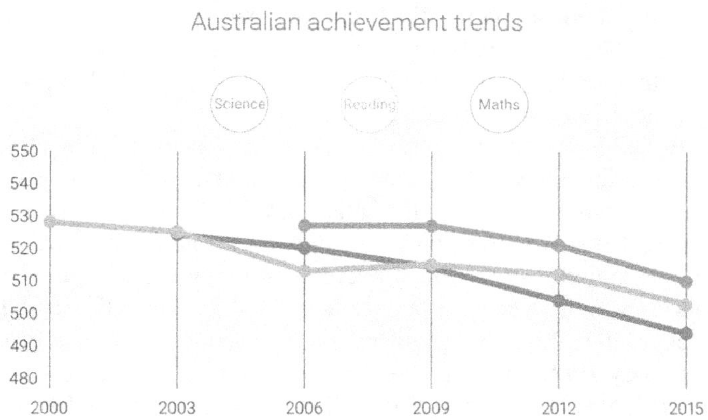

FIGURE 2.3. Australian PISA Achievement Trends.
Figure reproduced with permission from Thomson et al 2017.

and Reporting Authority, ACARA 2016).[13] Student performance on these tests is closely correlated with students' family disadvantage and school disadvantage. Most worrying is the fact that gaps between the most disadvantaged students and least disadvantaged students *widen* as they progress through Australia's schooling system (Goss et al., 2016).

When we turn to look at secondary school completion, similar equity gaps are revealed across all States and Territories. Nationally, 74 per cent of young Australians finish Year 12 or gain a Higher School Certificate or equivalent qualification by age 19. This overall number, however, masks enormous State differences: 84.8 per cent of those in the Australian Capital Territory reach this milestone, compared to 59.6 per cent in Tasmania and a woeful 47.2 per cent in the Northern Territory. 78.2 per cent of young people in major cities gain Year 12 qualifications compared to only 43.3 per cent of young Australians in very remote locations. This reflects the historical structure of their schooling systems—only going to 10th grade until recently in Tasmania, the remoteness of much of the Northern Territory, the high Indigenous population in the Northern Territory, who continue to experience effects of decades of bad policies, and ACT which has a small and relatively socio-economically advantaged population. Those from the highest SES decile are 30 percent more likely to gain a Year 12 qualification than those in the lowest decile, and there is a gap of 32 per cent between Indigenous and non-Indigenous students (Lamb et al., 2015).

These patterns persist when examining tertiary education. Australia is the eighth most highly-educated nation in the OECD, with 45 per cent of adults between 25 and 64 years old having attained tertiary qualifications (mostly Bachelor Degrees or equivalent), trailing Canada, the US and the UK (OECD, 2016, p. 37). However, parental educational attainment continues to influence children's educational attainment strongly. For example, children whose parents did not complete secondary school are half as likely to gain a tertiary qualification compared to those with tertiary-educated parents (OECD, 2016, p. 82). Low educational attainment is the principal risk factor for young people (age 15–29 years old) not being in education, employment or training.

Strikingly, and in contrast to most other countries discussed in this book, Australia does exceptionally well at meeting the educational needs of an increasingly diverse school population. Over half of all Australians were either born overseas or have a parent that was born overseas, making it one of the most culturally diverse nations included in this book and around the world. Yet, unlike in most other countries with high migrant and refugee intakes, Australian children with migrant backgrounds from non-English speaking countries complete Year 12 and undertake tertiary study in far greater proportions than the rest of the student population. This may be attributed to cultural or family factors. Many migrant

[13] This means that a third grader in 2016 was found to have the same literacy and numeracy levels as a third grader in 2008, which is unsurprising. But what is concerning is that the proportion of students failing to meet the minimum benchmarks has not reduced over time despite significant policy efforts.

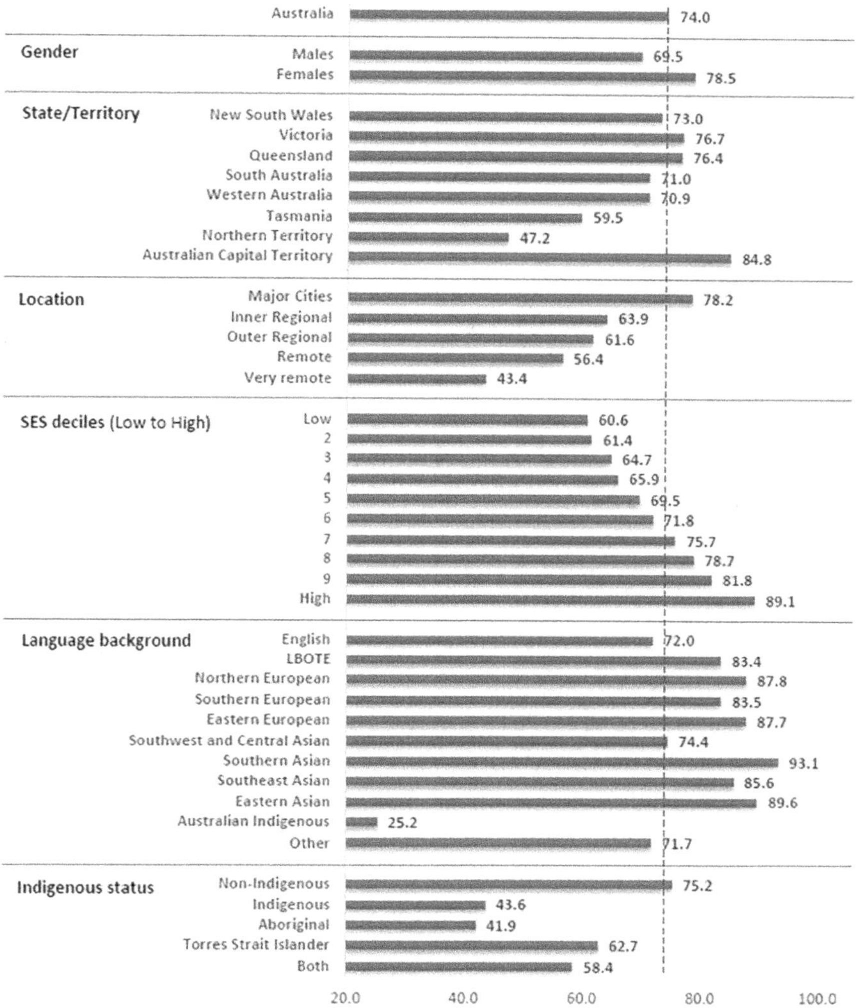

FIGURE 2.4: Proportion of Young Australians Completing Year 12 or Equivalent by Age 19. Figure reproduced with permission from Lamb et al., 2015, p. 42.

and refugee parents have risked their lives or made enormous sacrifices to come to Australia and increase their children's opportunities in life. They, thus, are extremely invested in seeing their children succeed in school and beyond. Many come from regions such as South-East Asia and East Asia where there is very strong emphasis placed on school instruction, homework and exam performance (Zhao, 2014). Another factor could be Australia's efforts since the 1970s to reframe itself as a multicultural nation, including a plethora of State and Commonwealth initiatives in schooling and beyond to enhance the economic and social participation of those facing language and cultural barriers, such as funding for translators at schools and free English language tuition provided at many worksites, increasing the uptake of such services (Hinz, 2009).

Figure 2.4 provides a graphical representation of how well Australia's education system meets the educational needs of different children across the nation. The significant differences in schooling outcomes between different Australian jurisdictions indicate the impact that different policy settings can have. They also indicate geographic and demographic factors beyond a State's control. For example the Australian Capital Territory, which consistently outperforms other jurisdictions, also has the most geographically-condensed and socio-economically advantaged population, while the reverse is true for the Northern Territory.

RECENT POLICY ACTIVITY TO ADDRESS PERFORMANCE CONCERNS

Concerns about increasing inequality and poor performance led to the Gillard-Rudd (Labor) Commonwealth Government in 2012 pursuing a largely unilateral National Plan for School Improvement, underpinned by the National Education Reform Agreement (actually a set of bilateral agreements with State governments). At the agreement's core was an A$6.5 billion increase in school funding, of which the Commonwealth pledged to pay two-thirds if the States paid one-third. Funds were to be distributed to schools (via State governments and school system authorities) using a needs-based funding system consisting of a base amount plus top-ups for different forms of concentrated disadvantages faced by schools (including remoteness, students with disabilities, indigenous students and low SES background).

These reforms had two key weaknesses. The first stems from a pledge made by Gillard that all students would benefit and no school would lose a dollar in federal funding. Consequently, money was spread too thinly to alleviate concentrated disadvantage. The second key weakness was that half of the pledged funding increase was allocated five and six years into the future—beyond the 4-year budget cycle and beyond the next federal election, which Labor lost. The incoming Coalition government refused to honor the deals struck by the Labor government with the States, arguing that there were more effective ways to improve schooling results than more funding—such as better teaching, parental engagement, a strengthened curriculum and greater autonomy for schools—and has pursued these via programs funded by tied grants, rhetoric and the council of education ministers. The irony is that these four strategies had been key tenets of the Commonwealth Labor government's broader National Plan for School Improvement and built into the legislation and intergovernmental agreements that the Coalition rejects. These strategies also been pursued for decades by the States.

In 2017, the Coalition Commonwealth government surprised many by reversing its longstanding position, introducing its own 'needs-based' reforms to school funding, and with support from minor parties and independent politicians, boosted school funding and amended the 2013 Australian Education Act to reflect revised formula and conditions. While the increase was less than Labor had pledged, it was much more than the Coalition had previously agreed to, was more closely aligned to a school's need, and—radically—also involved reductions in federal funding to some of the most affluent private schools. It is too soon to know whether the conditions attached to this modest increase in Commonwealth funding could lead to more or less federal intervention in schooling policy. At the time of writing the states are still demanding that the more generous deals struck with the Commonwealth Labor government in 2013 be honored, while the Commonwealth Coalition government is advising the states to revise their own funding allocations between public and private schools, to reduce the over-funding of private schools and under-funding of public schools. The conditions in tied grants could also be influenced by the recommendations of the Review to Achieve Educational Excellence in Australian Schools, established by the Commonwealth Coalition in 2017 at the time of their policy reversal on school funding. Several members of this review—including the Chair, David Gonski who chaired the landmark review of school funding to inform Labor's policy—have publicly espoused for the principle of subsidiarity and recommended the return of greater policy autonomy to the States, recognizing that with their direct connections to schools and extensive experience designing, managing and reforming school systems, the States are better placed to develop and implement school improvement initiatives. Similar positions were also advocated in the short-lived White Paper on the Reform of the Australian Federation (Department of Prime Minister and Cabinet, DPMC, 2014) and other prominent publications.

POLICY DEBATES AND TENSIONS

Since the establishment of the first schooling systems by the Australian colonies in the mid-1850s, Australian schooling policies have been profoundly shaped by two central and competing principles: choice and equity. The relative influence of each principle has waxed and waned over time and between governments. Generally speaking, Commonwealth governments and Coalition governments have given prominence to choice, while the policies of State and Territory governments and Labor governments have emphasized equity. For example, the original and overriding principle underpinning the debut of general, recurrent funding for schools from the Commonwealth under the Whitlam (Labor) Government in the 1970s was the principle of need: schools would be topped up to reach a funding benchmark (equity). Yet, choice was also supported by providing some funding to all students regardless of the school they attended.

At State level, the Victoria's Kennett (Coalition) Government devolved 93 per cent of the State's school education budget to individual schools to spend as they thought best (within an expanded, State-wide accountability and curriculum framework). This increase in school autonomy, along with relaxation of school enrolment zones, was thought to enhance educational choice, increase the capacity of schools to respond to the needs of their students, and drive system-wide innovation and excellence through competition. But equity was also a central component of these Victorian reforms, with each school's funding allocation based on their size and relative need. While both principles continue to dominate policy debate, the weight given to choice appears to be strengthening relative to equity, with school choice seen by Australian governments as an untouchable right, and enabled by generous public funding for private schools, which retain the ability to select their students and charge fees.

The other major tension in Australian schooling policy pertinent to this volume is State diversity and innovation versus national consistency. Australian schooling continues to be characterized by a lack of coherence, which means that reform efforts tend to be disjointed, resulting in unnecessary complexity, wasted resources and inconsistencies (Bolt 2014; CEDA, 2016). This lack of cohesion is exacerbated by the competing principles driving school policy in Australia. Moves for greater consistency and/or coherence have been growing since the 1970s, pushed largely by Commonwealth governments—Labor and Coalition. The States have generally gone along with these efforts, and at times led them (such as state-led moves towards national curriculum statements in the early 1990s) or organically moved towards greater consistency and homogeneity of their school systems, without pressure from the Commonwealth (for example, in the decade following Victoria's school decentralization reforms, all other States increased autonomy for their public schools to varying degrees).

There is strong support among the States for the new national institutions such as ACARA, notwithstanding perennial resentment at intermittent Commonwealth funding cuts or attempts to dominate. The States continue to be able to innovate, though arguably there is less scope than in previous decades. Australia's State governments are restricted by an increasing number of highly-prescriptive tied grants and a paucity of comparable, fine-grain, timely data to compare the successes and failures of small and medium level program innovations in other States. The Education Council, ACARA and individual States are working on all these issues. They are also working to modernise school curriculums and pedagogy to develop in students the skills and capabilities recognized as vital to meeting the complex and unknown challenges of the twenty-first century, such as creativity, resilience, problem solving and communication skills.

CONCLUSION AND OVERALL ANALYSIS

As this chapter has demonstrated, it is not wholly accurate to describe Australian federalism as having either a converging (homogenizing) effect or a diversifying effect (catering to different needs, cultures, preferences or both). These terms do not capture the nuance and complexity present in Australia's dynamic and politically-charged school policy sphere. Commonwealth policies pursued through tied grants, and intergovernmental initiatives pursued through the Education Council and ACARA have resulted in some convergence, for example a national curriculum framework, greater consistency in the compulsory ages of schooling, and national testing as a tool for 'yardstick comparisons' between jurisdictions and tracking of progress and change over time. But States still retain primary responsibility for schooling, and these tied grants and intergovernmental agreements have also been sufficiently flexible to allow for States continue to make school funding allocation decisions, program decisions and to pursue their own policy priorities and strategies. Indeed, some of these intergovernmental agreements actually sought to return some power and policy autonomy (and capacity to diverge) to the States. The States continue to be the engine of innovation in Australian schooling, and this innovation continues even within these new national frameworks—for example, Victoria's pioneering developments to its own curriculum, notwithstanding the Australian Curriculum; or South Australia's early years' policy framework which unites historically separate infancy, family, early childhood and schooling policies in a cohesive birth-to-eight years old policy framework centred on the needs of children and their families.

Concurrent responsibilities subject to centripetal forces is a more accurate description of this contested policy space. This reality reflects are growing public preference among Australians for national approaches, national consistency and greater role for the Commonwealth government, which has been eager to oblige. This is in contrast to Switzerland and Germany, where concerns of democratic deficit saw strong moves and pressure from citizens to push responsibilities away from the centre.

Australia is doing well to meet the education needs of an increasingly diverse population, and is slowly reducing the educational gaps between its Indigenous and non-Indigenous populations, although this gap remains unacceptably large and more work is needed by all governments in collaboration with each other and Indigenous communities.

But despite serving an ethnically diverse population fairly well, Australia is failing to harness the potential of all of its young people, especially those born into less fortunate circumstances. Policy decisions over the last few decades have entrenched rather than alleviated socio-economic disadvantage.

What role will federalism play to promote educational quality and progress in the future? It depends on whether government roles are realigned with functional capacity, experience and expertise. For schools, national and international evidence suggests that the States are best placed to design and implement policies, programs and regulatory regimes, and to allocate funding among schools, due to their greater expertise, experience and administrative capacity. The Commonwealth can play a valuable role supporting State and national initiatives, gathering and analyzing data from all school systems in all States and making it readily available and usable by educators and researchers across the nation. Such a transformation of government roles and responsibilities is unlikely in the near future, especially when schooling remains such a hot topic for Australian families and voters, and where education is more important than ever for individual and national success. As long as education remains vitally important to Australians, it is likely that governments at all levels will seek to maintain or increase their involvement. In this more likely scenario, greater coherence is needed to ensure resources—time and money—are invested in places and in ways that amplify educational development, and minimise inequities, to enable each student and the nation to realize its potential and meet the complex challenges of the future.

APPENDIX 2.1 AUSTRALIAN PRIME MINISTERS SINCE 1973 (WHEN COMMONWEALTH GOVERNMENT SHARPLY INCREASED ITS ROLE IN SCHOOLING)

Year	Party	Prime Minister
1973 – 1975	Labor	Gough Whitlam
1975 – 1983	Coalition of the Liberal "conservative" Party and National (formally Country) Party	Malcolm Fraser
1983 – 1991*	Labor	Bob Hawke
1991 – 1996	Labor	Paul Keating
1997 - 2007	Coalition	John Howard
2007 – 2010*	Labor	Kevin Rudd
2010 – 2013*	Labor	Julia Gillard
2013*	Labor	Kevin Rudd
2013 – 2015*	Coalition	Tony Abbott
2015 – current (2017)	Coalition	Malcolm Turnbull

*Indicates that the change to following prime minister occurred without an election

REFERENCES

Australian Bureau of Statistics. (2017). *Schools Australian 2016, ABS.* Canberra, Australia. Retrieved March 20, 2017, from www.abs.gov.au

Australian Curriculum Assessment and Reporting Authority. (2016). *National Assessment Program: Literacy and Numeracy. National Report for 2016.* Sydney, Australia: ACARA.

Bita, N. (2015). Private school funding grows 23 pc, public schools 12.5pc. *The Australian,* 6 July. Retreived on October 5, 2016, from http://www.theaustralian.com.au/national-affairs/education/private-schools-get-twice-funding-of-government-institutions/news-story/43a9669a53ff9a5b5aa9a6c45cb09ed2

Bolt, R. (2014). *Speech and comments.* Melbourne Institute's Economic and Social Outlook Conference, Melbourne.

Buckingham, J., & Jha, T. (2016). *One school does not fit all.* Research report 9, 31 January. Sydney, Australia: Centre for Independent Studies.

Committee for the Economic Development of Australia (CEDA). (2016). *Australia's economic future: An agenda for growth, Melbourne, Australia: CEDA.* Retrieved from https://www.ceda.com.au/Research-and-policy/All-CEDA-research/Research-catalogue/Australia-s-economic-future-an-agenda-for-growth

Commonwealth Department of Education, Employment and Workplace Relations. (2011). *Review of School Funding—Final Report.* Canberra: Australia: DEEWR.

Connors, L., & McMorrow, J. (2015). Imperatives in schools funding: Equity, sustainability and achievement. *Australian Education Review, 60.*

Department of Prime Minister and Cabinet. (2014). *Reform of the Federation White Paper: Issues Paper No. 4: Roles and Responsibilities in Education. Part A: Childcare and Early Childhood Education and Schools.* Canberra, Australia: Department of Prime Minister and Cabinet.

Fenna, A. (2008). Commonwealth fiscal power and Australia federalism. *University of New South Wales Law Journal, 31*(2), 509–29.

Goss, P., Sonnemann, J., Chilsolm, C., & Nelson, L. (2016). *Widening gaps: What NAPLAN tells us about student progress.* Melbourne, Australia: Grattan Institute.

Hinz, B. (2009). *Many hopes one dream: The story of the Ethnic Communities' Council of Australia.* Melbourne, Australia: Australian Scholarly Publishing.

Hinz, B. (2010). *Australian federalism and school funding: Exploring the nexus in Victoria's devolution reforms.* Refereed paper presented at the Australian Political Studies Association Annual Conference, Melbourne, Australia, 26–29 September 2010.

Hinz, B. (2016). *Federalism and Australian Schooling Reforms.* Unpublished PhD thesis, School of Social and Political Sciences and Melbourne Graduate School of Education, University of Melbourne, Australia.

Independent Schools Council of Australia. (2016). *Recurrent funding, ISCA.* Retrieved on October 5, 2016, from http://isca.edu.au/about-independent-schools/recurrent-funding-for-independent-schools/

Jensen, B., Weldmann, B., & Farmer, J. (2013). *The myth of markets in education.* Melbourne, Australia: Grattan Institute.

Jones, S. (2008). Cooperative federalism? The case of the Ministerial Council on Education, Employment, Training and Youth Affairs. *Australian Journal of Public Administration, 67*(2), 161–172.

Kemp, D. (1990). *Address-in-reply to governor-general's speech.* House of Representatives Hansard. Canberra, Australia: Parliament of Australia. This speech is available online at http://parlinfo.aph.gov.au/parlInfo/search/display/display.w3p;query=Id%3A%22chamber%2Fhansardr%2F1990-05-15%2F0007%22

Knott, M. (2016). Gonski funds skewed to aid the Catholic school system. *Sydney Morning Herald,* 12 October.

Lamb, S., Jackson, J., Walstab, A., & Huo, S. (2015). *Educational opportunity in Australia 2015: Who succeeds and who misses out. Mitchell Report 09/2015.* Centre for International Research on Education Systems, Victoria University, for the Mitchell Institute. Mitchell Institute, Melbourne, Australia.

Ministerial Council for Education, Employment, Training and Youth Affairs (MCEETYA) (2008). *Melbourne Declaration on Educational Goals for Young Australians.* December, Melbourne. Retrieved on March 23, 2016, from http://www.curriculum.

edu.au/verve/_resources/National_Declaration_on_the_Educational_Goals_for_Young_Australians.pdf

National Catholic Education Commission. (2016). *Media Release: Funding certainty a genuine need for parents and schools, NCEC 27 September*. Retrieved on October 5, 2016, from http://www.ncec.catholic.edu.au/news-events/media-releases/420-funding-certainty-a-genuine-need-for-parents-and-schools/file

National Centre for Vocational Education Research. (2016). *Australian vocational education and training statistics: VET in Schools 2015, Adelaide*. Retrieved on October 17, 2016, from https://www.ncver.edu.au/__data/assets/pdf_file/0017/60380/VET-in-Schools-2015.pdf

Nghiem, H. S., Nguyen H. T., Khanam R., & Connelly, L. (2015). Does school type affect cognitive and noncognitive development in children? Evidence from Australian primary schools. *Labour Economics, 33*, 55–65.

Organization for Economic Cooperation and Development (OECD). (2016). *Education at a Glace 2016*. OECD Publishing, Paris, France. Retrieved on October 5, 2016, from http://www.oecd-ilibrary.org/education/education-at-a-glance-2016_eag-2016-en

Pyne, C. (2014). Address to Christian Schools Australia celebration dinner. Canberra, Australia. Retrieved on January 29, 2016, from http://www.csa.edu.au/resources/csnpf-2014/ministers-address-christopher-pyne

Ramamurthy, V. L. (2012). Tied grants and policy reform in hospitals and schools. In P. Kildea, A. Lynch, & G. Williams (Eds.), *Tomorrow's federation: Reforming Australian government* (pp. 114–130). Leichhardt, NSW, Australia: Federation Press.

Richardson, H. (2016). Election a sure victory for Gonski plan. *The Mercury*, 6 July.

Savage, G. (2016). Who's steering the ship? National curriculum reform and the reshaping of Australian federalism. *Journal of Education Policy, 31*(6), 833–850.

Steering Committee for the Report on Government Services. (2017). *Chapter 4: School education. Report on Government Services*. Productivity Commission, Canberra, Australia. Retrieved on February 8, 2017, from http://www.pc.gov.au/

Thomson, S., De Bortoli, L., & Underwood, C. (2017). *PISA 2015: Reporting Australia's results*. Australian Council for Educational Research, Camberwell, Australia. Retrieved on March 16, 2017, from http://research.acer.edu.au/ozpisa/

Thomson, S., Wernert, N., O'Grady, E., & Rodriges, S. (2016). *TIMSS2015: A first look at Australia's results*. Australian Council for Educational Research, Camberwell, Australia. Retrieved on March 20, 2016, from http://research.acer.edu.au/cgi/viewcontent.cgi?article=1000&context=timss_2015

Victorian Auditor General. (2015). *Additional school costs for families,* Melbourne, Australia: Victorian Auditor General's Office.

Watson, L. (1998). *Intentions, opportunities and outcomes: The impact of Commonwealth involvement in Australian schooling*. Unpublished PhD thesis. Crawford School of Public Policy Australian National University, Canberra, Australia.

Whitlam, G. (1985). *The Whitlam Government 1972–1975*. Ringwood, Victoria, Australia: Viking.

Zhao, Y. (2014). *Who's afraid of the big bad dragon. Why China has the best and worst education system in the world.* San Francisco, CA: Jossey-Bass.

CHAPTER 3

FEDERALISM AND EDUCATION IN AUSTRIA

Peter Bußjäger

INTRODUCTION

Austria's education system is strongly centralized compared to other federalist systems. The federal powers dominate the division of competences or functions between the Federation and the states (*Länder*) in the various fields of education. Moreover, the distribution of competences is very casuistic and complicated. As will be shown, this dominance of the Federation prevails not only in legislation but also in the administration of laws. Interestingly, recent reform projects tend to strengthen the dominating role of the Federation. This chapter aims to explain the difficult relationship between Federalism and Austria's education system at the present time.

EVOLUTION OF THE FEDERAL AND EDUCATION MODEL

Austria's education system has been contested for many years. With the beginning of Austria's federal system in the 1920s, the leading political parties could not reach agreement on the distribution of competencies in educational matters between federation and the *Länder*. Therefore only provisional regulations were

Federalism and Education: Ongoing Challenges and Policy Strategies in Ten Countries, pages 43–61.

implemented due to a tense political reality that included disputes between the Social Democrats and the Catholic Church as well as uncertainty about the future political developments in the *Länder*.

Art. 14 of the Federal Constitution (*Bundes-Verfassungsgesetz* [B-VG]) finally stipulated that matters of the school system, education system and vocational training would be regulated in a separate federal constitutional law. Until this specific constitutional law would be set into force, the school laws of the Monarchy would persist.

For a better understanding of the Austrian school system, it is therefore necessary to go further back in Austrian history and take a brief look at its historical development.[1]

The Austrian school system sprung from the Theresia School Reform of 1774, which introduced a public state school with a 6-year compulsory attendance. However, this reform was implemented slowly and did not include all regions. The basis for a modern educational system was first created in the second half of the 19th century through the Reich Public School Law (*Reichsvolksschulgesetz*) of 1869, which established for the first time a universal compulsory school system on a uniform basis. At that time Austria was not a federation but a decentralized unitary state. Nevertheless, the crown lands had a small sphere of their own competences and had their own parliaments, which were called the *Landtage*. The crown lands were able to pass laws without regard to the laws of the central state's educational system.

With the end of the Austro-Hungarian Empire and the founding of the First Republic (1918), development of the educational system was politically influenced by the Social Democrats. Their impact resulted in a school reform movement, based on the principle of giving community assistance to the weak and needy, most notably in Vienna. This period introduced free teaching and learning aids into the compulsory schools. This positive development was aborted by the establishment of a fascist regime in Austria and the Second World War.

With the beginning of the Second Republic, the two major political parties in Austria, the Austrian People's Party (ÖVP) and the Socialist Party (SPÖ), entered into negotiations to relegislate the Austrian school system. The final product of these negotiations was the "School Law" (*Schulgesetzwerk*) of 1962, which still remains the statutory basis for the entire Austrian school system. The provisory regulation of Art. 14 B-VG was abolished and replaced by a very detailed distribution of competences in educational matters (see in detail below 2).

The statute incorporated the *Contract between the Holy See and the Republic of Austria*, the first concordat to have been ratified by a freely-elected parliament. The concordat provided, among other things, for the extension of religious instruction to vocational schools and for statutory government subsidies to private

[1] This chapter follows partly Pelzelmayer Herbert, Development of the Austrian School System http://www.oecd.org/edu/research/1818705.pdf. See also Juranek, 1999, p. 54.

parochial schools at 60% of the costs of teachers' salaries, which was extended to 100% in 1972.

In order to assure its continued force, the School Law was elevated to the status of a constitutional provision, with the effect that from then until 2005, all modifications of the educational system had to be passed by a 2/3 majority vote in parliament.[2] By seeking a stable school system, Austria paid the price of a pronounced rigidity with regard to the implementation of innovations. This condition characterizes Austrian school development until today, despite the fact that in 2005, this provision was abolished.

The School Law of 1962 was a suitable basis at the time for appropriate contemporary innovations, inasmuch as the goal was a nation-wide harmonization of the educational system and improvement of the education and viability of the youth.

This goal subsequently took the form of successive dismantling of the often primitively organized upper level *Volkschule* (an intermediate level form), the extension of compulsory schooling to nine years, the establishment of a "music-oriented Realgymnasium" (as an independent upper level form leading to the Matura exam; later Upper Level Realgymnasium) as well as a Pedagogic Academy (now: college of education) to train public school teachers (as a post-secondary facility). In vocational middle schools and higher level schools, the vocational and general education (*allgemeine Bildung*) curricula were co-ordinated, while in compulsory vocational schools, technical education took precedence. The expansion of general education as the additional province of the vocational school was first established in 1975 and put into practice after 1990 with the introduction of "Technical English" and "German and Communications" into the curriculum.

In the late 1960s, Austria was swept up in the reform movement resulting from findings of various OECD conferences and resulting recommendations triggered in nearly all industrialized countries. Perspectives from the first OECD Report, *Educational Planning in Austria*, was one of the primary foundations for the subsequent intensive educational planning and school development policy. As a complement thereto, the School Reform Commission was set up in 1969, followed by the "Centre for School Experiments and Development" (*Zentrum für Schulversuche und Schulentwicklung*) two years later.

The first SPÖ non-coalition government (minority cabinet, 1970/71) announced the following goals: *Gesamtschule*, full-day school, changes in dual-track apprentice training and teacher training as a university discipline. These educational policy programs enjoyed positive resonance among the public. Comprehensive school experiments were launched to prepare the necessary reforms. The most important evaluation projects primarily concerned:

- Pre-school and pre-school classes (assistance for children held back from school attendance)

[2] Art. 14 para. 10 B-VG, as amended by BGBl. I 31/2005.

- *Grundschule*, a better match of learning opportunities in accordance with the individual child's abilities by the creation of appropriate organizational forms and application of specific methods, the mainstreaming of the handicapped, foreign language orientation classes, and all-day day care.
- At the Secondary Level I, the testing of various features of integrated school forms (integrative, supplemental, orientation level) and forms of all-day care.
- In the polytechnical curriculum, the testing of performance groups and remedial courses in compulsory subjects such as German, mathematics and technical drawing, so-called *seminars* (fairs for those interested in agricultural or technical fields) and electives, improved vocational orientation with respect to transition from the Secondary Level I to Secondary Level II, in particular with regard to dual track vocational education,
- Finally, in the institutes of general higher education the testing of new curricula, new performance groups (including lift and support courses), the concept of electives, and the reform of the college entrance exam (*Reifeprüfung*).

These centrally-organized expansive school experiments were efficiently implemented in the regulated school systems and yielded success. Examples are the care in pre-school classes of school-age children who were not ready for school, the foreign language orientation classes in the elementary school, the all-day day care programs, the elective courses, and the reform of the Matura in the institutes of general higher education. Additionally, they implemented various remedial and assistance measures through adjusted subject and teaching methods.

Of course, expectations of a fundamental organizational change at the Secondary Level I (*Gesamtschule*) were not fulfilled; even today, the lower level of the institutes of higher general education and the *Hauptschule* or *Mittelschule* are operating in parallel.

After the mid-1980s, a certain paradigm shift occurred with regard to Austrian educational planning and school development. Up until then, emphasis was on comprehensive and wide-ranging structural measures in schools. Since then, the accent has been on internal school reform, greater accessibility, autonomy, and quality of the school (without rendering structural changes obsolete) and the increased professionalism of those directly and indirectly involved in education and education policy (administration, monitoring, teachers).

To follow up on the resulting impetuses and challenges, a Department for Education Research and Planning was set up within the Federal Ministry for Education. The Research and Planning commission attempts to capitalize the existing potential of school research, by cooperation with national and international research institutes and sponsorship of expert forums for educational policy discussions. This takes place in close cooperation with the Centre for School Experiments and School Development, which has been assigned with new goals and agendas and whose mission is to serve as liaison for scholarship, planning, school administration and school realization.

The present emphases in education are founded on the conviction that future school development must be geared more closely towards the needs of those directly affected by education. One consequence of this attitude has been to design measures to allow more discretion for individual schools (School Autonomy). A related law from 1993 (14th Revision of the School Organization Law) takes a first step towards the offering all schools the voluntary option of submitting curriculum proposals to the school community committee or school forum (a board composed of objective faculty, pupils and guardians) for approval by a 2/3 majority vote. Alterations to required courses create an individual school profile (Curriculum Autonomy) and within certain parameters, each school can decide on the size of classes. However, changes in the curriculum for each school type can be made only to the extent of 15% of the instruction hours. In vocational middle and higher schools, school autonomy measures are implemented by electives within course areas. The funding requisitions process for all federal schools has been simplified (financial autonomy).

Since this idea is designed to gear school development more closely towards the individual school, an issue arises with broader school system functioning and ultimately with their (measurable) quality. This concern is especially pertinent because the eventual degrees awarded by schools with differing profiles must be comparable.

In attempt to move towards greater school autonomy, the Federal Ministry for Education and Art has begun to reduce the intensive organizational rules restricting the autonomy of schools. Alongside the now very pronounced organizational-functional emphases, new approaches in comprehensive Austrian school developments aim to continue to improve equal opportunity and access to education in the Austrian school system.

Points which have been realized in recent years include:

- Relaxation of school entrance requirements and introduction of alternative forms of performance measuring in the primary school,
- Improvement of the horizontal transition (Primary level to Secondary Level I to Secondary Level II to post-secondary area) and the creation of greater mobility in vertical interfaces (*Neue Mittelschule* to General High School Lower Level; vocational compulsory school to vocational intermediate schools to vocational upper-level schools to Academic High School Upper Level)
- Continuing the integration of the handicapped pupils at the Secondary Level I (schools for ages 10 to 14) and
- Improved internationally-oriented education (measures for mobility and exchange, foreign language offensive, intensification of intercultural learning).

In 2017, a school reform bill has passed the Austrian parliament. It intends to strengthen school autonomy and increase funds for all day schools (see nearer below 6.). According to the law, from 2017 to 2025, a total of EUR 428 million are to be allocated to infrastructure and after-school programs, EUR 248 million to teachers at compulsory schools, and EUR 74 million to teachers above all at secondary schools. The law also includes reforms for the Austrian school administration (see nearer below).

This legislation is an important achievement of the past federal government, which is formed by the Social democrats and the Conservatives, the Austrian People's Party. Nevertheless, it is more of a compromise than an engaged project with a new approach. As the bill needed a two-third majority in the National Council (because of restructuring of the school administration), the consent of the opposite party of the Greens was necessary. The Greens gave their consent after a compromise for the introduction of projects testing a compulsory comprehensive school system was achieved.

CONSTITUTIONAL DISTRIBUTION OF POWER IN EDUCATION[3]

General Remarks

The distribution of powers in Austria's education system is very centralistic and complicated. The federal level withholds clear influence over the autonomous competences of the *Länder*.

The division of competences in the Austrian federal constitution (B-VG) is generally described as very complicated and casuistic. There are four main types of competences: Art 10 contains the competences of the federation in legislation and execution, Art 11 comprises competences of the federation in legislation and of the *Länder* in execution, and Art 12 lays out framework legislation for the federation and the competences of the *Länder* in legislative implementation and execution. Finally, according to Art 15 B-VG, the general or residual clause declares that the *Länder* are competent for all matters which are not explicitly transferred to the federation in legislation or execution.

Regarding matters of education, the competences are enumerated in two broad articles, namely Art 14 (education in general) and Art 14a (education in the fields of agriculture and forestry) mirroring the instruments of Art 10, 11, 12 and 15 in these matters. This very complex distribution of competences mainly is the residual result of the school reform of 1962. However, as previously described, the centralization of Austria's school system has its roots in the monarchy of the 19th century. Those roots remain powerful today.[4]

[3] See also Juranek, 199, p. 377; Kröll, 2012, p. 686.

[4] For the Austrian education system see http://www.bildungssystem.at/en/footer-boxen/isced/international-standard-classification-of-education/.

Early Childhood Education

Early childhood education encompasses programs for the very young (up for three years) as well as formal childcare for children before they enter primary education (ages three to six). It corresponds to the ISCED level 0. The elementary level (ISCED 0) in Austria refers to cribs, kindergartens, after-school care facilities and children's groups. Playgroups and nannies can also provide this service. Additionally, elementary schools provide pre-school education programs for children of school age who are not ready for elementary education yet. Early childhood education is legislated and administrated autonomously by the *Länder*, as laid out in Art. 14 para. 4 lit. b) B-VG (Kindergarten-System and day-homes-System). In practice, however, early childhood education is carried out by the municipalities.

Still, the Federation and the *Länder* have made various agreements that supply the *Länder* with federal funding to improve early education services. These agreements are based on Art. 15a B-VG and are a typical instrument of Austrian federalism intending to harmonize the legal system.[5] Legislation from the federal level dictates professional-employment qualifications for kindergarten teachers and educational assistants to be employed by the provinces, municipalities or municipal associations. Implementation and execution of these tasks, however, are the business of the *Länder* (Art. 14 para. 3 lit. d] B-VG).

Primary and Lower Secondary Education

In Austria, primary School begins at the age of compulsory education, which starts at the age of 6 and lasts for nine years. The primary level lasts four years and corresponds to the ISCED level 1. Schools of this level are primary/elementary schools, special needs schools, and schools designed for integrative/inclusive education.

Lower secondary education encompasses the first 4 years after primary education and corresponds to the ISCED level 2. Pupils can choose between General Secondary School (*Hauptschule*), New Secondary School (*Neue Mittelschule*), Academic Secondary School Lower Level (AHS *Unterstufe*), as well as special needs schools and inclusive education. Many of these options have differing admission requirements.

Generally, legislation concerning school principles lies in the hands of the Federation while the implementation and execution of those principles remain tasks of the *Länder*. Such is the case in both primary and lower secondary education, with Art. 14 para. 3 lit. b) and c) B-VG providing that the issues of maintenance, dissolution, local districts, size of classes and instruction periods of public compulsory schools will be legislated by the federation but carried out by the *Länder*.

---

[5] Presently in force: Vereinbarung über den Ausbau des institutionellen Kinderbetreuungsangebots, BGBl. I 120/2011 with amendment BGBl. I 85/2014.

In addition, Art 14 para. 2 B-VG dictates that while legislation lies in the hands of the Federation, it will be executed by the provinces in matters concerning service code and staff representation rights at public compulsory schools.

Upper Secondary Education

Secondary level I is followed by secondary level II (9th school year), which encompasses educational institutions focusing on general or vocational education. In Austria, these include Pre-Vocational School (*Polytechnische Schule* preparing pupils for an apprenticeship or a job), Vocational school and Apprenticeship (dual system), School for Intermediate Vocational Education (BMS), Colleges for Higher Vocational Education (BHS—excluding the 4th and 5th forms), Academic Secondary School Upper Cycle (AHS *Oberstufe*), as well as the Pre-Vocational Year (*Berufsvorbereitungsjahr*) and Integrative Vocational Training.

The competences for BMS, BHS and AHS are exclusively competences of the Federation in legislation as well as in execution (Art 14 para. 1 B-VG). The federation and the *Länder* share authority in matters regarding the *Polytechnische Schule* and the dual system (Art. 14 para. 3 B-VG).

Post-Secondary Non-Tertiary Education

Post-secondary non-tertiary education encompasses qualifications that are considered to be beyond secondary education, but are not included in the tertiary sector. These courses include Schools of Nursing, certain Continuing Education Courses at universities, universities of Applied Sciences, and University Colleges of Teacher Education. It corresponds to the ISCED level 4. According to Art. 14 para. 1 B-VG, all matters concerning universities and other institutions of tertiary education (for example, *Fachhochschulen*) are competence of the Federation in legislation and execution.

Short-Cycle Tertiary Education

Short-cycle tertiary education covers all post-secondary qualifications that teach graduates professional knowledge, skills and competences typically in a practice-oriented way, focusing on specific occupations. It includes Colleges for Higher Vocational Education (BHS) from the 4th Grade, Schools for People in Employment, Add-on Courses (*Aufbaulehrgänge*), Post-secondary VET Courses, Industrial Master College, Building Craftsperson, and Master Craftsperson School. It corresponds to ISCED level 5.

Tertiary Level Education

After having completed a general or vocational education pupils are allowed to study at a university, a university of applied sciences, or a university college of teacher education. All institutions of tertiary education are competence of the federation both in legislation as in execution. Besides some private universities, which play no significant role, universities are also maintained by the Federation. The *Länder* may influence the tertiary level only by maintaining *Fachhochschulen*, which are also subject of federal legislation and administration. The tertiary level encompasses Bachelor's, Master's, or Doctoral educational levels or equivalents. These are the highest attainable levels of formal education and correspond with ISCED levels 6–8 (6: Bachelor's or equivalent; 7: Master's or equivalent; 8: Doctoral or equivalent.)

FUNDING RESPONSIBILITIES[6]

In the case of public compulsory schools (primary level and lower secondary level), regions (*Länder*), municipalities, or associations of municipal corporations are obliged to maintain school buildings and to finance their own equipment. For general compulsory schools, these bodies are usually municipalities or associations of municipal corporations, whereas, the *Länder* hold these responsibilities for vocational schools.

School maintenance and financing (*Schulträgerschaft*) includes the establishment of a school, the maintenance of the building, responsibility for operating costs, the acquisition of equipment and teaching materials, provision for the school doctor, and the appointment of the necessary support staff (cleaners, caretakers, etc.). The provision of teachers in compulsory schools, however, is always the responsibility of the *Länder*. Teachers at public compulsory schools are therefore employed and paid by the *Länder*. However, the federal government reimburses the costs incurred by the *Länder* due to the system of equitable adjustment of revenues and expenditure between the territorial authorities in Austria, according to federal regulations.

The costs of equipping and maintaining vocational schools, specialist schools, and colleges for agriculture and forestry are borne by the *Länder*. The costs for the teaching staff at these schools, however, are divided between the federal government and the individual *Länder*.

Public compulsory schools are not allowed to charge school fees and even travel to and from school by public transport is free of charge. School books are provided by the public sector and become the property of the pupils. Over the last few years, a contribution of 10% has been introduced for both free transport for pupils as well as for schoolbooks. Transport costs are paid from a fund which is financed by employers' and employees' social security contributions and which is administered by the Federal Ministry for Social Security and Generations.

The federal government bears all costs, including teachers' costs, for those medium-level and higher-level schools (upper secondary level) which are established and maintained by the federal government. In this case too, the teachers' employment contracts are not made with the school; the teachers are employed by

[6] See also Juranek, 1999, p. 472.

TABLE 3.1. 2012–2013: Public Education Expenditures by ISCED 2011: Fields of Education and regional administrative bodies 2012 to 2013 (in mil. Euro)

	ISCED 2011 Level 0	ISCED 2011 Level 1	ISCED 2011 Level 2	ISCED 2011 Level 3	ISCED 2011 Level 4	ISCED 2011 Level 5	ISCED 2011 Level 6/7/8	
Year	**Elementary Sector**	**Primary Sector Grade 1–4**	**Secondary Sector I Grade 5–8**	**Secondary Sector II Grade 9 And Above**	**Post-Secondary Sector (Non-Tertiary)**	**Tertiary Sector (Non-University)**	**Tertiary Sector (University)**	**Public Education Expenditures Overall**
Federation Including Other Public Corporations								
2012	8.6	274.4	1,238.6	2,373.0	32.8	927.2	4,711.7	9,568.3
2013	5.8	310.2	1,281.0	2,436.5	19.3	873.8	4,757.1	9,683.8
Länderr Including Vienna								
2012	788.7	1,904.9	2,057.8	878.4	39.5	38.5	116.8	5,824.7
2013	853.6	2,031.6	2,134.7	888.5	38.6	42.1	113.8	6,103.0
Municipalities Including Municipalities Assoociations								
2012	873.7	525.9	539.3	110.7	—	2.4	19.4	2,070.5
2013	907.1	587.3	568.8	94.2	—	4.4	19.1	2,180.9
Overall								
2012	1,670.0	2,705.2	3,835.7	3,362.2	74.3	968.1	4,847.9	17,463.5
2013	1,766.4	2,929.2	3,984.5	3,419.2	57.9	920.3	4,890.0	47,967.6

TABLE 3.2. Public Education Expenditure 2014: Regional Differentiation And Educational Institutions, In Mil. Euro

Federation, Länder and Municipalities	Overall	Daycare Centers	Schools of General Education	AHS	Vocational Schools	BMS BHS	Teacher Training Colleges	Colleges	Universi-ties	Government Department, Administration
					Total Expenditure					
Public Sector	18,168.84	2,224.56	5,305.61	1,747.03	572.49	2,202.12	221.41	338.93	3,885.32	1,671.37
Federation (incl. universities)	9,518.29	—	54.64	1,733.03	7.12	1,840.74	221.03	255.40	3,868.58	1,537.75
Länder	4,442.31	391.90	3,108.24	3.10	446.13	338.68	0.38	79.92	16.73	57.22
Burgenland	146.35	6.26	120.76	—	11.50	4.26	0.32	2.90	—	0.34
Carinthia	414.42	39.29	264.77	—	42.44	49.22	—	10.98	0.36	7.36
Lower Austria	1,085.05	177.07	716.00	—	78.95	88.70	—	4.69	10.42	9.22
Upper Austria	1,013.42	89.30	689.64	1.16	112.25	77.81	0.06	24.74	3.58	14.88
Salzburg	345.62	18.66	248.85	0.03	41.42	19.71	—	4.92	2.37	9.66
Styria	698.15	34.98	508.17	—	73.90	64.29	—	15.84	—	0.96
Tyrol	471.16	12.63	351.04	1.80	57.50	26.31	—	12.15	—	9.73
Vorarlberg	268.15	13.71	209.01	0.12	28.16	8.38	—	3.70	—	5.07
Municipalities	2,535.53	1,159.98	1,253.53	10.89	41.36	8.47	0.00	—	—	61.30
Burgenland	116.77	65.94	46.46	0.01	4.16	0.09	—	—	—	0.11
Carinthia	176.83	72.43	92.13	4.33	0.01	0.92	—	—	—	7.01
Lower Austria	579.30	231.09	320.57	2.50	15.30	2.46	—	—	—	7.37
Upper Austria	544.67	268.79	243.98	0.56	14.50	0.78	—	—	—	16.07
Salzburg	211.75	104.86	100.23	0.19	1.60	1.19	0.00	—	—	3.69
Styria	468.75	212.53	236.83	0.25	3.88	1.25	—	—	—	14.01
Tyrol	283.41	130.94	138.91	3.05	1.86	0.93	—	—	—	7.71
Vorarlberg	154.06	73.40	74.41	0.00	0.07	0.84	—	—	—	5.32
Vienna (Land and municipality	1,672.71	672.68	889.21	—	77.89	14.23	—	3.61	—	15.10

(continues)

TABLE 3.2. Continued

Federation, Länder and Municipalities	Overall	Daycare Centers	Schools of General Education	AHS	Vocational Schools	BMS BHS	Teacher Training Colleges	Colleges	Universi-ties	Government Department, Administration
					Personnel Expenditure					
Public Sector	11,227.82	1,097.54	3,948.55	1,400.69	378.75	1,728.61	113.97	2.35	2,347.44	209.93
Federation (incl. universities)	5,541.00	—	0.01	1,399.75	0.00	1,495.99	113.97	—	2,347.44	183.84
Länder	3,751.02	168.91	3,042.38	—	314.88	219.50	—	2.35	—	3.00
Burgenland	129.18	0.12	117.79	—	8.03	3.24	—	—	—	—
Carinthia	311.65	—	254.56	—	26.54	29.73	—	0.82	—	—
Lower Austria	983.68	168.15	703.22	—	56.80	53.84	—	—	—	1.67
Upper Austria	828.95	0.01	681.52	—	85.79	61.63	—	—	—	—
Salzburg	279.53	0.21	244.74	—	24.96	9.62	—	—	—	—
Styria	603.67	0.43	504.94	—	54.07	44.18	—	—	—	0.05
Tyrol	381.26	—	329.59	—	37.11	13.03	—	1.52	—	—
Vorarlberg	233.11	—	206.02	—	21.58	4.23	—	—	—	1.28
Municipalities	944.02	660.60	264.27	0.94	4.58	1.88	—	—	—	11.76
Burgenland	59.26	45.92	13.15	—	0.18	—	—	—	—	0.01
Carinthia	71.08	47.46	23.07	—	—	—	—	—	—	0.56
Lower Austria	184.25	118.87	63.33	0.44	0.15	0.73	—	—	—	0.73
Upper Austria	206.94	141.61	55.65	0.05	2.46	0.19	—	—	—	6.98
Salzburg	93.92	68.14	24.35	—	—	—	—	—	—	1.44
Styria	153.40	109.49	42.50	0.03	—	0.15	—	—	—	1.23
Tyrol	108.76	78.41	27.07	0.42	1.78	0.79	—	—	—	0.29
Vorarlberg	66.40	50.70	15.15	—	—	0.03	—	—	—	0.53
Vienna (Land and municipality)	991.78	268.02	641.89	—	59.29	11.24	—	—	—	11.33

the federal government. And as with compulsory schooling, students are exempt from school fees, enjoy free transport, and are provided with school books.

Schools in Austria receive overall budgets as well as a budget guarantee over 3–4 years. However, the amount of the funds which they manage themselves is by comparison relatively small. There are, however, models to increase financial autonomy, some of them are already in use. For example, under certain conditions which are laid out in schooling laws, schools may lease rooms or parts of the property (e.g. the gymnasium or sports ground) to third parties as a way of raising extra funds. They may spend the income at their discretion under the condition that the money is used for school purposes. The same applies to external resources collected at the school by means of sponsorship or advertising activities. In addition, since 1998, so-called institutions with partial legal capacity may be established in schools maintained by the federal government, which are authorized to carry out legal operations as listed under legislation.

In 2013, the overall school system expenses amounted to nearly 18 Bill. Euros (exactly 17.967,6 Mio €) according to Statistics Austria.[7] The Federation covered 9.683,8 Mio €, the *Länder* including Vienna, which is both Land as well as municipality, 6.103,0 Mio € and the municipalities 2.180,9 Mio €.

Tables 3.1 and 3.2 show the expenditure in Austria's educational system at all levels of government and levels of education:

INTERGOVERNMENTAL RELATIONS AND ADMINISTRATIVE STRUCTURES[8]

Federal Level

Concerning matters administrated by the Federation, the Federal Minister of Education is the supreme executive authority. The Federal Minister for Education is the political head of the Ministry of Education and Women's Affairs, which is responsible for drafts of legislation and execution of all matters pertaining to compulsory education, teaching and curricula, private schools, the structural set-up of the educational authorities, and thus of the entire school inspectorate. Furthermore, the Ministry is competent for the system of higher-level secondary general education (age 10–18, grades 5–12) and for the entire system of intermediate and higher level technical and vocational education (age 15–19; grades 9–13). This responsibility includes matters pertaining to the service code and staff representation for teachers at all of these institutions. The Ministry is also responsible for teacher education/training and in-service training establishments.

The federation's responsibility for framework legislation and the province's responsibility for implementing and executing legislation includes the external organization of public compulsory schools. External organization contains mat-

[7] See Statistik Austria, 2015, http://www.statistik.at/web_de/statistiken/menschen_und_gesellschaft/bildung_und_kultur/formales_bildungswesen/bildungsausgaben/index.html.

[8] See also Juranek, 1999, p. 508.

ters such as the structure, organizational forms, establishment, maintenance and closing, the setting of the number of pupils per class, and the regulation of teaching time (Art. 14 para. 3 B-VG).

Federal administration at the regional level is presently still provided by separate federal authorities, i.e. the so-called province school boards (*Landesschulräte*). In all of Austria's nine *Länder*, a province school board is installed, which is made up of a president (province governor), a collegiate board and an office. The boards issue ordinances and general instructions and have a wide-ranging say in hiring teachers and school heads at secondary intermediate and higher-level schools. This system will be replaced by the *Bildungsdirektion* in 2019.

Responsibilities at Regional Level

In accordance with the constitutional allocation of responsibilities in education, the provinces are responsible for school maintenance and for staffing matters in compulsory education, secondary intermediate schools for agriculture and forestry, and part-time compulsory vocational schools for agriculture and forestry (Art. 14 para. 3 B-VG und Art. 14a B-VG).

These tasks are carried out by the offices affiliated with the provincial governments. Normally, separate departments exist that operate under the province governor. Almost all matters pertaining to the maintenance of general compulsory schools (*Allgemein bildende Pflichtschulen*) with the exception of staffing, have been assigned by Land legislation to the municipalities. In fulfilling those duties, they are supported by the associated province. The provinces themselves are in charge of maintaining establishments of vocational compulsory schools (*Berufsbildende Pflichtschulen*) and schools of agriculture and forestry.

Tertiary education at public universities (*Universitäten*), universities of applied sciences (*Fachhochschulen*) and at private universities (*Privatuniversitäten*) are regulated by federal law, although all of these are organized as autonomous self-governing bodies (Art. 14 para. 1 B-VG).

Universities are subject to legal supervision by the Federal Minister of Science, Research and Economy. The Minister's supervision is complemented by additional legal supervision of university councils which also monitor financial management. There is no *Landër* competence in this area. Under the provisions of the Federal Ministries' Act (*Bundesministeriengesetz*), the Federal Ministry for Science, Research and Economy is responsible for matters concerning universities, universities of applied sciences, the student representative bodies, study grants and scholarships, the promotion of the construction of student hostels, and for the promotion of research at universities. The Federal Ministry of Science, Research and Economy's manages issues concerning science, research, and economy (which includes innovation and technology, external affairs and European integration, company policy, tourism as well as energy and mining issues).

The Universities Act 2002 (Universitätsgesetz, 2002) gave universities a new legal basis combing organizational and study law. The Act has transformed universities from federal institutions into legal persons under public law, removing them from the scope of federal administration (decentralization effort) and introducing full legal capacity (autonomy).

Universities of Applied Sciences Studies and Universities of applied sciences institutions are governed by federal law according to the Universities of Applied Sciences Studies Act (*Fachhochschul-Studiengesetz*, FHStG). Universities of Applied Sciences may be maintained by the federal government, other corporate bodies and by private legal entities. The Agency for Quality Assurance and Accreditation Austria (AQ Austria) is the central organization responsible for accreditation in the universities of applied sciences sector. It is responsible for accreditation and for developing quality assurance guidelines for this sector.

The administration of universities of applied sciences lies with the legal entities providing these study programs and has to be exercised in accordance with legal regulations and guidelines issued by the AQ Austria University Colleges of Teacher Education. University Colleges of Teacher Education may either be public establishments maintained by the federal government or private institutions.

The federal government maintains eight university colleges of teacher education plus the University College of Agrarian and Environmental Pedagogy; private organizations maintain five university colleges of teacher education.

PISA RESULTS AND OECD REPORTS

Key findings of the OECD PISA Reports 2012 and 2015[9] on Austria included:

- While Austria's mean performance in mathematics, reading and science in 2012 returned to the levels found in 2003 and 2006, it dropped down in 2015.
- Austria performs above the OECD average in mathematics (ranks 2015 between 14 and 22), below average in reading (ranks between 23 and 28), and around average in science (ranks between 18 and 24) among the 65 countries and economies that participated in PISA 2012.
- The 15-point increase in the gender gap concerning mathematics performance between 2003 and 2012 is the largest increase observed among all countries with data for both years.
- Austrian students are among those who enjoy mathematics the least, and girls tend to have particularly low levels of joy in learning mathematics and motivation to pursue the subject. This may be linked to practices that group students into different schools based on their ability, which may include gender-based biases.

[9] See for OECD, 2012, http://www.oecd.org/austria/PISA-2012-results-austria.pdf and for PiSA 2015 http://www.oecd.org/austria/pisa-2015-austria.

- In Austria, some 82% of students are satisfied with their school and more than three in four students (77%) find the conditions in their schools ideal, compared to the OECD average of 61% (2012).

In 2015 the OECD reported in respect of Austria: [10]

- Early childhood education in Austria was almost universal for 4–5 year-old children, but was still below the OECD average for the 2 and 3-year-olds. More than two out of three 3-year-olds (71%) were enrolled in an early childhood education programme, slightly below the OECD average of 74%.
- Some 90% of young adults (25–34 year-olds) have attained at least upper secondary education in Austria (the OECD average is 83%). The majority of students (70%) in Austria are enrolled in a vocational track at the upper secondary level (the OECD average is 46%).
- Tertiary attainment of young adults has steadily increased in Austria, from 31% in 2005 to 38% in 2014. Even though tertiary attainment rates are rising, they still remain slightly below the OECD average (32% in 2005 and 41% in 2014).
- Educational upward mobility remains remarkably rare. Only 21% of young adults in Austria have attained higher educational qualifications than their parents, one of the lowest rates of upward educational mobility across OECD countries.
- In Austria, 12.0% of 20–24 year-olds were NEET in 2014, well below the OECD average of 17.9%.
- Austria maintains a high level of expenditure per student at all levels in an education system characterized by public funding and fiscal federalism. Austria devoted a particularly large amount of funding to secondary students; its spending of USD 13.806 per student is among the highest across OECD countries.
- Austria has a rapidly aging teaching workforce. In recent years, it has seen a 19 percentage-point rise in the proportion of secondary teachers aged 50 or older, from 26% in 2005 to 45% in 2013.
- Austrian teachers have some of the highest statutory salaries, among the highest across OECD countries at all levels of education. In 2013, upper secondary teachers at the top of their salary scale, for example, were paid USD 74.195, well above the OECD average of USD 52.822.

Finally in 2016 the OECD stated that "the governance of school education in Austria is characterized by a complex distribution of responsibilities between the federal and the provincial levels based on a split between federal and provincial schools, a complex distribution of federal funding for teacher salaries of provin-

[10] See http://gpseducation.oecd.org/CountryProfile?primaryCountry=AUT&treshold=10&topic=EO.

cial schools, and limited school autonomy for their staff and finances" (Nusche, Radinger, Busemeyer, & Theisens, 2016, p. 13).[11] The present arrangements create structural challenges impeding on the capacity for efficient management of school resources. As clear lines of accountability and integrated monitoring systems are lacking, governance arrangements set incentives to misspend, obfuscate the flow of resources, and nourish a culture of mistrust.

The distribution of responsibilities leads to the establishment of inefficient parallel structures in personnel management (including provincial school boards and school departments of the provinces). Furthermore, the present distribution of responsibilities prevents a more integrated approach to the governance of the school system evident in the existence of multiple information systems (which hampers a comprehensive approach to monitoring the performance of the system), the lack of strategic planning resulting in inefficient organization small school networks, the lack of a comprehensive approach to controlling the supply and demand for teachers, and the lack of a comprehensive approach to human resource allocations (leading to a lack of administrative and pedagogical support staff).

At the lower secondary level, important steps have been undertaken to harmonize the regulatory regime with the New Secondary School reform, a reform of initial teacher education, and the introduction of a new teacher service code. However, besides changes in the political willingness of stakeholders, a full move to comprehensive schooling seems unlikely as long as the split between federal and provincial schools is maintained.

The OECD perspective comes from a very centralistic point of view. In principle, it is true that dual structure of federal school boards in the *Länder* and school departments in the *Landër* governments should be transformed into a unitary structure. This would, in the words of the OECD "eliminate inefficiencies in the current system and create the conditions for integrated and strategic policy making, especially at the lower secondary school level. It would thus also facilitate moving to a more comprehensive school system in the future" (Nusche et al., 2016, p. 14).

According to the results of the working group on reforms of the educational system, the new institutions are likely to have a hybrid character with shared responsibilities between the federal and the provincial levels. The new institutions replacing the provincial school boards and the school departments of the provincial governments should be responsible for recruiting and assigning all teachers to individual schools. The employment of other pedagogical support staff and possibly also of administrative support staff should also be transferred to the new institutions responsible for teacher recruitment. This would facilitate a broader view of the human resource needs in schools and help to harmonize and equalize levels of support staff in different schools. Schools should gradually receive more

[11] See http://www.oecd-ilibrary.org/docserver/download/9116061e.pdf?expires=1465823092&id=id&accname=guest&checksum=3AA18EDB62D5C41860219A628D54D0AA

autonomy in choosing their personnel, accompanied by effective accountability mechanisms, investments in school leadership capacity, and steps to increase school size.

In the opinion of the OECD "Austria should explore different ways to introduce more elaborate and needs-based formula funding which takes into account additional factors besides student enrolment to address inequities in a more targeted way and take steps to improve its accountability and controlling instruments. Both these measures would contribute to greater transparency of resource flows and help create greater levels of trust between different levels of government" (Nusche et al., 2016, p. 15).

RECENT REFORM PROJECT: EDUCATIONAL REFORM 2017

Austria's educational system is presently undergoing changes. With the end of 2015, the Federal Government presented the results of a working group on educational reform composed by representatives of the Federation and the *Länder*.

The proposed reforms intended to enhance the autonomy of schools, and to introduce the chance that they may function as a test-region of a comprehensive school system for secondary level. However, these regions may not include more than 15% of the population of one single *Länder*.

The 2017 education reform bill includes a special focus on the administrative structures of education and the consultation process of the draft lasted until the end of April 2017.

The draft intends to strengthen school autonomy by giving the school principals more flexibility in hiring teachers and to regulate the number of pupils educated in one class. Another important aspect of the reform is to introduce a model merging small schools into larger units, so-called school clusters, through maintaining the single locations in the various municipalities. Finally, it includes a model in which all pupils up to age 14 are tested in certain regions.

The aspects that deal with school administration combine the two pillars of federal and *Länder* administration in educational matters with the existing federal authority *Landesschulrat* and administration bodies of the *Länder* in a new authority called *Bildungsdirektion* (educational council) in each Land. It is a compromise formula to avoid the decision of transferring school administration either to the federal competences or transferring them into Land execution. The new authority should be a "common authority" of the federation and the *Länder* and should execute both federal legislation and land legislation—a hybrid concept that is completely new in Austria's constitutional system. Consequently the federal law on establishing the new educational councils needs the consent of all *Länder*.

Critics not only from the opposition parties in parliament, but also from the teachers' union and from parents' association fear that directors of schools and respective the head of the school clusters will receive more power and might make decisions regardless of objections coming from parents or teachers.

The *Länder* are criticizing the enormous complicated regulations concerning the new administrative authorities and the fact that the new authority is increasing the influence of the federal government in education matters. On the other side, opposition parties in parliament are criticizing that the *Länder* have still too much influence in Austria's educational system.

From the experts' point of view, the reform contains some important ideas, for example the school clusters or the strengthening school autonomy nevertheless on an administrative front, the project has failed to establish clear structures and will bring probably more centralization and more regulation in Austria's school system.

OUTLOOK

Recent debates about educational policy in Austria are the result of differing views on what has worked and not worked of the traditional education system. Proponents of the two-track secondary system, for example, defend it as performance-oriented and criticize the levelling of achievement or lowering of standards that the introduction of a single compulsory middle school would involve. On the other hand, opponents of the two-track system criticize its rigidity and inherent absence of equal opportunity. Consequently, such bipolar terms as performance and levelling, elite and mass education, and achievement and equal opportunity prevail in educational debates. Such language inhibits the possibility of compromise.

The 2017 school reform bill is still strongly contested. With the beginning of 2019, the new *Bildungsdirektion* will be established. It remains unclear if this administrative reform will last for a long period of time.

REFERENCES

Juranek, M. (1999). *Schulverfassung und Schulverwaltung in Österreich und Europa, Das österreichische Schulrecht* (vol. 1). Vienna, Austria: Verlag Österreich.

Kröll, T. (2012). Schulrecht. In E. Pürgy (Ed.), *Das Recht der Länder* (vol. II/1, pp. 677–794). Vienna: Jan Sramek Verlag.

Nusche, D., Radinger, T., Busemeyer, M., R., & Theisens, H. (2016). OECD *reviews of school resources: Austria*. Retrieved from http://www.oecd-ilibrary.org/education/oecd-reviews-of-school-resources-austria-2016_9789264256729-en;jsessionid=5nbil7kjnoqqt.x-oecd-live-03

OECD. (2012). *Results from PISA*. Retrieved from http://www.oecd.org/austria/PISA-2012-results-austria.pdf

Pelzelmayer, H. (n.d.). *Development of the Austrian school system*. Retrieved from http://www.oecd.org/edu/research/1818705.pdf

Statistik Austria. (2015). *Öffentliche Bildungsausgaben*. Retrieved from http://www.statistik.at/web_de/statistiken/menschen_und_gesellschaft/bildung_und_kultur/formales_bildungswesen/bildungsausgaben/index.html

CHAPTER 4

THE ORGANIZATION OF EDUCATION POLICIES:

A Mirror of Belgian Political History and Federalism

Peter Bursens, Petra Meier, and Peter Van Petegem

INTRODUCTION: EDUCATION POLICIES IN THE BELGIAN FEDERAL MODEL

Education policies have been a core feature of the Belgian federalization process. In large part, reforms to the education system drove that federalization process as in the case of the Flemish push to include Dutch as an official language (alongside French) in public schools and other matters of public administration. Demands from the Flemish part of the country to heighten the use of the Dutch language coincided with a Flemish autonomy movement to decide upon policies related to language themselves, instead of leaving such decisions to the central state, which had been dominated by French-speaking elite for decades after its foundation in 1830. Although the population in Flanders, including the capital city of Brussels, primarily spoke Dutch, the Belgian political system was, at the outset, entirely run

Federalism and Education: Ongoing Challenges and Policy Strategies in Ten Countries, pages 63–79.

by a French-speaking elite that dominated all political, financial and economic matters.

Initially, the Flemish movement was culturally oriented, striving for the recognition of Dutch. This led to a series of language laws regulating the use of Dutch in courts (1873), public administration (1878), the army (1887), but also public schools (1883) and the educational system in general, except for higher education (1895) (De Winter & Baudewyns, 2009; see also Witte, Creaybeckx, & Meynen, 2005). Flemish demands for autonomy were strengthened by the brave sacrifices Flemish soldiers made during WWI, but subsequently hampered by part of the Flemish movement's collaboration with the German occupation during WWII. The economic and industrial dominance of Flanders (the Dutch-speaking northern part of Belgium) from the 1960s onwards again fortified Flemish claims. These demands have dominated the political agenda ever since. The center-periphery cleavage constituted the start for the federalization of the country. Due to a growing deadlock between the French-speaking and now emancipating Flemish political elite and a request of the latter for the autonomous organization of several culture-related competencies, four state reforms (1970, 1980, 1988–89, 1992–93) transformed the Belgian unitary state into a federation, which were further fine-tuned in two more recent state reforms (2001–02, 2011–13). The underlying logic was (and still is) to organize separately what was difficult to run as a joint venture (Deschouwer, 2012).

After a long process, the third constitutional reform (1988–89) transferred competence for education to the sub-state level. However, before this policy, education had been one of the first competences to be split along linguistic lines, even before the first state reform (1970) laid the foundation for the current federal state architecture. In the heat of political turmoil over language, the national Ministry of Education split in 1965, resulting in two Ministers of Education (one for each language) until the regional parliamentary elections in 1995 led to the formation of sub-state governments comprising portfolios on education.

While education was an important issue in the negotiations on the organization and financing of the Belgian federation, it was also a politically salient topic for other reasons. The initial political struggle regarding education was part of the so-called church-state cleavage. This non-confessional religious divide has always been one of the three constituting factors of Belgian politics, together with the center-periphery and socio-economic cleavages. Belgium, and especially Flanders, has a strong catholic tradition, granting the Catholic Church an important stake in the organization of public life, including education (see, for instance, the history of the oldest university in Belgium, the Katholieke Universiteit Leuven). The foundation of the Belgian state in 1830 was—amongst other conflicts—characterized by a struggle between catholic and liberal forces over the separation of church and state. This struggle has long focused on the question of which actors should be entitled to organize education and to appoint teaching staff, to what extent religious matters were to be part of the school curriculum, and whether the state had to finance religious curricula.

The outcome of this struggle was the School Pact of 1958, which settled the main principles and still regulates the organization of education today, as it is integrated in the Constitution. Freedom in organizing education is a constitutional right (article 24 of the Belgian Constitution), which means that private actors are allowed to engage in offering education. The state must satisfy the demand for non-confessional education, and even more, it must organize non-confessional education. The state must also provide education to all, meaning that under a number of conditions, the state must subsidize other organizers of education, both local authorities and private (often catholic) initiatives. The law seeks to ensure that parents across the country must be able to opt for a school of their preference—either catholic or non-confessional—close to their home (Draelants, Dupriez, & Maroy, 2011).

Cuts in public spending in the 1980s put the School Pact in danger but also facilitated the transfer of education to the sub-state level with the third state reform in 1988–89. This constitutional reform marked the translation of core elements of the School Pact into constitutional provisions on education policy. While the church-state cleavage led to the development of two fully fledged school networks (*netten / réseaux)*, a catholic and a non-confessional one, the center-periphery cleavage led to a separation of each of these systems along linguistic lines. As we explain in the next section, the religious cleavage triggered some shared competencies between the federal and the sub-state, while the territorial cleavage inspired a centrifugal dynamic. The outcome of both is a complex system of education policies and underlying political structures bearing the traces of Belgian political history. Evolutions in education policies, such as strategies to cope with cultural diversity and to enhance upward social mobility take place in, and are partially shaped by, this unique constitutional set-up.

Intriguingly few scholars of federalism focus on education in Belgium (exceptions are De Rynck, 2005; De Rynck & Dezeure, 2006; Erk, 2003). Most of the current literature deals with the performance of the education system or approaches the issue sociologically, focusing on the socio-demographic background of pupils and how this relates to mechanisms of social exclusion. More recently, there has also been some work on the added value of bi- or multilingual education starting from a young age, which is a politically salient issue given the Flemish struggle to ensure education in Dutch (Van De Craen, 2014).

In the light of this rather scarce academic attention, this chapter unpacks today's organization of primary and secondary education in the Belgian federation, first focusing on two crucial issues of federalism defining the institutional context of education policies: competencies and financing. We then address quality assurance policies as part of the overall focus of the volume. The following section describes the division of competencies between the Belgian federation and the sub-state level in matters of primary and secondary education, including the institutions and processes in place to solve conflicts. This section also discusses how these traits relate to the underlying features of Belgium as a federal system, and whether and how federalization has brought divergent evolutions in education policies in the Flemish and French Communities. The subsequent section presents the financing model of primary and secondary education within the Belgian federation, set against some background information on the organization of fiscal federalism in Belgium. The last section addresses the topic of quality assurance of primary and secondary education within the Belgian federation, with a focus on the organization of competencies and the European context.

THE DISTRIBUTION OF COMPETENCES REGARDING PRIMARY AND SECONDARY EDUCATION

In Belgium, education is a Community-level competence. Three Communities in conjunction with three Regions comprise the Belgian federation's double sub-state level governmental organization (Deschouwer, 2012). This double sub-state architecture is the outcome of a compromise between opposite aspirations of the Flemish and French-speaking political elites regarding federalization in the 1960s. The Flemish, striving for the recognition and political adaption of the Dutch language, wanted a part of the territory to be governed in Dutch while the French-speaking branch argued for the free use of language by citizens (Van Dijck, 1996). The Flemish request came because French held a dominant position in state matters and the population in Brussels and surroundings were undergoing continued francization. Growing numbers of municipalities were switching from a Flemish to a bilingual status (De Winter & Baudewyns, 2009). The French-speaking elite, on the other hand, aspired to conduct more autonomous economic policies in their region, irrespective of cultural or language concerns. The final compromise, enshrined in the first state reform of 1970, was a double sub-state structure comprising Communities and Regions. This agreement laid the basis for the federal state architecture characterizing Belgium today. Regions are competent for territorially bound matters and, thus, the country is divided into three geographically confined entities: Flanders, Wallonia and the Capital Region of Brussels. Communities, on the contrary, oversee person related policies and for that purpose the population is divided into three groups: the Flemish Community, the French Community, and the—relatively small—German-speaking Community. Notwithstanding the person-related character, however, the Communities are confined to specific territories: the Flemish Community and the French Community respectively to Flanders and Wallonia, while the Capital Region of Brussels has a bilingual status, and the German-speaking Community is located within the Eastern Cantons of the Walloon Region along the border with Germany. Correspondingly, the Flemish Community organizes education in Flanders, the French Community in Wallonia, both in Brussels, and the German-speaking Community in the Eastern Cantons (for an extensive account on Regions and Communtities, see Deschouwer, 2012).

Education is a quasi-exclusive competence of the Communities, except for the determination of compulsory school age (6–18), minimum conditions to issue diplomas, and teachers' pensions. The latter falls under the remit of the federal state, still in charge of most of social security policies. Especially the French-speaking parties in Belgium are strongly in favor of keeping such competencies at the federal level in order to maintain a level of interpersonal solidarity across the country that they fear could be lost if social welfare provisions are transferred to the regional level. Even if transferred, however, the Regions rather than the Communities would likely obtain pensions given the complex double structure of the sub-state level and its financing. In short, while education is now mostly an exclusive competence of the Communities, there are still rules stipulated in the School Pact of 1958 and enshrined in the Constitution that restrict community power.

The quasi-exclusive character of education as a competence of the Communities must be seen in the light of the overall federalization of Belgium. As mentioned in the introduction, the Belgian federal system is characterized by a centrifugal dynamic in which competences have increasingly been pushed down to the sub-state level as a strategy to overcome deadlock at the central level. Federalism in Belgium is first and foremost based on the incapacity to cooperate, even though the argument of efficiency is also put forward, especially by some Flemish parties. As a result, shared competencies are reduced to a minimum. The Belgian federation is characterized by a high degree of policy autonomy at the state level with minimal and underutilized mechanisms for cooperation (Swenden & Jans, 2006). And in education policy specifically, no mechanisms for cooperation exist, meaning that if sub-state actors would wish to cooperate, they have to rely on general intergovernmental consultations and cooperation agreements. The obligation to establish such cooperation agreements was part of the political deal on the transfer of competencies. However, to date, the Communities do not formally cooperate in matters of education (EU policy-coordination being the exception, see Beyers & Bursens, 2006).

This absence of any form of cooperation is well illustrated by the fact that the Communities do not engage in joint education in the Brussels Capital Region. Each Community organizes its own education and parents can opt for schools in their own language across the Brussels Capital Region. However, since education is unilingual, bilingual families (e.g. one parent is Flemish and the other French-speaking) must choose one single language for the education of their children. Theoretically, it is possible to swap systems. In practice, this is increasingly difficult given the priority access rules (such as language spoken at home, language of the former school, etc.). Such rules have been established to address social segregation and the growing number of pupils; however, having schools maintain a Flemish character also serves Flemish authorities because most of the population in Brussels with a lower level of education, lower socio-economic level, etc., speaks French rather than Dutch. In recent years, bilingual education (*immersion*) has emerged, but mainly on the initiative of the French Community. Initiatives in Flanders remain scarce and are still in the experimental phase, while bilingual education is booming in the French Community.

Outside of mechanisms for cooperation, the Belgian federation does create mechanisms to solve conflicts of interest or competence disputes. Regarding conflicts of competences, ex ante checks of new legal initiatives emanating from the federal or sub-state level are carried out by the Council of State (*Raad van State /Conseil d'Etat)*, while ex post reviews of competences are in the hands of the Constitutional Court. Political conflicts of interest, on the other hand, are dealt with by the Federal Consultation Committee (*Overlegcomité / Comité de concertation*) which is composed of the prime-ministers from the governments of the different state levels. Finally, a set of rules protect the language minorities both at the federal level and in the Capital Region of Brussels. Most of these also apply to matters of education but are not used in practice. The main reason for this minimal federal role is the highly exclusive character of education as a competence of the Communities. Education policies have been transferred so completely that no common dependence remains that could raise conflicts of interest across the Communities.

Traditionally three kinds of institutions organize education: the state, provinces, and other public bodies and private actors. Within each Community these different school networks organize education and create their own coordinating structures serving as an interface between the state and the schools.

After the transfer of education by the 1988–89 state reform, the organization, policies, and financial capacity regarding education started to diverge between the two main Communities. Although the principles of the School Pact were reiterated in the new constitutional provisions on education policy and thus were to be applied in all parts of the country, the Communities developed their own approach regardless (De Rynck, 2005; De Rynck & Dezeure, 2006; Erk, 2003). One of the triggers for divergence were the austerity policies by the federal government in the 1980s, as these caused a decrease in the federal grants to the Communities. These cuts made Flemish education relatively better off because the Flemish Community could transfer budget from the Region to the Community, which was not possible for the French Community (cf. next section). This resulted in a higher increase in the education budget in Flanders as compared to the French Community.

The 1990s brought the start of this differentiation between Communities (De Rynck, 2005). Essentially, the French Community continued the former Belgian approach while the Flemish Community implemented substantial reforms. Flanders created ARGO (*Autonome Raad voor het Gemeenschapsonderwijs*), an autonomous public agency outside the education ministry charged with the organization of public education (with a heavily politicized management securing the Christian-Democrats a say in the organization of public education). At the same time, a new organizational structure was set up, much more decentralized and with extensive participation of parents, civil society representatives and professionals (directors and teachers), with clear incentives to cooperate across systems. The decoupling between minister and administration and the creation of the agency offered an opportunity to reform quality control. A committee of experts (without unions or schools) inspired a decree that made the government responsible for performance targets, but granted autonomy to the schools to choose the way to reach those targets. The inspectorate was organized at the regional level with recruitment from Catholic and non-confessional backgrounds. All this was accepted by the powerful Catholic network of schools because of the large degree of autonomy it was granted in exchange.

The French Community, on the other hand, stayed much closer to the Belgian tradition: the dominant *Parti Socialiste* (PS) stuck firmly to its agenda: equality must be assured and can only be assured by a strong central government organizing and controlling education. No structural changes were made. Attempts to do so failed, largely because socialist trade unions and local politicians feared loss of power as education providers. All power remained in the hands of the centralized regional state administration, fully controlled by political parties (de facto the PS). Some authors link the differential developments in financial capacity and organization between communities to their diverging performances.

De Rynck (2005) attributes many differences in educational results to differences in adaptation between the two social-democrat parties. While the Flemish social-democratic party lost voters and had to accept the diversification of the educational landscape, the French-speaking PS became stronger and kept firmly to the state (i.e. the region) controlling education policies. This explanation aligns with the widely shared understanding that both social-democrat parties evolved differently, the Flemish developing into a more open and modern social-democrat version, the French-speaking PS remaining much more classically socialist. According to De Rynck (2005), the decision to establish ARGO represents a critical juncture made possible by the coordination between all major Flemish parties to install an 'enabling state,' by including external quality control in exchange for the reconfirmation of freedom of education. The French Community remained largely in favor of the 'controlling state.' In this respect, the federalization of education was highly interesting (especially for the PS) as it enabled the community government to continue its preferred national policies at the sub-state level. However, divergence in education policies should not be exaggerated as political actors were (and still are) limited by the legacy of the School Pact principles.

Other features, such as the disintegration of dual federalism, have also been put forward as explanatory factors for divergent policy outcomes in Belgium (Deschouwer, 2012; De Rynck & Dezeure, 2006). When neither problems nor solutions are clear-cut, competitive federalism becomes more likely, meaning that regions will use their autonomy to experiment in an uncoordinated way, which can often lead to further policy divergence (Dente, 1997, in Keating & McEwen, 2005). In this respect, regions may choose to race to the bottom, to compete in the single market, or to opt for a race to the top aiming at creating shared identification at the regional level through generous spending schemes and new education policies (Beyers & Bursens, 2013). This differential evolution matches the main findings of Europeanization research, arguing that similar EU pressures result in divergent outcomes at the member state level due to domestic differences (Börzel & Risse, 2000; Featherstone & Radaelli, 2003; Graziano & Vink, 2006). These national differences can be quite diverse, of course, and can include both preferences (party ideology) and hard institutions (financial capacity, administrative structures) in discussion regarding education policies.

FINANCING PRIMARY AND SECONDARY EDUCATION

While the Communities, like the Regions, maintain a high level of political autonomy, they have, contrary to the Regions, no fiscal power of their own. This is yet another crucial characteristic of the Belgian federation (Deschouwer, 2012; Swenden & Jans, 2006) and is highly relevant for matters of education, as education is the most important part of the Communities' budgets. Traditionally, both Communities and Regions depend primarily on federal grants based on financial transfers, enshrined in a special majority law of 1989. While the latest state reform to date (2011–2013) considerably increased the fiscal power—and financial responsibility—of the Regions, this was not the case for the Communities, which continue to rely on federal grants. The Communities' lack of fiscal power is due to the bilingual status of the Brussels Capital Region. It is impossible to grant Communities taxation powers in the Brussels Capital Region because the linguistic identity of its citizens is not established. This bilingual status goes back to 1963 when language censuses were abolished as the Flemish feared an increasing francization of especially Brussels and surroundings. Instead, a language border was drawn, later codified in the first State reform of 1970, which established that the Brussels Capital Region would remain bilingual.

One of the consequences of this decision is that the Communities solely rely on federal grants financed through personal income related taxes and value-added taxes (VAT). The share of the personal income tax each Community receives has been fixed in the special majority law of 1989 and is annually adapted to the index of consumer prices and to the growth of the GNP. It furthermore depends on the contribution of the Communities in the amount of personal income taxes raised. Given the fact that the number of Flemish and French-speaking citizens in the Brussels Capital Region is not officially established, a fixed repartition key has been set, with 20% of tax revenue for the Flemish and 80% for the French. This distribution considerably overestimates the real number of Flemish (Dutch-speaking) people in the Brussels Capital Region as compared to the number of votes cast for Flemish candidates at elections (the latter serving as an informal indicator for the number of Dutch–speaking Flemish in the Brussels Capital Region). The share of the federal grant based on VAT is indexed in a similar way as the share of person income related taxes and is based on the birth rate and the number of pupils (Decoster & Sas, 2012; Vanpraet, 2014).

Calculating a portion of the federal grant to the Communities based on VAT income is more favorable for the Flemish Community given the economic prosperity of Flanders. However, there is another more important factor as to why the Flemish Community is financially better off. The fact that the Flemish Community and Region were merged when the sub-state level was set in place has allowed for a smooth transfer of financial resources from territory bound matters (associated with the Region) to person related matters such as education (associated with the Community). A similar merging of institutions in the French Community and the Walloon Region is politically less feasible. The French-speaking citizens in Brussels make up more than 25% of the total French speakers, which makes it politically difficult for Wallonia to govern their cultural affairs. Furthermore, French culture in Belgium is traditionally associated with Brussels. While the Flemish government steadily invested resources in education beyond that of the federal grant spending levels attributed to the Communities, the French Community did not make that same investment. With growing numbers of school-aged children (many of whom require supplementary resources), an increasingly old and underfinanced infrastructure, and the need to adapt to a modern knowledge economy, resources for education have been a constant worry for French Community political elites. This concern was partly met during the fifth state reform (2002–2003) in which leaders allocated an extra grant to the Communities for education purposes (adjusted to income tax levels).

Overall, the Flemish Community stands well off while resources for education remain a permanent worry for the French Community. Nevertheless, both Flanders and the French Community adopted policies that make education (almost) free of charge until the end of secondary school. For Flanders, this means free education for primary schools, almost free education in secondary schools (only costs for trips and materials), and—importantly—no cost to register in a school. Also, higher education tuition fees are kept very low. The French Community's policy is one of 'free access to education,' which boils down to a similar system as the Flemish. Both Communities finance schools of the Catholic and the non-confessional systems equally, according to the constitutional provisions. However, both Communities have put in place differential financing based on objective needs of schools. For instance, in Flanders, public schools receive 4,5% more because they must provide educational programs to satisfy all religious and philosophical denominations. Similarly, schools organized by the municipalities receive 3,5% more to guarantee the freedom of school choice. Other differential financing occurs based on the social background of the pupils (e.g. language spoken at home, educational qualification of the mother) or the type of education (e.g. technical schools get more money for equipment than general schools).

All in all, the financing of education, as of the Communities in general, might be described as ad hoc, reflecting Belgium's process of incremental reform. While the constitutional provisions limit divergence between the Communities, some differences nevertheless occurred, due to differences in financial means, regional institutional environments, and policy preferences.

THE ORGANIZATION OF QUALITY ASSURANCE OF PRIMARY AND SECONDARY EDUCATION

As mentioned above, according to Article 24 of the Belgian Constitution, freedom of organization of education is a constitutional right. In the context of quality assurance, this means that schools are free to develop their own policy regarding education quality assurance within the boundaries set by the regulatory framework. To guarantee the overall quality of education in the country, the federal level sets the bar for the minimum conditions to issue a diploma. However, because no single institutional body controls the compliance of this provision, the de facto reality is that the Flemish, French and German-speaking Communities organize quality assurance separately. This practice stands for all other educational legislation without overarching mechanisms at the federal level. Already in 1991, the OECD published a review study on educational issues in Belgium, entitled '*Education in Belgium: The Diverging Paths.*' To understand the manifestation of this divergence, one must consider the development of curricula, the evaluation at system level, and external and internal evaluation of schools.

The Development of Curricula

In contrast to the residual competence regarding the minimum conditions to issue diplomas, the Communities (and entities within the Communities) also formally have full control over the curricula of primary and secondary schools. In the case of Flanders, this means that the Flemish Government imposes minimal standards of educational quality through the setting of attainment targets and developmental objectives. The educational umbrella organizations (or individual schools) translate these targets and objectives into school curricula that (ideally) attain the targets and objectives imposed by the government. A similar approach is used in the French Community. Since 1997, all schools have been required to pursue the same objectives, which means that students are expected to acquire the skills prescribed in governmental standards. In the same way as in Flanders, each education organizing authority and umbrella organization defines its own curricula in compliance with these governmental standards. While the content of the governmental targets and objectives is not necessarily the same in the two Communities, nor subject to common regulations, the approach and rationale is similar: the central level (i.e. the Community) creates a framework with minimum standards and within this framework the lower policy making levels (umbrella organizations, individual schools, and organizing authorities) are given the pedagogical freedom to develop school curricula.

System Level Evaluation

At the system level, the Communities collect evidence about the overall educational quality as a means for quality assurance. Both Flanders and the French Community have experience in participating in international comparative research programs based on student outcomes or on educational processes. Comparative data from these types of international surveys provide a framework that helps educational policy-makers gain insight in the strengths and weaknesses of their system. In the context of Belgium's divergent systems, however, an intra-country comparison is also relevant.

The International Association for the Evaluation of Educational Achievement (IEA) and the Organization for Economic Co-operation and Development (OECD) have a long tradition of organizing comparative studies based on the assessment of 8 or 15-year old pupils. Examples are the Progress in International Reading Literacy Study (PIRLS), Trends in International Mathematics and Science Study (TIMSS), the International Civic and Citizenship in Education Study (ICCS) organized by the IEA and Program for International Student Achievement (PISA), organized by the OECD.

Given the long common history of the educational system in Belgium, one would expect more or less similar results for the two Communities, but the opposite holds: substantial differences appear when student outcomes in both Communities are compared. Take, for instance, the triennial PISA-survey, involving 15-year old students, focusing on reading, mathematical, and scientific literacy. In 2012, Belgium as a country scored above the OECD average in mathematics. However, Danhier et al. (2014) took a closer look at the breakdown between Communities and found remarkable differences. Flemish pupils scored consistently above the OECD average, while the French-speaking score consistently below the average. Danhier et al. (2014) also report that in the French Community, 21.2% of all students did not reach a basic level of mathematical literacy, while in Flanders, the percentage of students failing to achieve the standard was only 15.4%. On the other side of the spectrum, 12% of the French Community students performed in the two highest levels, while in Flanders, 25.3% achieved those results. Such differentials make two systems among the most unequal within a single country.

TABLE 4.1. Breakdown of Belgian PISA Results.

	OECD average	Belgium	Flanders	French Community
Mathematics	494	515	531	493
Reading	496	509	518	497
Science	501	505	518	487

Source: Danhier, Jacobs, Devleeshouwer, Martin, & Alarcon, 2014.

Many researchers have analyzed possible causes of those differences of outcome. Previous research shows that differences in socio-economic or migration background are insufficient explanations. Hindriks and Verschelde (2011) argue that socio-economic differences or the number of migrants attending the schools cannot explain educational differences, as these pupils follow the trend of divergent scores between the two Communities. The researchers excluded autonomy in salary policies, teaching methods, textbook choice, grouping of pupils or pupil assessment, all referring to operational autonomy and operational empowerment of principals and teachers. Perelman, Pestiau, and Santin (2011), using another type of measurement, find that autonomy nor skills of teachers or gender ratio have significant effects.

Hindriks and Verschelde (2011) point to identity economics, i.e. whether individuals identify with the organization and with the goals of the organization, as the missing link. If parents and pupils identify with the school, they will perform better and drop out at a lower rate because students will strive towards meeting the goals of the organization. However, they don't provide hard evidence for this hypothesis. Other hypotheses proposed by Danhier et al. (2014) cite the better financial conditions of schools in Flanders, the different quality of school management, and different levels of autonomy in personnel and financial policies as the factors most responsible for differential outcomes. Yet another alternative hypothesis is that the difference in performance already existed before the federalization of education (Vandenberghe, 2011), but there is little empirical evidence to prove the latter either.

Next to the participation in international surveys, the Communities can also apply other approaches to get an indication of the educational quality at system level. In Flanders, the Ministry of Education organizes wide-scale tests in the framework of the National Assessment Program (NAP). The program aims to screen to what extent students obtain their prescribed attainment targets. The results of the NAP offer insight in the overall performance at system level. It also serves as a basis to critically question the feasibility and quality of the attainment targets and to gain insight in the way schools implement those targets.

External Evaluation of Schools

Belgium has a long tradition of controlling the quality of education by the so-called Inspectorate, which serves as 'the eye and the ear' of the Minister of Education. For a long time, the work of the Inspectorate focused on monitoring the quality of the functioning of individual teachers. The teacher was seen as the main actor in the teaching and learning process and therefore needed to be controlled in order to guarantee a high quality of education. At the end of the 19th century, however, evidence was growing that a teacher cannot be seen apart from the system in which (s)he functions. In both Communities, the legislation changed and a similar shift took place in the focus of the Inspectorate's work. The overall aim remained the monitoring of educational quality, but instead of focusing on the individual teacher, a more holistic approach that targets the whole school, is now employed in both Communities.

In 1991, quite soon after federalization, the Flemish Community voted to implement a first important Decree regulating the focus and role of the Inspectorate. The Decree restricted the Inspectorate's control and created a new, separate body of pedagogical advisors responsible for supporting and guiding teachers and schools in their professional development process. The inspection no longer monitors the implementation of pedagogical projects, nor does it control the educational, artistic or counseling methods used at schools—responsibility for those decisions lies with each individual school. In contrast to the public character of the Inspectorate, the pedagogical advisors are part of the specific educational network of the school (e.g. the Catholic or municipal network). The legal inspection regulations regarding each school subject's 'religion' and 'non-denominational ethics' remained unchanged; they still are controlled by separate non-governmental inspection bodies affiliated with the corresponding ecclesiastical authorities or a specific Inspection Board in the case of ethics. In 2009, a new Decree assuring quality operation was adopted. It stipulates that the Inspectorate remains responsible for advising on the recognition of schools (which allows them to issue degrees), to carry out inspections of schools, and to carry out other tasks if asked directly by the Flemish Government.

The distribution of responsibilities and roles is somewhat different for the French Community. According to the Decree of 2007, Inspectors represent one entity responsible for evaluating and controlling the level of studies in schools. The Decree specifically tasks them with ensuring compliance with government curricula, ensuring that teaching materials and school equipment adequately meet educational needs, and ensuring consistency in teaching and assessment practices. Next, the Inspectorate is responsible for detecting possible segregation mechanisms in schools and supporting the removal of such mechanisms. Where needed, inspectors also must monitor compliance of neutrality. Furthermore, they may draft opinions and make proposals, on their own initiative or at the request of the Government, on all matters within their jurisdiction. As in Flanders, there are separate inspection bodies to monitor the quality of the religion classes of officially recognized religions.

The exact responsibilities of the Inspectorate in the French Community become clearer when compared to the legislation in the Flemish Community, for example, in relation to control of segregation mechanisms or regarding the issue of 'neutrality.' Differences in cultural traditions may play a role, as historically there is a majority of Catholic education in Flanders, while in French-speaking Belgium there is an extensive network of public education with a more secularized tradition.

While the level of exactness in laying out the Inspectorate's responsibilities is somewhat higher in the French Community compared to the Flemish Community, the opposite can be said about the procedures and protocols for school visits, with the Inspectorate in the French Community having greater autonomy. Further, the there is no protocol for school visits and the frequency of school evaluations is not specified. These procedures and protocols are described more precisely in the Flemish Community where different stakeholders demand a clear picture of exactly what the Inspectorate is and is not allowed to do. Each school must be inspected at least once in every ten years. Depending on the previous assessment of the Inspectorate, certain schools may be inspected more frequently than others. This practice means that there is a differentiated approach, not only in frequency, but also in the focus of school investigations.

A very important principle for the Flemish Inspectorate is the assurance of an equal treatment of all schools in tandem with a respect and consideration of the specificities of each school. The different foci of investigation are based on specific school profiles. One can conclude that it is a matter of balancing the guarantee of equal treatment for everyone while aiming to fairly represent the differences between schools in denomination, pedagogical approach, assessment policy, and more.

Internal Evaluation of Schools

Internal evaluation of schools refers to the process initiated and carried out by the schools themselves to evaluate their own quality. School self-evaluation is not obligatory in Flanders nor in the French Community (as it is in the German-speaking Community), but tends to occur informally through regular school processes.

In the Flemish Community, article 6 of the Decree on Quality Assurance (2008) stipulates that schools must examine and monitor their own quality in a systematic way. It is the freedom of the school to determine how this should happen. This means that schools must prove that they use procedures that allow them to monitor their quality. The Inspectorate monitors if schools have a system that satisfactorily fulfills this requirement. A review team from the OECD (2011) identified two emerging trends influencing the school self-evaluation procedures in Flanders: an emphasis on policy making capacities (the extent to which schools enact reforms to improve educational quality (Van Petegem & Vanhoof, 2009)) and on collegial visits (schools visiting and peer reviewing each other).

In the French Community, school councils (including the school head and representatives from the organizing authority, staff, parents, students and the social, economic and cultural environment of the school) are responsible for the internal evaluation process, looking at the school's achievement in relation to the school's objectives. The focus of this internal evaluation is different from the focus of external evaluation: the former examines the implementation of the school project and the latter evaluates the subjects.

CONCLUSION

In the Belgian federation, education policies are almost exclusively in the hands of the three Communities. The gradual transfer from the national level to the Communities reflects the long journey of a unitary state moving towards a full-fledged federal political system. The resulting autonomy has presented the Communities with ample opportunities to develop organizational structures and policies as they see fit. At the same time, however, the Belgian constitution is characterized by several provisions and legacies of earlier compromises that shape the margins within which autonomous policies can be created and implemented. Combined, these two features explain why the Communities' educational organization and policies, despite differences in some areas, have, on balance, developed rather similarly.

Freedom of education is a central principle of the Belgian Constitution, a principle that has a thorough impact on the educational system, both before and after the federalization of the country. In addition, the Communities do not enjoy taxation competences, but are financed by grants from the federal level and are therefore limited in financial leverage with respect to education policies. Hence, even though educational policy became a realm almost exclusively of the Communities in Belgium more than 25 years ago, current policies maintain many similarities to pre-federalization policies.

With respect to finances, both Communities fund education through federal grants. This structure means that the two Communities are faced with similar budgetary opportunities and constraints (though not exactly equal because the institutional merger of Region and Community at the Flemish side gave the Flemish education sector somewhat more financial power). This has not, however, caused divergence in the basic principles that determine the financing of the different school networks. The policy space for the latter is close to zero as constitutional provisions clearly stipulate the freedom to organize education and the equal treatment of all those who provide education.

Overarching principles and responsibilities regarding quality assurance are also largely comparable across the Communities (e.g. a government-mandated curriculum with minimum attainment goals, an inspection as 'eye and ear' of the Minister of Education, and the role of internal evaluation of schools). At the same time, concrete regulations do differ (e.g. specification of the role of the inspection, the application of school self-evaluation). We observed that the list of responsibilities is longer in the French Community while the inspection procedures are more precisely described in the Flemish Community. These differences can partly be explained by a historical perspective given the majority of Catholic schools and the strong Catholic educational network in the Flemish Community—which highly stresses the importance of free initiative of education, and a more freemason and socialist dominance in the French Community with a cultural link to the more centralized system in France.

But despite overarching similarities, OECD studies report substantial differences in performance of secondary school pupils between the two Communities. Authors disagree about what exactly causes this divergence, but some argue that the different organization of education, induced by the autonomy and the different party positions, is part of the explanation.

Overall, our analysis adds up to a rather messy picture. While education policies are almost exclusively in the hands of the Communities, a common historical legacy as well as certain constitutional stipulations prevent the Communities from drifting completely apart. Clear differences in terms of organization and performance co-exist with rather similar systems of quality assurance.

REFERENCES

Beyers, J., & Bursens, P. (2006). The European rescue of the federal state: How Europeanisation shapes the Belgian state. *West European Politics, 29*(5), 1057–1078.

Beyers J., & Bursens, P. (2013). How Europe shapes the nature of the Belgian Federation: Differentiated EU impact triggers both co-operation and decentralization. *Regional and Federal Studies, 23*(3), 271–291.

Börzel, T., & Risse, Th. (2000). When Europe hits home: Europeanization and domestic change. *European Integration online Papers (EIoP), 4*(15). Retrieved from http://dx.doi.org/10.2139/ssrn.302768

Danhier, J., Jacobs, D., Devleeshouwer, P., Martin, E., & Alarcon, A. (2014). *Naar kwaliteitsscholen voor iedereen? Analyse van de resultaten van het PISA 2012-onderzoek in Vlaanderen en in de Federatie Wallonië* [Towards quality schools for all? Analysis of the PISA2012-results in Flanders and the Walloon Federation]. Brussel, Belgium: Koning Boudewijnstichting.

Decoster, A., & Sas, W. (2012). *De nieuwe financieringswet: Anders, maar ook beter?* [The new financing law: Different, but also better?]. Leuven, Belgium: KULeuven.

De Rynck, S. (2005). Regional autonomy and education policy in Belgium. *Regional and Federal Studies, 15*(4), 485–500.

De Rynck, S., & Dezeure, K. (2006). Policy convergence and divergence in Belgium: Education and health care, *West European Politics, 29*(5), 1018–1033.

Deschouwer, K. (2012). *The politics of Belgium. Governing a divided society*. Basingstoke, UK: Palgrave.

De Winter, L., & Baudewyns, P. (2009). Belgium: Towards the breakdown of a nation-state in the heart of Europe? *Nationalism and Ethnic Politics, 15*(1), 280–304.

Draelants, H., Dupriez, V., & Maroy, Ch. (2011). *Le système scolaire* [The school system] CRISP dossier nr. 76. Brussel, Belgium: CRISP.

Erk, J. (2003). 'Wat we zelf doen, doen we beter' [What we do ourselves, we do better]. Belgian Substate Nationalisms, Congruence and Public Policy. *Journal of Public Policy, 23*(2), 201–224.

Featherstone, K., & Radaelli, C. (2003). *The politics of Europeanization*. Oxford, UK: Oxford University Press.

Graziano, P., & Vink, M. (2006). *Europeanization: New research agendas*. Basingstoke, UK: Palgrave.

Hindriks, J., & Verschelde, M. (2011). Examining the educational gap between Flemish an French-speaking schools. In P. De Grauwe & P. Van Parijs (Eds.), *Educational divergence—Why do pupils better in Flanders than in the French-speaking community* (pp. 36–40). Brussels, Belgium: Re-Bel Initiative.

Keating, M., & McEwen, N. (2005). Introduction: Devolution and public policy in comparative perspective. *Regional and Federal Studies, 15*(4), 413–421.

Organisation for Economic Cooperation and Development (OECD). (2011). *School evaluation in the Flemish-speaking community of Belgium 2011.* OECD Reviews of Evaluation and Assessment in Education. Paris, France: OECD Publishing.

Perelman, S., Pestiau, P., & Santin, D. (2011). Why is the performance of Flemish and French speaking students so different? In P. De Grauwe & P. Van Parijs (Eds.), *Educational divergence—Why do pupils better in Flanders than in the French-speaking community* (pp. 27–35). Brussels, Belgium: Re-Bel Initiative.

Swenden, W., & Jans, M.T. (2006). Will it stay or will it go? Federalism and the Sustainability of Belgium. *West European Politics, 29*(5), 877–894.

Van De Craen, P. (2014). Le défi du multilinguisme dans l'enseignement: Enjeux, solutions et résultats [The challenge of multilingualism in teaching: issues, solutions and results]. In H. Bijleveld, F. Estienne, & F. V. Linden (Eds.) *Multilinguisme et orthophonie. Réflexions et pratiques à l'heure de l'Europe* [Multilingualism and orthophony. Current reflections and practices in Europe] (pp. 41–57). Issy-les-Moulineaux, France: Elsevier Masson.

Vandenberghe, V. (2011). Inter-regional educational discrepancies in Belgium. How combat them? In P. De Grauwe & P. Van Parijs (Eds.), *Educational divergence—Why do pupils better in Flanders than in the French-speaking community* (pp. 5–25). Brussels, Belgium: Re-Bel Initiative.

Van Dijck, R. (1996). Divided we stand.' Regionalism, federalism and minority rights in Belgium. *Res Publica, 38*(2), 429–446.

Van Petegem, P., & Vanhoof J. (2009). *Zelfevaluatie als motor voor schoolontwikkeling. Succesfactoren en valkuilen* [Self-evaluation as engine for school development. Success factors and stumbling blocks]. Mechelen, Belgium: Plantyn.

Vanpraet, J. (2014). De financieringswet na de zesde staatshervorming: Een overzicht van de Financieringstechnieken [The finance law after the sixth state reform: An overview of financing techniques]. In J. Velaers, J. Vanpraet, Y. Peeters, & W. Vandenbruwaene (Eds.), *De zesde staatshervorming: instellingen, bevoegdheden en middelen* [The sixth state reform: Institutions, competences and resources] (pp. 871–912). Antwerpen, Belgium, and Cambridge, UK: Intersentia.

Witte, E., Creaybeckx, J., & Meynen, A. (2005). *Politieke geschiedenis van België* [Political history of Belgium], Antwerpen, Belgium: Standaard Uitgeverij.

CHAPTER 5

FEDERALISM AND EDUCATION

The Canadian Case[1]

Jennifer Wallner

INTRODUCTION

Federal systems are centred on the principle of 'shared-rule' and 'self-rule,' where political and societal actors attempt to find a balance between the value and benefit of collective decision-making and central oversight, contrasted with the value and benefit of independent decision-making and subnational autonomy. Finding such a balance, however, can be a challenge in any policy arena; nowhere is this more apparent than in the field of education. In general, the power over schooling in federations is allocated to the subnational level. As documented in this volume, most federations have nevertheless instituted a variety of centralizing practices to afford the central government some influence over education policy in the name of increasing equity, efficiency, and effectiveness. In other words, the tendency

[1] This chapter was produced with the generous support of the SAIC, Government of Quebec and the Faculty of Social Sciences at the University of Ottawa. A version of a portion of this chapter has appeared in Idée Fédèrale's newsletter *The Federal News*, July 2015, Vol. 6. No. 2. The author wishes to acknowledge the excellent research assistance provided by Aaron Rudkin.

Federalism and Education: Ongoing Challenges and Policy Strategies in Ten Countries, pages 81–99.

has been to tip towards shared rule and compromise the principle of self-rule in the design and management of schooling systems.

Canada is a notable exception to this pattern. Provinces jealously guarded their autonomy in the field, rejecting any effort by the federal government to establish a central Ministry of Education. Instead, in 1967, they created their own Council of Ministers of Education, Canada to bring together the senior education officials from the 13 jurisdictions. What is more, without federal intervention, the provinces and territories devised their own system of Pan-Canadian assessment to collectively monitor academic standards and quality assurance, and took some tentative—albeit now largely abandoned—steps towards developing common curricular standards. Neither of these initiatives, however, compromised subnational autonomy in the field. Consequently, there is little evidence of a centralizing trend in the Canadian education system as political and societal actors have prioritized self-rule over shared-rule.

Interestingly, calls for centralization and the establishment of a federal department of education were long heard throughout Canada's history. The concern centred around the fear that since all provinces (and now the territories) could choose their own practices for schooling, Canadians were unlikely to have access to comparable systems of education and the system as a whole could suffer from a host of problems including inefficiencies, ineffectiveness, and inequalities. Two factors could further exacerbate the potential for major interprovincial and territorial differences in elementary and secondary schooling. The first are the various and significant asymmetries that set the provinces and territories apart from one another. Political trajectories and economic profiles are markedly different from coast to coast to coast, which could in turn lead to different educational practices. The second is Canada's diverse population with multiple nations working to coexist within a shared—but contested—political framework. Given the strong cultural component associated with schooling, such internal diversity could encourage alternative, if not contradictory, schooling practices. Thanks to these factors, Canada's 13 elementary and secondary schooling systems could be riddled with major differences undermining educational equality across the federation.

The evidence reveals, however, that this is not the case. Regarding equity, the substance of provincial and territorial education policies and practices are quite similar. What is more, the difference in educational investments between richer and poorer provinces is relatively narrow. Differences between the territories and the provinces, moreover, stem from the considerable cost differentials associated with delivering services in the north, which are in part addressed through supplemental unconditional funds from the federal government. Regarding efficiency, relative to other countries, Canada does not spend more on elementary and secondary education. Regarding effectiveness, Canada has strong high school completion rates and does extremely well in such performance-based accountability assessments such as the Program for International Student Assessment (PISA) run by the OECD. Most striking from Canada's results is the fact that inter-school and interprovincial equity in the results of such assessments have been appreciably high, outstripping results from other federations with greater central oversight. In other words, despite the absence of central control, Canada's education system is equitable, efficient, and effective.

These findings can lead us to conclude that there are considerable strengths to Canada's system of education. Two factors seem to underpin this success. Firstly, if we look *within* each province and territory, we uncover a high degree of centralization whereby local school boards and concomitantly individual schools exercise little autonomy free from their respective Ministry of Education. As a result, the overwhelming majority of schools within each subnational jurisdiction are tightly regulated with strong levers of oversight to confirm the implementation of common curriculum, comparable levels of funding, and the staffing of schools with certified and highly qualified instructors.[2] Furthermore, thanks to the centralization at the provincial level, if one province experiments with a new strategy, the other provinces can learn from the innovator and draw lessons to improve their own systems, implementing changes with relative ease. As such, it thus is better to describe Canada's schooling system as *deconcentrated* rather than decentralized. Secondly, Canada has a relatively decentralized fiscal architecture that features considerable taxation autonomy for the provinces and a robust system of *unconditional* equalization to redistribute funds throughout the federation. This fiscal arrangement helps to ameliorate the impact of economic inequalities among the jurisdictions without compromising autonomy through the imposition of central conditions and regulations to gain access to the funds, thus indirectly translating into greater inter-territorial equity in education inputs and outcomes.

Despite these strengths, Canada's education system nevertheless faces its own challenges. Fortunately, all of these can be addressed within its deconcentrated system and does not require the creation of a new bureaucracy housed in the federal capital. To start, as revealed in the PISA of 2012, interprovincial performance and equality across the Canadian federation slipped, specifically in mathematics. Secondly, the educational achievements of Aboriginal Canadians lag significantly behind that of non-Aboriginal Canadians. As such, these are problems that the jurisdictions face in common and need to be addressed. Finally, as this review demonstrates, the territories continue to lag behind their provincial counterparts. As the territories are now taking on greater responsibilities for education, additional supports are necessary to nurture policy capacity in the name of educational advancements. The important point in the context of this book, however, is that these weaknesses *do not* emerge from the deconcentrated institutional configuration of the education sector. In other words, instituting measures of centralization,

[2] In Canada, according to data released in 2012, only between five and six percent of children attend private elementary or secondary schools. See : *Statistics Canada, Summary Elementary and Secondary School Indictors for Canada, the Provinces and Territories, 2006–2007 to 2010–2011*, available at http://www.statcan.gc.ca/pub/81-595-m/81-595-m2013099-eng.pdf; and http://www.cbc.ca/news/canada/private-school-success-due-to-better-students-not-better-schools-statscan-says-1.3016123

akin to those deployed in other federations, would not addressed these challenges. What is more, this configuration does not intrinsically prevent the weaknesses from being addressed. Rather, provinces and territories must continue to build on the strengths of the deconcentrated system and work collaboratively to address both provincial performance in mathematics and these important challenges.

This chapter advances in five parts. It opens with a brief overview of the main features of the Canadian federation and the education sector. This is followed by a description of the provincial and territorial elementary and secondary education systems, documenting the degree of equality, efficiency and effectiveness today by detailing the substance of education policy itself in the 13 schooling systems. The third section then considers the educational investments offered by each province and territory, to determine the relative fiscal equality of education across Canada. The fourth section then considers the educational achievements realized by each system demonstrating the relative degree of inter-provincial-territorial comparability. The fifth section concludes this chapter with a discussion of the factors that have contributed to the success of schooling in Canada while also outlining the three challenges that need to be addressed.

FEATURES OF CANADA'S FEDERATION

The education sector of any federation can be influenced by such structural factors as geography, political institutions, and demographics. It is therefore important to acknowledge these features of Canada's federation prior to delving into the details of the country's education sector.

Geographically, Canada is the second largest country in the world, but it ranks just 36th in terms of population. Moreover, almost 90% of the population resides close to the 49th parallel bordering the US. The four largest provinces, both in terms of territory and population, are British Columbia, Alberta, Ontario, and Quebec (Statistics Canada, 2012b). In fact, 86% of Canadians reside in these four provinces. In the meantime, the three northern territories of the Yukon, the Northwest Territories, and Nunavut account for over a third of Canada's landmass, but are home to only 0.3% of the population. It is this fact that translates into Canada's skewed population density of 3.5 persons per square kilometer, one of the lowest population densities in the world. The issue for education is that such disparities in geography relative to population density intensify the costs associated with providing schooling to Canadians from coast to coast and could translate into significant regionally-based educational inequalities. Staffing schools in the northern territories and regions of each province, for instance, is a persistent challenge. Similarly, infrastructure costs for the construction and maintenance of schools are high across the country and building deficiencies such as mould are a common occurrence (see for example: CBC News, February 28, 2012; CBC News, April 19, 2012). Finding effective economies of scale to ensure high educational achievements has thus been a constant priority for provincial and territorial education policymakers.

Relative to most federations, Canada is classified as highly decentralized due to the fact that the provinces enjoy considerable autonomy free from federal oversight (Lecours, 2017; Watts, 2008). Furthermore, beginning in the 1990s, the territories started to gain province-like status and autonomy from the federal government through processes of formal and informal devolution (Government of Canada, 2015). Motivated in part to assure Canadian sovereignty in the Arctic, federal and territorial decision-makers realize that social and economic conditions of Northerners must be addressed to advance the sustainability of the region (Government of Canada, 2013). Clarified in further detail below, concrete steps include supplemental unconditional funds allocated to the territories to address the stark differences regarding the relative economies of scale between the southern and northern jurisdictions.

The subnational jurisdictions are responsible for the vast array of social services that together constitute the welfare state. In terms of the constitutional division of powers specific to education, provisions for schooling include the allocation of power to the provinces, with the stipulation that religious minority school boards established prior to Confederation in 1867, are protected by the Constitution. The responsibility for schooling Aboriginal peoples living on reserves, however, falls to the federal government. As of 1982, under the terms of Section 23 of the Charter of Rights and Freedoms, a provision was added protecting the educational rights of minority francophone and Anglophone communities across the country.

Drawing from its British heritage, Canada is also governed by a parliamentary system replicated at both the federal and subnational orders. The policy making process is therefore relatively centralized led by the political executive and supported by a strong professionalized public service (Radin & Boase, 2000; Wallner, 2012). Furthermore, in terms of intergovernmental relations, negotiations among the orders of government are dominated by political and bureaucratic executives and occur behind closed doors. The Council of Ministers of Education, Canada (CMEC) is used to facilitate interactions and collective initiatives among the senior education officials from across the country. Of all the intergovernmental tables in Canada, the CMEC is the most institutionalized and active facilitating the establishment of such things as a pan-Canadian assessment program.

The final, if arguably, the most significant factor that can shape an education system in a federation is demographics. Canada is a multinational state divided between the two official languages of English and French. Quebec maintains a majority Francophone population with smaller minority Anglophone communities throughout its territory, while the remaining nine provinces are majority Anglophone with minorities Francophone communities unevenly dispersed. In addition to linguistic dualism, Indigenous peoples constitute a third 'nation' within Canada, comprised of First Nations, Métis, and Inuit peoples. According to the National Household Survey, in 2011, 4.3% of the total Canadian population have an Aboriginal identity.[3] The largest numbers of Indigenous peoples live in Ontario, Manitoba, Saskatchewan, Alberta, and British Columbia. A recent study produced by the Assembly of First Nations (AFN, 2012) reported that in 2010, there were approximately 515 First Nations elementary and secondary schools for students living on-reserves, providing education for 64% of those students. The remaining First Nations students receive their education in provincial schools where the majority of the population is non-Aboriginal. Looking at the three northern territories, the majority of the population in the Yukon are non-Indigenous Canadians whereas the majority of the populations in the Northwest Territories and Nunavut—a public Aboriginal government—is majority Aboriginal.

With these details on the geography, political structures, and demographics of the Canadian federation in hand, the subsequent section begins the assessment of the degree of equity, efficiency, and effectiveness of the 13 schooling systems. It starts by examining the substance of provincial and territorial education policies.

THE SUBSTANCE OF PROVINCIAL AND TERRITORIAL EDUCATION SYSTEMS

To map the substance of education policies in the Canadian provinces and territories, the sector is broken down into a series of components: education governance, finance, curriculum and evaluation.[4] Each dimension opens with a brief discussion of key debates and policy options that decision-makers face before outlining the current practices that are in place. The conclusion that can be drawn from this overview is that the substance of provincial and territorial education policies share marked affinities and demonstrate minimal variation thus producing a relatively comparable schooling system.

Education Governance

Education governance includes the policies and practices that establish the managerial parameters and organizational attributes of the education sector, from the central authority that oversees the system to the management of individual schools at the local level. Looking at all the jurisdictions, a parallel administrative structure exists in each of the provinces and territories with an individual minister responsible for overseeing a department (or ministry) of education. These ministries of education are extremely powerful with such responsibilities as setting provincial and territorial curricula, hiring provincial superintendents to oversee local school boards, and overseeing the certification of teachers for all publicly funded schools. Teachers employed in the public system in all provinces and territories are required to have a university degree and complete a university level teacher-

[3] See https://www12.statcan.gc.ca/nhs-enm/2011/as-sa/99-012-x/99-012-x2011003_3-eng.cfm

[4] Components of this discussion are drawn from Wallner (2014). Due to space considerations, the policies pertaining to the teaching profession are excluded from this survey.

training program. Such practices help certify the standardization of schooling within each of the 13 jurisdictions.

In each province, intermediary bodies known as school boards or districts provide another layer of regional administration overseeing collections of individual schools. In Newfoundland, for example, there is one Anglophone school district that manages 261 schools and one Francophone school district that manages 5 schools. Responsibilities of the districts include such things as general policies on bussing, employment equity, professional development, and discipline. Mirroring its southern counterparts, the Northwest Territories also has 9 school boards (7 public, one Catholic and one Francophone); due to their smaller populations, however, Nunavut and the Yukon opted for a different administrative structure without intermediary school boards instead splitting the administrative responsibilities between the central government and the local schools themselves.

One key difference among the provinces and territories nevertheless persists: publicly funded religious school boards operating under the umbrella of the public system. Three provinces—Alberta, Saskatchewan, and Ontario—and the Northwest Territories have separate Catholic school boards that operate alongside the public school boards. In return for public funds, however, these boards must adhere to provincial standards in curriculum, assessment, and teacher credentialization. Therefore, while the inclusion of such boards may diminish religious equality across the country and the secular nature of society,[5] they do not directly contribute to or translate into inequalities in educational outcomes across the federation.

Education Finance

In education finance, the key question involves determining "the acquisition, allocation, and arrangement of funds to support formal educational institutions and programs" (Lawton, 1996, p. 1). Some systems, for example, may require individual citizens to cover the costs entirely with schools charging tuition for each student. Others may grant taxation powers to either individual schools or—perhaps more reasonably—to school boards in order to collect revenues from the local population to cover educational expenses. A third approach combines elements from the first, with local taxes offset by conditional grants from the central government thus instituting a shared-cost arrangement. The fourth and final option calls for the full centralization of education finance where one authority covers the total costs for public schooling. By exercising complete control over the purse strings, this model would maximize the authority of the central administrators.

Today, all of the provinces and territories deploy—either formally or informally—the fourth model of education finance. Some explicitly centralized education finance by officially terminating any historical legacy of local taxation autonomy. Others, like Saskatchewan and Manitoba, gradually introduced this

[5] For more on these debates, please see : Bramadat & Seljak 2009.

model by stealth: local taxation powers are left in place on paper, but it is the provincial government that sets the rate. In this arrangement, local boards thus do not enjoy the necessary autonomy to make independent tax choices. Consequently, the financial arrangements for the provincial and territorial schooling systems are highly centralized at the expense of local control.

Curriculum

There are different pedagogical outlooks that inform the organization of curriculum and high school. According to a *traditional* approach, courses are separated into individual silos with mandatory textbooks and instructional activities prescribed to teachers. Then, depending on identified abilities, students are streamed into programs that are largely isolated from one other with little opportunities to move between tracks. An alternative model, which rests on the principles of *progressive education*, calls for flexible content where subject matter is more integrated and children are given a greater opportunity to grow over time (Davies, 2002). In its ideal form high school, for example, would be organized in a composite fashion where students could move seamlessly between various options rather than the stratified tracks that are a hallmark of the traditional approach. A recent iteration of the progressive approach has coalesced into the idea of outcomes-based learning (OBL), where decision-makers specify particular learning targets and determine the desired goals and objectives of a particular course or program. It is then up to the educator herself to decide how the materials should be instructed.

For course content, all of the provinces and territories use the OBL approach such that curriculum developers specify the learning outcomes students are expected to have achieved by the end of a particular grade cycle. Looking at high school, 12 of the 13 jurisdictions deploy the composite model for high school, albeit with some challenges. After attempting to completely eliminate streams, students in Ontario for example, do choose between general or advanced course offerings and they can still get locked into a particular trajectory, thus limiting accesses to post-secondary schooling. Adhering completely to the composite model of secondary schooling thus remains an elusive goal in the education system and some research suggests this negatively impacts the transition from secondary to post-secondary institutions. Given that nine of the 10 provinces are similarly organized, such negative effects would be evenly experienced across the provinces. More pertinently, however, as outlined in further detail below, Canada has one of the highest post-secondary completion rates in the world, signaling that the transition between secondary and post-secondary schooling is being well managed.

The one exception to this arrangement is found in Quebec. That province has fashioned a unique hybrid model that integrates aspects of both the composite and traditional approach to secondary schooling. Where Grade 12 marks the end of high school in the rest of Canada, composite secondary schooling ends at Grade 11 in Quebec. At that time, students wishing to continue their schooling attend a

College d'enseignement general et professionnel (CEGEP) that is operated by the province. A fully funded provincial program, CEGEP bridges secondary schooling with the post-secondary world, preparing students for university, entry into a technical profession, or the broader workforce. While recent reports indicate that the system may be under threat due to financial pressures (Chouinard, 2015), other provinces and territories in the federation could learn from this model and adapt it to help manage the secondary to post-secondary transition for their own respective students. What is significant in the context here is that Quebec's system neither hinders the transfer of those students to other provinces to pursue, for example, post-secondary education, nor interfere with students from the rest of Canada from participating in Quebec's schooling. Students from other provinces simply need to complete four years of university-level education as opposed to three years for those educated within the CEGEP system. As such, educational equality and effectiveness is not undermined by this policy differences within the Canadian federation.

Evaluation

Evaluation can be subdivided into two elements: examinations and assessments. Examinations are a key means for instructors to determine whether or not individual students have learned the necessary content and skills to advance to the next level of schooling. Assessments, on the other hand, came on the Canadian policy agenda in the 1990s, aligned with the standards-based reform movement and performance-based accountability. While taking the form of a test, assessments attempt to provide decision-makers with information regarding student achievement that is publicly reported through an index, hopefully providing a gauge of some strengths and weaknesses of a specific education system of interest (Earl, 1995).

All of the provinces and territories, except PEI, have some form of mandatory high school exams. These examinations, however, vary considerably in terms of their scope and importance. For students in Alberta, 50% of their marks in the final year of high school are derived from provincially set exams. In British Columbia, 40% of students' marks in Grades 10, 11, and 12 are generated from results on provincial exams. In New Brunswick and Ontario, however, the only mandatory exam is a literacy assessment that all students must successfully complete in either Grade 9 or 10 respectively, to graduate from high school.

All of the provinces and territories, save Saskatchewan, have internal assessment regimes to track the progress of either samples of students or the entire population over time. Results from these assessments are either published on the provincial level or down to the individual schools. Independent think tanks, like the Fraser Institute, moreover, use the data to provide comparative report cards of schools within the provinces of Alberta, British Columbia, Ontario and Quebec.[6] In 2014, after moving back and forth on the issue, the Government of Saskatchewan decided to shelve its standardized testing program and re-work the regime in collaboration with the twenty-eight school boards and representatives from the First Nations and Métis communities (Stinson, 2014). In all jurisdictions, however, the stakes associated with the assessments are relatively low as results are either used to identify and ameliorate certain schools or constitute only a portion of individual students' grade advancement. There are neither major penalties, sanctions, and/or funding reductions for poor results, nor accolades and increased compensation for individual teachers or schools associated with positive results in provincial assessments (Klinger & Saab, 2012).

In addition to these internal assessment regimes, the Council for Ministers of Education Canada (CMEC) in collaboration with Statistics Canada runs the Pan-Canadian Assessment Program (PCAP) conducted in both official languages. Administered at regular intervals to students in the provinces who are 13 years of age at the beginning of the school year, in the domains of reading, mathematics, and science, PCAP is designed "to determine whether students across Canada reach similar levels of performance in these core disciplines . . . and to complement existing jurisdictional assessments with comparative Canada-wide data on the achievement levels attained by Grade 8-Secondary II students across the country" (CMEC, 2014, p. 1). Consequently, without direct federal intervention, the provinces have managed to formally cooperate and establish a program to provide ministers of education a tool to examine and compare the curriculum and achievements of other members of the federation in a relatively systematic fashion.

INVESTMENTS IN CANADIAN SCHOOLING

Before delving into the details, a few broad observations of education finance in Canada are necessary. First, it is important to note that according to the OECD, Canada is ranked 11th overall in terms of educational spending as a percentage of GDP, and thus only slightly above the OECD average (OECD, 2011). As such, despite the lack of central oversight, Canada appears to be relatively efficient in terms of educational expenditures. Second, the overwhelming majority of education finance comes from the provinces and territories. Looking at school board revenues, for example, Statistics Canada reported that in 2008, the federal government provided $113,545 total funds, municipal governments provided $192,312 in total whereas the provinces and territories provided $35,771,485 of funds for school boards (Statistics Canada, 2010). Consequently, these figures confirm the preeminence of the provinces and territories as the financial *and* administrative drivers of schooling in the Canadian federation.

[6] The right wing think tank, the Fraser Institute, uses provincial assessment data to provide a report on individual schools and then rank those schools with others. These reports also track schools' performance over five years. See https://www.fraserinstitute.org/school-performance

Two measures are used in this section to assess the comparability of educational investments across the 13 schooling systems: (1) per pupil spending; and (2) total public spending as a percentage of GDP. Data is drawn from recent reports produced by the Council of Ministers of Education Canada and Statistics Canada.

Expenditures per student typically include all direct operational and maintenance costs of running schools, such as school-based staff, materials, supplies, maintenance, and security. According to the most recent figures compiled by the CMEC, for all levels from pre-primary to upper secondary, the average per-pupil spending in Canada was $11,044 in 2008/2009 (Statistics Canada, 2014a, p. 48). What is more, spending across the provinces was relatively consistent, ranging from a high in Alberta of $12,751 to a low in Prince Edward Island of $9,817.[7] Looking between the provinces and territories in the federation, however, we find a major difference where per-pupil spending rises to $15,428 in Nunavut before jumping to $19,499 in Yukon and $22,784 in the Northwest Territories. These more substantial funding differences between the northern and southern jurisdictions are reflective of the marked differences in the costs associated with schooling in the remote territories.

Looking at total public spending as a percentage of GDP, Statistics Canada reports that Canada as a whole dedicated 6.7 percent of its GDP to all educational institutions (primary, secondary and tertiary) in 2009 (Statistics Canada, 2014a, p. 43). Once we break provincial and territorial spending down, a different pattern emerges from what was reported above. Provincial and territorial financial outlays to educational institutions as a percentage of GDP vary from highs in Nunavut (8.8%), Prince Edward Island (8.6%), Nova Scotia (8.3%) and Yukon (7.0%) to a low in Alberta (5.5%). In other words, the province that spends the most per-pupil does so despite allocating the least of its overall GDP to education. What this signals is that some provinces and territories in the federation are driven—either by choice or by circumstances—to dedicate a greater share of their GDP to schooling than what is required in other jurisdictions. Left unchecked, such fiscal imbalances could translate into regional inequalities across the federation. Fortunately, as detailed below, features of Canada's fiscal architecture helps to monitor and ameliorate these fiscal imbalances.

THE ACHIEVEMENTS OF CANADIAN SCHOOLING

Three indicators are used to measure Canadian educational achievements: (1) the number of adults with tertiary education; (2) the proportion of individuals with high school diplomas; and (3) the results of Canadian students on a leading international standardized assessment.

---

[7] As documented by Wallner (2012), the differences among the provinces in per pupil spending are less than that recorded in other federations with greater central oversight like Germany and the United States.

As of 2011, at 51 percent, Canada has the highest proportion of adults (aged 25 to 64) with tertiary education—or the equivalent of college and university completion—among OECD countries. What is more, between 2001 and 2011, the proportion of individuals who did not complete high school decreased from 18 percent to 11 percent. Breaking this measure down among the provinces and territories, troubling differences nevertheless appear in the proportion of the population with tertiary education with rates ranging from almost 65 percent in Ontario to less than 35 percent in Nunavut (Statistics Canada, 2014b, p. 26).

Focusing on adults aged 25 to 34, 92 percent of Canadians have at least a high school diploma with relatively small differences among the provinces. According to Statistics Canada, 2011 figures for all provinces ranged from 90 percent to 94 percent, indicating a high degree equality and parity across the jurisdictions. At 90 percent, the Yukon Territory also performed on par with the provinces. For the two other territories, however, the statistics are not as high. Dropping below the OECD average of 82 percent, Northwest Territories lags behind its other counterparts and, with less than 55 percent of the population aged 25 to 34 holding high school diplomas, the proportion of adults in Nunavut with upper secondary education is significantly below that of the rest of Canada (Statistics Canada, 2014b, p. 24).

One of the most prominent international assessments of school-aged children is the Programme for International Student Assessment (PISA) run by the Organisation for Economic Cooperation and Development (OECD). In place since 2000, the PISA assesses the knowledge of 15-year old students from participating countries every three years in reading, mathematics, and science on a rotating basis.[8] In the most recent round, students from sixty-five countries were assessed, including all 34 OECD countries. Whereas most countries only provide samples of between 5,000 and 10,000 students, Canada's sample totals 21,000 15 year-olds from approximately 900 schools over the 10 provinces. The large sample enables reliable data that is representative of each province and of both francophone and Anglophone school systems in certain regions.

In the first four rounds of the PISA, Canada performed extremely well. Canadian students were consistently ranked in the top ten of participating countries and all of the provinces performed better than the OECD's average score. Furthermore, according to the OECD, Canada demonstrates strong performance in terms of equity as socio-economic factors matter less than in many other countries. To quote from the 2006 PISA report: "Parents in [Canada] can be less concerned about school choice in order to enhance their children's performance, and can be confident of high and consistent performance standards across schools in the entire education system" (OECD, 2006, p. 9). In the 2012 round of PISA, the average score across participating countries was 494 and Canada's average was

[8] Unfortunately, students from the territories are not included in Canada's sample for either the PCAP program or the PISA program.

518. Once again, Canada also stood out in terms of its high equity in student performance, as reported by the CMEC (2013a). Among OECD countries, Canada was only outperformed by Korea, Japan, and Switzerland.

Looking over the nine-year time span, the performance of Canadian students in mathematics has nevertheless declined by 14 points, which is statistically significant (CMEC, 2013a, p. 30). "Scores decreased in all provinces except Quebec and Saskatchewan," reports the CMEC, "the largest declines occurred in Manitoba (36 points), Alberta (32 points), and Newfoundland and Labrador (26 points)" (CMEC, 2013a, p. 30). Building from this second finding, for the first time since the assessment was launched, in 2012, appreciable differences among the provinces have appeared. Students in Quebec performed significantly above the Canadian average, students in Ontario, Alberta, and British Columbia performed at the Canadian average, while the remaining provides were below the Canadian average (Richards, 2014). In the meantime, Prince Edward Island ended up with a score below that of the OECD's average. Fortunately, results from 2015, which focused on science, rebounded with the provinces gaining across the board and high results for the country as a whole (CMEC, 2016). Consequently, it seems that the decline is contained exclusively to mathematics.

OUTLOOK: EVALUATING CANADA'S DECONCENTRATED EDUCATION SYSTEM

The previous sections documented the ways in which the substance, financing, and outcomes of the 13 elementary and secondary systems in Canada's federation are relatively equal, efficient, and effective, despite the fact that the federal government plays virtually no role in the management and oversight of the schooling of Canadian children. Whereas other federations, such as Australia and the United States, have witnessed considerable trends that favour centralizing the education sector with the respective federal governments taking a greater role directing schooling policy, there has been no similar shift in Canada. How has Canada achieved this feat preserving the tradition of self-rule in the field?

Two factors underpin this result. Focusing exclusively for the moment on the provinces, through the mechanisms of informal learning and formal cooperation, policy makers adopted strategies from one another thus nurturing the policy comparability identified today (Wallner, 2014). Such information exchanges are facilitated by the fact that within each province the administration and financing of schooling is highly centralized. As such, when a premier, minister of education, or senior education policy maker wishes to institute a change inspired by one of the other jurisdictions, they are capable of doing so. Hence why it is more accurate to describe Canada's 13 schooling systems as deconcentrated rather than decentralized. Local school boards and individual schools exercise little autonomy from the ministries, in contrast to the system in place in such federations as the United States. Furthermore, unlike such countries as Australia where 34 percent of students attend non-government schools (Australian Bureau of Statistics, 2016; Perry, 2015), the overwhelming majority of Canadian students receive their schooling in public institutions, further reinforcing ministerial control over the direction and management of the system.

The value of such intergovernmental relations and administrative structures can be better appreciated through a comparison with the United States. There, interstate differences in the governance of American education begin at the peak of the hierarchy where some state boards of education are completely autonomous from the governors office and there is no office of education within the governor's executive. Furthermore, local boards and individual schools in the United States enjoy considerably greater autonomy than their Canadian counterparts as the tradition of local control is more highly valued, even to the point of being recognized by the Supreme Court. As a result, intergovernmental interactions in the US are fragmented and more difficult to coordinate thus impeding the transfer of information and the amelioration of interstate differences across the federation.

The second factor that underpins the success of Canada's deconcentrated system of education is the financial arrangements between the two orders of government, also known as the fiscal architecture of the federation. Robin Boadway writes that "The Canadian federal system represents the textbook best-practice system of fiscal federalism" (2014, p. 99). Thanks to its design, the provinces exercise considerable fiscal autonomy from the federal government, greater than that of subnational governments in most federations (Shah, 2014) The federal government also oversees a largely unconditional transfer program that moves funds to the provinces and territories, which further prioritizes the principle of self-rule in lieu of hierarchical accountability. These arrangements stand in stark contrast with the fiscal architecture of such federations as the United States where Washington earmarks virtually all of its transfers to the states. There are four major transfers to the provincial and territorial governments: the Canada Health Transfer (CHT), the Canadian Social Transfer (CST), the Territorial Formula Financing (TFF), and equalization. Arguably, the keystones of Canada's fiscal architecture are the TFF and equalization. The TFF "provides territorial governments with funding to support public services, in recognition of the higher cost of providing programs and services in the north." (Department of Finance, n.d.). Created in 1957, equalization is designed to enable 'less prosperous provincial governments to provide their residents with public services that are reasonably comparable to those in other provinces, at reasonably comparable levels of taxation' (Department of Finance, n.d.). Given structural economic inequalities among the provinces and territories, without such a redistributive fiscal architecture, it is highly unlikely that the 13 education systems would have achieved such a strong level of equitability, efficiency, or effectiveness.

These two features—namely education governance and the federal fiscal architecture—have enabled Canada's 13 schooling systems to capture one of the classic benefits of federalism; namely, the idea that each subnational unit can act as a laboratory of innovation as Justice Louis Brandeis famously described in the 1930s. The deconcentrated design, moreover, has even generated regional collaborations without requiring the engagement of all 13 systems. For example, in the late 1990s, the four provinces of Atlantic Canada set in motion a plan to harmonize curriculum in the region, which was achieved within 10 years.

Despite these strengths, however, schooling is not perfect in Canada. Three concerns are outlined here: Canada's achievements in mathematics, the schooling for Aboriginal peoples, and the quality of education in the territories. First, as revealed in the 2012 round of PISA, educational achievements in mathematics slipped and some inequalities were observed (Richards, 2014). While results from the most recent round of PISA are more positive, with Canada recording strong scores in science, the provinces should take a close look at their approaches to math. While the cause of these declines remains unclear, some observers noted that many of these provinces had made adjustments to their mathematics curriculum, which may have contributed to the slipping scores. Informed by the positive results in Quebec, moreover, additional analysis suggests that modifications must be made to teacher training to guarantee that instructors have higher and more specialized qualifications in math instruction. Given that such interprovincial learning was used to forge the pillars of the education system, and contributed to the strong results at the outset of the PISA assessment, policymakers are well positioned to make the necessary adjustments within the existing arrangements and work to continue improving schooling in mathematics for Canadians.

Schooling for Aboriginal peoples also continues to lag behind that of non-Aboriginal peoples. Although many factors contribute to this failure, including social and economic conditions as well as the legacy of the residential schools policy, one leading cause is the fractured, fragmented, and complicated governance and administrative arrangements that oversee this segment of the population to the point that some scholars have characterized it as a 'policy vacuum' (Mendelson, 2008). While the federal government is responsible for the education of First Nations peoples living on-reserves, the remaining Aboriginal populations living off reserves fall under the auspices of provincial and territorial regimes.

Some First Nations have secured self-governance agreements to take control of the schooling of their people, but these agreements vary dramatically from region to region and to date little research has been done to track the changes and their implications to further educational advancement.[9] This situation, moreover, for many First Nations communities dovetails with certain challenges faced in the three territories, including social and economic isolation. The Canadian federation is only beginning to take concrete steps to address this failing. For example, in its 2016 budget, the federal government allocated $300 million in additional funding for on-reserve school operation, adding about 20 percent to the existing arrangement (Canada, 2016). A recent report identified marked progress in such

[9] One effort to track the various agreements can be found online at https://www.aadnc-aandc.gc.ca/eng/1308840098023/1308840148639

provinces as British Columbia and Ontario where Aboriginal students achieve results much better than the national average. Additionally, within all provinces "specific band-operated on-reserve and provincial off-reserve schools and particular school districts have been diligently tackling Aboriginal education for decades, and are achieving impressive results that deserve to be known far more widely" (Richards & Scott, 2009, p. iv).

Finally, results continue to show that the territories lag behind their provincial counterparts. One positive sign, nevertheless is that these results have been improving as the territories have gained greater autonomy. Addressing this inequality is a key priority of the northern territories. A recent study confirmed that poor social conditions and limited educational opportunities correlate with poor educational outcomes in the north (Conference Board of Canada, 2012). Efforts to improve educational opportunities include the establishment of a Masters of Education program, delivered in Nunavut, such that potential teachers can now receive their training in the north, partnerships with other southern universities for on-line learning enabling "Northern students to remain in their Northern communities while they study, and after graduation when they join the workforce" (Conference Board of Canada, 2012, p. 32). Furthermore, the territories are also reforming their curricula to include specifically local topics and expand the programming for traditional ecological knowledge, indigenous knowledge, and traditional knowledge (Ayres, 2012). As the territories are increasingly taking control of their respective education systems, they are also engaging as full members in the CMEC. In principle, through such engagement, the territories should be able to build their own policy capacity while borrowing strength from the other jurisdictions thus leveraging the benefits of a deconcentrated system of education.

The important point in the context of this book is that none of these problems arise from Canada's deconcentrated education sector and all can be resolved within the confines of the arrangement. Due to the combination of centralized administrative structures at the subnational level and the largely unconditional system of fiscal redistribution, Canada has largely resolved the dilemma between shared rule and self-rule in schooling. A balance has been struck between over centralization in the hands of the federal government and the risk of regional ineffectiveness, inequality and inefficiency in Canadian education.

REFERENCES

Alphonso, C., & Grant,T. (2013). A tale of two schools: The correlation between income and education in Toronto. *Globe and Mail*. November 16. Retrieved on March 9, 2016, from http://www.theglobeandmail.com/news/national/time-to-lead/a-tale-of-two-schools-the-correlation-between-income-and-education/article15463950/?page=all

Assembly of First Nations. (2012). *A portrait of First Nations and education*. Report produced by the Chiefs Assembly on Education. Presented in Gatineau, Canada, October 1-3, 2012. Retrieved on February 21, 2016, from http://www.afn.ca/uploads/files/events/fact_sheet-ccoe-3.pdf

Australian Bureau of Statistics. (2016). Summary of findings: Commentary on student numbers. Retrieved on March 15, 2016, from http://www.abs.gov.au/ausstats/abs@.nsf/mf/4221.0

Ayres, M. (2012). *The impact of Inuit Qaujimajatuqangit on formal education in Nunavut.* Masters Thesis. Royal Roads University, Victoria, British Columbia, Canada.

Boadway, R. (2014). Canada. In A. Shah (Ed.), *Global Dialogue on Federalism Series: The Practice of Fiscal Federalism: Comparative Perspectives* (pp. 98–125). Montreal and Kingston, Canada: McGill-Queen's University Press.

Bramadat, P., & Seljak, D. (Eds.). (2009). *Religion and ethnicity in Canada.* Toronto, Canada: University of Toronto Press.

CBC News. (2012, February 28th). *Quebec woman says mould in classroom made her sick.* Retrieved on March 2, 2016, from http://www.cbc.ca/news/canada/ottawa/quebec-woman-says-mould-in-classroom-made-her-sick-1.1153737

CBC News. (2012, April 19th). *Walls crumble, mould infects First Nations School.* Retrieved on March 2, 2016, from http://www.cbc.ca/news/canada/thunder-bay/walls-crumble-mould-infects-first-nation-school-1.1283304

Chouinard, T. (2015, January 17th). Le quart des cégeps en déficit [A quarter of CEJEPs are in deficit]. *La Presse.* Retrieved on June 15, 2016, from http://www.lapresse.ca/actualites/education/201501/16/01-4836002-le-quart-des-cegeps-en-deficit.php

Conference Board of Canada. (2012). *Lessons learned: Achieving positive educational outcomes in northern communities.* Ottawa, Ontario: Conference Board of Canada.

Council of Ministers of Education Canada (CMEC). (2011). *PCAP-2010: Report on the Pan-Canadian assessment of mathematics, science, and reading.* Toronto, Canada: CMEC. Retrieved on April 29, 2014, from http://www.cmec.ca/Publications/Lists/Publications/Attachments/274/pcap2010.pdf

Council of Ministers of Education Canada (CMEC). (2013a). *Measuring up: Canadian results of the OECD PISA study.* Toronto, Canada: Council of Ministers of Education, Canada. Retrieved on June 16, 2016, from http://www.cmec.ca/Publications/Lists/Publications/Attachments/318/PISA2012_CanadianReport_EN_Web.pdf

Council of Ministers of Education Canada (CMEC). (2014). *PCAP 2013: Report on the Pan-Canadian assessment of science, reading, and mathematics.* Toronto, Canada: CMEC. Retrieved on June 8, 2015, from http://www.cmec.ca/Publications/Lists/Publications/Attachments/337/PCAP-2013-Public-Report-EN.pdf

Council of Ministers of Education Canada (CMEC). (2016). *Measuring up: Canadian results of the OECD PISA study: Performance of Canada's youth in science, reading, and mathematics.* Toronto, Canada: CMEC. Retrieved on March 1, 2017, from http://cmec.ca/Publications/Lists/Publications/Attachments/365/Book_PISA2015_EN_Dec5.pdf

Davies, S. (2002). The paradox of progressive education: A frame analysis. *Sociology of Education, 75,* 269–286.

Earl, L. (1996). Accountability and assessment: Ensuring quality in Ontario schools. In N. Watson, J. Scane, & G. Bedard (Eds.), *For the love of learning: Background papers for the Royal Commission on Learning* (vol. 2, pp. 410–425). Toronto, Canada: Royal Commission on Learning.

Government of Canada. (2013). *Canada's north: Overcoming the challenges to leverage the opportunities.* Retrieved on February 28, 2017, from http://www.horizons.gc.ca/eng/content/canada's-north-overcoming-challenges-leverage-opportunities

Government of Canada. (2015). *Improving and devolving northern governance*. Retrieved on June 16, 2016, from http://www.northernstrategy.gc.ca/gov/index-eng.asp

Government of Canada (2016). *Growing the middle class*. Ottawa, Ontario: Department of Finance Canada.

Klinger, D. A., & Saab, H. (2012). Educational leadership in the context of low stakes Accountability: The Canadian perspective. In L. Volante (Ed.), *School leadership in the context of standards-based reform: International perspectives* (pp. 69–93). Dordrecht, The Netherlands: Springer.

Lawton, S. (1996). *Financing Canadian education*. Toronto, Canada: Canadian Education Association.

Lecours, A. (2017). *Dynamic de-centralization in Canada, 1867–2010*. Unpublished Paper.

Mendelson, M. (2008) *Improving education on reserves: A First Nations Education Authority Act*. Ottawa, Ontario: Caledon Institute of Social Policy.

Ministry of Finance, Canada. (n.d.). *Federal transfers to provinces and territories*. Retrieved on March 7, 2016, from https://www.fin.gc.ca/access/fedprov-eng.asp

Organisation for Economic Co-operation and Development (OECD). (2006). *Education at a glance*. (p. 77). Paris, France: OECD. http://www.oecd.org/edu/skills-beyond-school/educationataglance2006-home.htm

Organisation for Economic Co-operation and Development (OECD). (2011). *Education at a Glance 2009*. Paris, France: OECD Publishing. Retrieved on March 14, 2016, from http://www.oecd.org/edu/skills-beyond-school/48630884.pdf

Perry, L. (2015, February 18). The Lessons from Canada: Why Australia should have fewer selective schools. *The Conversation*. Retrieved on March 7, 2016, from http://theconversation.com/the-lesson-from-canada-why-australia-should-have-fewer-selective-schools-35534

Radin, B., & Boase, J. (2000). Federalism, political structure, and public policy in the United States and Canada. *Journal of Comparative Policy Analysis: Research and Practice*, *2*, 65–89.

Richards, J. (2014). Warning signs for Canadian educators: The bad news in Canada's PISA Results' Part 1. Retrieved on June 9, 2015, from http://www.cdhowe.org/pdf/e-brief_176_P1.pdf

Richards, J., & Scott, M. (2009). *Aboriginal education strengthening the foundations*. CPRN Research Report. Ottawa, Canada. Retrieved from(http://citeseerx.ist.psu.edu/viewdoc/download?doi=10.1.1.514.7421&rep=rep1&type=pdf

Shah, A. (2014). ComparativecConclusions on fiscal federalism. In A. Shah (Ed.), *Global dialogue on Federalism series: The practice of fiscal federalism: Comparative perspectives* (pp. 370–394). Montreal and Kingston, Canada: McGill-Queen's University Press.

Statistics Canada. (2010). *School board revenue and expenditures, by province and territory. Summary table*. Ottawa, Canada: Ministry of Industry. Retrieved on June 16, 2016, from http://www.statcan.gc.ca/tables-tableaux/sum-som/l01/cst01/govt43a-eng.htm

Statistics Canada. (2012a). *Summary elementary and secondary school indictors for Canada, the Provinces and Territories, 2006-2007 to 2010-2011*. Retrieved on February 26, 2017, from http://www.statcan.gc.ca/pub/81-595-m/81-595-m2013099-eng.pdf

Statistics Canada. (2012b). *Annual demographic estimates: Canada, Provinces and Territories*. Ottawa, Canada: Minister of Industry. Retrieved on April 29, 2014, from http://www.statcan.gc.ca/pub/91-215-x/91-215-x2012000-eng.pdf

Statistics Canada. (2014a). *Education indicators in Canada: An international perspective*. Ottawa, Canada: Minister of Industry. Retrieved on April 29, 2014, from http://www.cmec.ca/Publications/Lists/Publications/Attachments/322/Education-Indicators-Canada-International-Perspective-2013.pdf

Statistics Canada. (2014b). *The educational attainment of Aboriginal peoples in Canada*. Retrieved on June 9, 2015, from http://www12.statcan.gc.ca/nhs-enm/2011/as-sa/99-012-x/99-012-x2011003_3-eng.cfm

Stinson, W. (2014). Government of Saskatchewan eliminates plan for standardized testing. *Global News*. Retrieved on June 9, 2015, from http://globalnews.ca/news/1266875/government-eliminates-standardized-testing/

Wallner, J. (2012). Political structures, social diversity and public policy: Comparing mandatory education in Canada and the United States. *Comparative Political Studies, 45*, 850–874.

Wallner, J. (2014). *Learning to school: Federalism and public schooling in Canada*. Toronto, Canada: University of Toronto Press.

Watts, R. (2008). *Comparing federal systems* (3rd ed.). Montreal and Kingston, Canada: McGill-Queen's University Press.

CHAPTER 6

EDUCATIONAL FEDERALISM IN GERMANY

Tensions Between the States' Autonomy and Cooperative Unitarization

Henrik Scheller

INTRODUCTION

Over the past decades, Germany's educational federalism has constantly been an object of controversial public debate. The controversy stems from natural tensions between the constitutionally guaranteed autonomy of local educational actors (schools, universities, parents, educational participants etc.) and the political will of the sixteen states (*Länder*) in educational matters. The *Länder* are sheltered by a so-called 'cultural sovereignty' (*Kulturhoheit*), which is one of the key characteristics of German federalism. Many professional concepts and instruments developed in the educational science discourse over the past 20 years have neglected this particular federal division of powers. The numerous interests as well as the strained national education budget create conflicts of objectives and allocation. The lines of conflict do not only exist between the jurisdictional levels of government, but also between state and non-state actors. In recent years, the

Federalism and Education: Ongoing Challenges and Policy Strategies in Ten Countries,
pages 101–130.

public and media perception of education as a key factor for social and economic development, especially in a resource-poor country such as the Federal Republic, has grown considerably. The growing number of corresponding controversies is shaping the public perception of Germany's educational federalism. Different surveys (Association for Canadian Studies, 2010; Bertelsmann Stiftung, 2009; Institut für Demoskopie Allensbach, 2012) show an overwhelming majority of the Germans rejecting "educational particularism" (Edelstein & Allmendinger, 2012, p. 18)—understood as strong disparities between the *Länder*'s education systems. The political potential behind such assessments becomes clear when contextualized by the system's scale: In 2014, about 17 million people made direct use of the approximately 976,000 institutions of the formal education sector in the Federal Republic. They were supported and trained by approximately 2.4 million people (Autorengruppe Bildungsberichterstattung, 2016).

However, the question arises whether Germany's federal structure is the primary reason for the deficits in its education system. Comparative politics analyses reveal that other factors, such as party differences about educational concepts, political institutions and veto players, political culture, the socioeconomic environment and the distribution of public finance, as well as the professional training of the pedagogical staff in individual branches of the education system all have a strong impact on educational outputs and outcomes (Busemeyer, 2015). In Germany these factors are, of course, at least (indirectly) determined by the structural diversity of the education systems of the sixteen federal states. But the dynamics of German educational federalism do not result solely from the back-and-forth balance between centralizing/unitarizing and decentralizing developments that can be common in federations (Benz 1985; Benz & Broschek, 2013; Benz, Detemple & Heinz 2015). Other driving forces are the massive expansion of education, especially since the end of the Second World War (Hadjar & Becker, 2006; Lörz & Schindler, 2011), as well as a slow but sustained change in the understanding and public perception of education over the last fifteen years. Since the PISA shock of 2001 showing disappointing performance, *Bund* and *Länder* implemented numerous reforms. Wilhelm von Humboldt's idea of a general humanistic education, which had been the dominating leitmotif for education in Germany for almost two hundred years (Humboldt, 1903), is being increasingly overlaid by an approach that promotes competences in the sense of individual employability and benefit maximization (Graßl, 2014; Neumann, 2014; Reinberg, 2001; Wößmann, 2011). In line with this change, the states, for example, pushed for the expansion and professionalization of early-childhood education, an increase of study places, the shortening of school-based training, as well as the streamlining and harmonization of curricula through a standardization of learning and assessment matters (Bundesministerium für Bildung und Forschung, 2007; Hepp 2011; Herzog 2013;). The federal government (*Bund*) provides financial support for many of these reforms.

With the transition from a teaching-oriented input perspective to an output- or outcome-oriented understanding of learning success, the promotion of learning competences takes more and more space within the education of individuals (Cortina et al., 1997). The demand for a broad imparting of general knowledge and professional content is therefore pushed into the background. Not only in schools, but also in universities, individual scientific subjects are being marginalized—whether by time and/or financial constraints or the focus of specific funding programs. The conceptual reorientation of the German education system has in many areas been accompanied by the simultaneous implementation of new public management concepts (Altrichter, 2007; Hildebrandt & Wolf, 2016; Kamm & Köller, 2010). This fundamental governance change goes along with a change in the mentality of the educational participants: since individual success is regarded as a criterion for social advancement and the associated economic success, claims against educational institutions to improve their teaching and research quality are increasing (Bude, 2011), even though as of yet, school and tuition fees could not be implemented across the country. By shortening school and training periods, the pressure on schools, colleges and universities is doubling—especially given an increasing tendency towards vocal student dissatisfaction.

The changes in Germany's educational federalism are aligned with changes in the constellation of actors over the last few years. Formerly sovereign tasks like the professional evaluation of study courses and pedagogical standards were transferred from the states' administrations to private actors like the newly created Accreditation Council (*Akkreditierungsrat*) as well as independent accreditation agencies. At the same time, the (university-based) educational sciences have been expanded by setting up new institutes or additional chairs. The network of educational stakeholders from the third sector (particularly foundations, associations, interest organizations etc.) has also grown steadily in recent years. Even though they do not hold formal veto-powers in the legislative process, they, nevertheless, publish expert reports and benchmarkings on current educational policies and finance their own programs and pilot projects. In doing so, they are lobbying both, *Bund* and *Länder*, although formal partnerships are unusual. Further, they are promoting the public discourse constantly. However, at the same time, the sequencing of educational reforms in Germany has become continuously shorter (Kaiser & Vogel, 2016; Münch, 2009; Wolf, 2006). Fundamental reforms are often modified shortly after coming into force. In some cases even the status quo ante—at least partially—was restored. In particular, reforms, which were implemented in the last few years with the intention to strengthen the autonomy of the *Länder* and individual educational institutions, have now been subject to broad political discussions (Immerfall, 2010; Münch, U., 2010; Welsh, 2014). The large number of reform activities lessens stability in the school environment—a prerequisite for the continuous and sustained learning processes of teachers and learners in all educational arrangements. Third sector initiatives in the field of education are above all, a response to a changed and still changing understanding of education, less to the specifics of German educational federalism, although in public debates it is blamed widely.

One of the main weaknesses of the German education system is the strong correlation between social origin and individual educational success (Bertelsmann Stiftung, 2014; Freitag & Schlicht, 2009: Organisation for Economic Co-operation and Development, OECD, 2016). Children from a socially disadvantaged environment, characterized by the social position of the parents as well as the school and urban catchment area, often show above-average deficits in their educational biography. They less frequently reach higher educational degrees, such as high school diploma or university degrees. Despite the many reform efforts undertaken since the release of the first PISA study, the successes in cutting these deficits has been limited (Hopf, 2003; Hoymann, 2005). The current challenges of German educational federalism clearly illustrate future needs for further action in this field: with the integration of around 1.1 million refugees from North Africa and the Middle East seeking protection in the Federal Republic in 2015 and 2016 alone, Germany's education and training system is facing one of its greatest challenges in recent years (KMK, 2016). The federal dimension of this migration movement becomes obvious with regard to the additional costs. *Bund* and *Länder* reached an initial compromise on a sharing arrangement between the jurisdictional layers of government only with great difficulties. A similar problem is limiting the implementation of the internationally binding UN Convention on the Rights of Persons with Disabilities from 2006 to 2008. *Länder* and municipalities are obliged to execute an inclusive education approach in childcare institutions and schools. However, the process has been sluggish so far (Klemm, 2015) since numerous *Länder* have not yet been able to reach an agreement with their municipalities to decide which level should bear the additional investment and personnel costs.

The differentiation of the sixteen education systems has caused the Länder, over the past decades, to be slow in adopting nationally and internationally defined standards and requirements. The original intention of having individual education systems in each federal state was not only to preserve cultural peculiarities of the regions, but also to ensure the best support for every individual. In addition, the constitutionally guaranteed room for maneuver in this field has always been used as an instrument for a political profiling of the parties (Benz, Detemple, & Heinz, 2015; Lanzendorf & Pasternack, 2008; Wolf, 2006). In the meantime, however, federal and institutional interfaces between the educational subsystems that are not compatible with each other carry the inherent danger of exacerbating the linkage between social origin and educational success. The heterogeneity of individual educational biographies and the mobility of the people have been increased in a way that obviously cannot be addressed by sixteen different education systems of the *Länder*, which formerly were aligned to a comparatively homogenous community of educational participants.

Keeping this in mind, this chapter briefly outlines the historical development of Germany's educational federalism since the founding of the Federal Republic. Subsequently, I will shed light on the constitutional distribution of power. The federalism reform I of 2006 represents a decisive road mark. Since it provided various changes in the distribution of competences between the federation and the states in the field of education, a before-and-after comparison should be carried out—even if single regulations have been already reversed. Subsequently, the constellation of actors, including the intergovernmental relations between *Bund* and *Länder*, is examined in greater detail. Section 5 is devoted to the funding responsibilities in German federalism. The cultural sovereignty of the *Länder* actually includes financing responsibilities for the corresponding policies. Nevertheless, the considerable increase in the national education budget over the last three decades is largely attributable to transfers of the *Bund*. In many areas, the *Länder* and municipalities benefit from various federal transfers and subsidies. The penultimate section sheds light on the problem of academic standards and quality assurance in the German education system. This example is particularly suited to discuss the thesis of my contribution, which underpins the fact that unitarization of the German federalism has been significantly promoted by a conceptually justified change in governance instruments: the results of monitorings, benchmarkings and peer reviews in all areas of the education system are now influencing the public perception. This encourages a political reform activism, which is often symbolic in nature. These developments reveal a second fundamental structural break (Lehmbruch, 1976), which roots back to two logics that are actually not compatible with one another: Reforms enforced by a growing number of comparative evaluation studies undermine the cultural sovereignty and the educational autonomy of the *Länder*. The development of pedagogical concepts within the educational science discourse, which is less oriented to the distribution of federal competences than to the individual, is promoting this trend. From a federal perspective, the actual stress situation is created by the institutional harmonization of standards and structures, undertaken in times of tight public budgets: such comprehensive governance reforms in an underfinanced system do not promote the acceptance and legitimacy of appropriate measures.

EVOLUTION OF THE FEDERAL AND EDUCATIONAL MODEL

The German educational federalism in its present form can be traced back to 1948: One year before the Federal Republic was founded, the Conference of the *Länder*'s Ministers of Culture was instituted. Up to now, roughly four development phases of German educational federalism can be identified (Anweiler et al., 1992; Hepp, 2011). The founding phase covers the years 1948 to 1964. A second phase was shaped by the student unrest in 1967/68, which was the starting point for fundamental reforms in the education system. In 1989, the Berlin Wall fell and the division of Europe came to an end. With the German reunification of 1990, Germany's educational federalism entered a third development phase. It lasted until 2001 and was mainly characterized by the transformation of the centralized education system of the GDR, which was federalized based on the model of the old Federal Republic. The release of the first PISA study at the end of 2001 was one of the most striking events in the history of German educational federalism. The public and media response to the report, with its comparatively bad results for the Federal Republic, was extraordinary. Shortly afterwards the term "PISA-Shock" was coined (Klieme, 2009; Kuhlmann, 2012). PISA thus was the starting point for a fourth phase, being defined by innumerable reforms by the federal and state governments in all areas of the education system, which continue today (Hepp, 2011; Münch, R., 2010; Scheller, 2010; Wolf, 2006). A further driver of these reform efforts was the so-called Bologna process, which was co-initiated by the Federal Minister of Education, Science, Research and Technology already two years in advance of the first PISA assessment study. This self-commitment aimed for a fundamental reorientation of the university system by 2010 through a declaration of the same name.

The first development phase of the German educational federalism—immediately after the end of the Second World War (1948–1964)—was characterized by a desire for rapid reconstruction of the destroyed infrastructure and the reeducation measures of the Allies. The latter urged Germany to be structured federally. Thus, a centralist enforced conformity (*Gleichschaltung*) of the education system, as in the Third Reich, should be prevented. This concern was in some ways undermined by the establishment of the Standing Conference of the Ministers of Education and Cultural Affairs of the *Länder* in the Federal Republic (Kultusministerkonferenz, KMK). Hardly any other institution has shaped the federal DNA of Germany as much as did this organization for horizontal coordination. The KMK was founded one year before the Basic Law (*Grundgesetz*) came into force on 23 May 1949. The federal government and the states still regularly use the reference to its early institutionalization in political debates, especially when the *Bund* is attempting to define the *Länder*s' agenda with its own educational initiatives. At the same time, the KMK is an example for the ambivalence characterizing German federalism. Even though the *Länder* still insist on their sovereignty, this institution is an important authority for horizontal coordination and harmonization (Füssel & Leschinsky, 2008; Scharpf, Benz, & Zintl, 1992; Wernstedt, 2005)—often called unitarization (Hesse, 1962).

1964 can be understood as the beginning of a second development phase of the German education system. It was triggered by the study *The German Education Catastrophe* by Georg Picht—a Southern German philosopher, theologian and pedagogue. In his book he warned with reference to internationally comparative school statistics about an education emergency (Bildungsnotstand), which could lead to an economic emergency in Germany (Picht, 1964). With his provoking analysis he caused a broad debate in the Federal Republic—especially since the economic miracle (*Wirtschaftswunder*) approached its climax and the common historical ignorance of the Nazi dictatorship led to first social tensions and generational conflicts. In 1967/1968 student protests at Western German universities partially brimmed over to the schools. But it was particularly Picht's analysis that gave the impulse for various educational reforms. In 1964, the prime ministers of the *Länder* had already adopted the so-called Hamburg Agreement (KMK, 1964), which provided a harmonization of the general education system. Determined during this period was a compensatory understanding of education: social disadvantages, due to the individual origin, should be compensated by comprehensive public education offers,thus encouraging social advancement. It was not without reason that various new universities and technical colleges were founded during this period. To the present date, this founding wave has financial implications: in order to ensure the viability of these universities after more than five decades of existence, the states now have to make substantial investments. Since their demographic and budgetary conditions have changed significantly, they are increasingly dependent on financial grants of the federal government.

The 1967/68 student protests formed the starting point for a third development phase of German educational federalism. This period was marked by a political planning euphoria (*Planungseuphorie*), which favored a further unitarization within German federalism (Abromeit, 1993; Hesse 1962; Lehmbruch, 2001). For the first grand coalition under chancellor Kurt Georg Kießinger (CDU) and vice chancellor Willy Brandt (SPD), the paradigm of a cross-cut-planning over different layers of government gained particular prominence. For this purpose the so-called "joint tasks" of the *Bund* and the *Länder* (*Gemeinschaftsaufgaben*) were institutionalized in the constitution in 1969. Therefore, Article 91b of the Basic Law, for example, clarified, "The federal government and the Länder may cooperate in the planning of education and the promotion of research facilities and projects of supraregional importance." For the annual implementation of this joint task, a *Bund-Länder*-Commission (BLK)—typical in Germany's cooperative federalism—was created. The main goal of educational planning was the coordination and financing of pilot schemes in the field of school and university education. Nevertheless, the commission also devised and supervised the various Higher Education Special Programs (*Hochschulsonderprogramme*). Originally, the federal government and the *Länder*, alongside experts, had also wanted to develop a so-called National Education Plan (*Bildungsgesamtplan*) within the framework of the joint education planning commission. These plans were supposed to include content and financial guidelines for all relevant areas of the education system (Poeppelt, 1978). Such a plan, however, was submitted only once in 1973. Regardless, its implementation became a victim of the economic recession in 1974/75: The federal and states governments lacked the financial resources for the implementation. In 1982 a new attempt was made and the draft for a second plan was drawn up. However, party political divergences between the federal and states level proved unbridgeable in adopting the plan. The political debate was dominated by a big polarization concerning the comprehensive school (*Gesamtschule*), questions of teacher trainings, and the expansion of the university landscape.

In 1990, German reunification took place. In the course of this historic event many conflicts that had existed in the old Federal Republic were frozen, since the first and foremost goal was to build up new administrative structures in the five new *Länder* as quick as was possible. With regard to the necessary restructuring measures in the educational field, considerable differences emerged between the various parties. While the SPD, for example, preferred the comprehensive school (*Gesamtschule*) as the main model for the organization of secondary education, the PDS—as the socialist successor party to the GDR state party—was committed to the maintenance of the unified school (*Einheitsschule*). In the end, the structure of the single states' school systems was laid down mainly by the parties, which were in charge of government from 1990 onwards. Since these *Länder* received administrative support from the former West German *Länder* in the years after reunification, the development of the education systems was oriented on the respective models of the old *Länder*. For example, the school systems in North Rhine-Westphalia and Brandenburg, in Saxony and Bavaria, as well as in Saxony-Anhalt and Lower Saxony, show certain similarities.

The development phase of the education system in unified Germany lasted for about ten years. At the same time, the scope and strength of the EU increased. Although the education systems of the member states have been strictly banned as subjects of harmonization in the Maastricht Treaty, the EU has continued to expand its efforts in this field. Similarly, the OECD has intensified its monitoring and benchmarking activities in its member states' education systems, always on the premise that economic growth and stable labor markets require high-qualified workers and employees. The OECD's efforts led to the first *Programme for International Student Assessment* (PISA) in 2000 (Klieme, 2009; Kuhlmann, 2012). For the Federal Republic, the results were so shattering that the federal government and the states subsequently agreed on various reforms (Schwager, 2005; Tillmann et al., 2008). One important milestone in this fourth and ongoing development period of Germany's educational federalism was the Education Summit (*Bildungsgipfel*) convened by chancellor Angela Merkel (CDU) in 2008. There, the federal government and the *Länder* agreed on a national education budget reaching 10 per cent of the GDP, even though a time frame and the expenditure parameters, which have to be taken into account in respective calculations, were not specifically defined (Wixforth, 2011). The educational finance reporting in Germany is, therefore, still facing some difficulties.

CONSTITUTIONAL DISTRIBUTION OF POWER

In the Federal Republic, education is subject to the states' cultural sovereignty. This is a constitutional abstraction since the Basic Law (BL) itself does not know the term. The competence rather arises from the constitutional division of power. Thus, Article 30 BL provides: "Except as otherwise provided or permitted by this Basic Law, the exercise of state powers and the discharge of state functions is a matter for the *Länder*." Article 70 para. 1 BL confirms that with a similar restriction. In the catalogs on the exclusive and concurrent legislation of the *Bund* (Articles 72 to 74 BL), there are no explicit references to cultural and educational matters, apart from a few exceptions in the field of higher education. This is why both policies are part of the *Länder*'s exclusive legislative power. With the federalism reform I from 2006, for the first time the cultural sovereignty of the *Länder* has found entry into the constitution. The new Art. 23 para. 6 BL provides: "When legislative powers exclusive to the *Länder* concerning matters of school education, culture or broadcasting are primarily affected, the exercise of the rights belonging to the Federal Republic of Germany as a member state of the European Union shall be delegated by the Federation to a representative of the *Länder* designated by the *Bundesrat*." As the *Länder* often cannot agree on a common position, the representatives sent by the *Länder* to Brussels must often abstain from voting.

Over the years, the federal government has encroached—partly with their consent—in various fields of the states' educational competencies. Until 2006, the federal government was held responsible for the following subjects: the framework legislation for the "principles of higher education" (Article 75 para. 1 no. 1a BL), the concurrent legislation for "the regulation of vocational training aid and the promotion of scientific research" (Article 74 para. 1 no. 13 BL), as well as the right to play its part in the joint tasks (*Gemeinschaftsaufgaben*) for "higher education constructions" and "educational planning and research promotion" (Article 91a para. 1 and Article 91b GG). In addition, the *Bund* executed the power to legislate the salaries and pensions for public servants (Article 74a para. 1 BL and Article 75 para. 1 no. 1 BL). In October 2003, *Bund*estag and *Bund*esrat set up a joint Commission for the Modernization of the Federal Order. The aim was to develop reform proposals to "improve the capacity for action and decision-making by the federal government and the *Länder*, to assign more clearly political responsibilities" and "to increase the expediency and efficiency of task fulfillment" (BR 750/03, own translation). The focus of the Commission's consultations was on the distribution of legislative powers, the participation rights of the states in the Second Chamber (*Bundesrat*), as well as the joint tasks of the *Bund* and the *Länder*. In December 2004, the negotiations of the commission failed in a first attempt because of a clash of interests over restructuring the responsibilities in the field of education (Sandberger, 2008). The *Länder* called for comprehensive competencies from kindergarten to university while the *Bund* also called—with reference to international benchmarkings—for increased competencies, especially for university admissions and degrees as well as the quality assurance in the tertiary education sector. After the federal elections in October 2005, the coalition agreement of the new grand coalition between the CDU/CSU and the SPD provided detailed recommendations for a federalism reform (CDU/CSU & SPD, 2005, p. 168). On this basis, a working group figured out a major compromise by summer 2006. After the *Bundestag* and the *Bundesrat* adopted these proposals, the Federalism Reform Act I with 25 amendments of the Basic Law came into force on 1 September 2006.

The federalism reform has resulted in the complete abolition of the framework legislation of the *Bund* (Article 75 BL). This had various consequences on the education policy area. The responsibility for "university admissions and degrees" has been transferred to the concurrent legislation of the *Bund* (Article 74 para. 1 no. 33 BL). The *Bund*, therefore, has gained an exclusive jurisdiction for this competence title. Since the so-called necessity clause is not applicable in this question, the *Länder* are allowed to deviate from federal laws in this field by issuing their own laws due to the newly created right of deviation (*materielles Abweichungsrecht*) (Münch, 2007). So, if the *Länder* do not agree with the regulations of a law passed by the *Bund*, they are allowed to make their own state law, which replaces the federation's legislative act. The "necessity clause" was tightened with the reform to some few, clearly defined matters, for which the *Bund* has the right to legislate, "if and to the extent that the establishment of equivalent living conditions throughout the federal territory or the maintenance of legal or economic unity renders federal regulation necessary in the national interest" (Article 72 para. 3 BL). To what extent this possibility of deviation is useful with regard to the question of "university admission and higher education degrees" (Article 72 para. 6 BL) and how it is actually used by the *Länder* in the light of the Bologna record is questionable. The compromise character of this decision therefore served primarily to save the face of both sides.

With the Federalism Reform I, the joint task under Article 91a para. 1 no. 1 BL has been abolished. The old regulation had allowed the *Bund* to "participate in the discharge of responsibilities of the *Länder*, provided that such responsibilities are important to society as a whole and that federal participation is necessary for the improvement of living conditions." Like the majority of the *Bund*'s funding programs, Article 91b BL was focused exclusively on constructional investments like new science, university and college buildings and the respective infrastructure. Additional personnel were not eligible. Despite the long lasting demand from academics for a comprehensive abolition of the joint tasks, *Bund* and *Länder* were only able to agree on the removal of the task "expansion and new construction of universities, including university hospitals" (Article 91b BL former version). In the past, the federal government had been financially involved in half of the corresponding states' expenditures. The concrete usage of the funds was debated and agreed upon each year in a joint planning committee by the *Bund* and the *Länder*. These institutions remain to this day the epitome of Germany's cooperative federalism, criticized by many academic and political observers (Abromeit, 1993; Kisker, 1971; Scharpf, 1985; Scharpf, Reissert, & Schnabel, 1976). With the abolition of the joint task of "higher education constructions" (Article 91b former version), the *Länder* have again received the sole responsibility for this area (Article 91b BL former version). Regardless, according to the newly introduced Article 143 c BL, they will receive guaranteed compensatory grants from the *Bund* until 2019.

In addition, the removal of the former joint task higher education constructions is actually only a restructuring. Article 91 b BL provides that "the Federation and the *Länder* may mutually agree to cooperate in cases of supraregional importance." This concerns "research facilities and projects apart from institutions of higher education" as well as "scientific projects and research at institutions of higher education." In the second case, however, a "consent of all the *Länder*" (Article 91b BL) is required. This stricter consensus quorum makes increased coordination efforts among the *Länder* necessary. Prior to this, decisions in the planning committee could be made only through a two-thirds majority. *Bund* or *Länder* could not be outvoted. With these new consensus requirements, the veto potential of the individual *Länder* has risen significantly. As a third funding priority, the new Article 91 b BL defines the "construction of facilities at institutions of higher education, including large scientific installations." The history of this new joint task demonstrates the extent to which the *Länder* actually depend on financial transfers by the *Bund*.

The Federalism Reform I also replaced the *Bund*'s legislation of the salaries and pensions of the public servants (formerly Art. 74a BL) with a new Art. 74 para. 1 no. 27 BL. According to it, the *Bund* has now only the competence to define "the statutory rights and duties of civil servants of the *Länder*, the municipalities and other corporations of public law as well as of the judges in the *Länder*, except for their career regulations, remuneration and pensions." Ten years after this regulation came into force, *Länder* benchmarkings show remarkable differentiations in the salary structures of civil servants and employees of the public sector (Jeffery & Pamphilis, 2016). For example, the range for the initial salary of primary school teachers varies between the *Länder* by around 500 euros. For teachers at secondary schools, the difference is even around 800 euros. So, the salary range between the *Länder* in the average gross salaries of teachers in 2015 was around 12 percent, ranging from about 4,100 euros in Hamburg to 3,700 euros in Rhineland-Palatinate. Since there has been an acute shortage of teaching personnel in the Federal Republic for several years, the range of variations in starting salaries has led to a competition among the *Länder* for teachers. Particularly in financially weak *Länder* such as Berlin and Brandenburg, potential job-seekers in the past often opted for their first position in Hamburg, Bavaria or Baden-Württemberg. In addition to a higher starting salary, these *Länder* lured the teachers with an appointment as a non-cancellable civil servant. The reciprocal enticement of teachers even led to a joint declaration of the *Länder*'s ministers of education in 2009, in which they agreed: "The *Länder* emphasize their shared responsibility for a fair competition and make a trustworthy vote in attracting teachers from other *Länder*" (KMK, 2009, p. 2). Since then, a joint advance planning has been carried out each year to forecast the demand for teachers (KMK, 2015). In addition, the *Länder* are now massively engaged in hiring lateral entrants and newcomers for the school service. The fact that they often receive the same salary as fully educated teachers has already led to protests by the trade unions. A competition between the *Länder* can be also observed with regard to university professors. For instance, the Western German *Länder* of Bavaria and Baden-Württemberg can offer their university professors in the highest income group (without special allowances) about 1,200 euros more than the financially weak *Länder* of Berlin and Saarland (Statistisches Bundesamt, 2016).

Although there are certain incompatibilities in Germany's educational federalism, neither the *Bund* nor the *Länder* have a competence-competence (*Kompetenz-Kompetenz*) or formal encroachment rights. This has also not been changed through the federalism reform, because neither one of the two jurisdictional levels has the authority to decide about the educational responsibilities of the other level alone. On the contrary, a rearrangement of competences requires a consensual, detailed, fact-based decision. Nevertheless, the federal government and the states can make use of various veto instruments. For example, it is possible for the *Länder* to deny approval of federal laws in the *Bundesrat*. Since 1994, they can also use the instrument of a competence-lawsuit (*Kompetenzklage*) at the Federal Constitutional Court (Article 93 para. 1 no. 2a BL). The federal government, on the other hand, can threaten to cut financial transfers to the *Länder*. The agenda-setting power is in the hands of the *Länder*'s governments—as far as their education systems are concerned. Nevertheless, the federal government also has possibilities to influence the educational policy agenda. The classical instruments for this strategy are monetary incentives, which are provided in the form of financial transfers for temporary funding programs or individual pilot projects in pursuit of innovative approaches to be imitated (Münch, 2009).

In the field of school politics and pre-school education, municipalities play a special role alongside *Bund* and *Länder*. While the *Länder* are responsible for the training, recruitment and remuneration of teachers at schools and universities, as well as an adequate provision of school and study places, the municipal school authorities are concerned about the maintenance, expansion and equipment of the local schools and the administrative staff. Therefore, they receive financial allocations within the frame of the municipal financial equalization schemes of the *Länder*. In addition to the investment funds for the municipalities, some *Länder* allow their schools to manage their own budgets for construction measures and personnel, too (Füssel & Leschinsky, 2008). These shared financing arrangements for staff on the one hand and structural investments on the other hand are often associated with a high bureaucratic burden for the responsible actors in schools and colleges. In addition, it often complicates the implementation of new conceptual approaches. For example, the integration of immigrants and refugees as well as the inclusion of people with disabilities cause specific needs both in terms of construction and personnel. Another example for this typical dilemma was the program for the expansion of full-time day schools (*Ganztagsschulen*) throughout Germany since 2003, the 4 billion Euros of the federal funding program could be used only for structural investments, but not for the employment of urgently needed staff. The hands of the *Bund* were tied: The costs for additional teachers and social pedagogical staff must be financed by the *Länder* and municipalities alone.

CONSTELLATION OF ACTORS AND INTERGOVERNMENTAL RELATIONS

The educational policy arena of the Federal Republic can be described as a non-hierarchical and closely coupled network with cooperative as well as competitive structural elements and negotiation patterns. The Federal Ministry for Education and Research (BMBF) and the Standing Conference of the Ministers of Education and Cultural Affairs (KMK) are the centers of this network structure. The tensions in this constellation are constituted through the cultural sovereignty of the *Länder* on the one hand and the harmonization efforts that have always existed in German federalism on the other hand. They have been pushed not only by the *Bund* but also by the *Länder* themselves. In the course of the European integration process, the *Bund* has come increasingly under pressure, particularly since the changing understanding of the resource education makes it necessary to represent the specificities of the federal education system outwardly: Due to its exclusive right of external representation the federal government has also to take a position on education policy initiatives of international organizations. Education is now understood as a key factor for economic growth, social cohesion and European identity formation. Not only the EU, but also other international organizations, such as the Council of Europe, the OECD, the UNESCO, the World Bank and the WTO, are forcing the international formation and convergence of a common educational understanding (Münch, R., 2010; Reuter & Linde, 1999; Scheller, 2007; Schemmann, 2007; Weymann & Martens, 2005). Education is progressively understood as a tradeable service: national education and science sites are competing against each other about new products and the academic elite. National education and science organizations have largely adopted this perspective. In education policy, the federal government and the *Länder* are thus under pressure from the outside as well as from the inside.

The Standing Conference of the Ministers of Education of the *Länder* (KMK) was founded in 1948, to address "education, higher education, research and cultural policy issues of supraregional significance, with the aim of forming a joint view and of representing common objectives" (KMK, 1955, p. 1). In addition to the horizontal coordination between the *Länder*, the KMK possesses a vertical coordination mechanism as well (Füssel, 1989), because the Federal Minister of Education and Research has a permanent guest status in the KMK-plenum. The KMK can be characterized as a multilateral compulsory negotiation system of the *Länder* executives (Reiter-Meyer, 2005; Scheller, 2010), although it was originally a voluntary alliance of the *Länder*. In case of the event in which only one of the sixteen *Länder* terminates the agreement on the joint KMK-Secretariat, the force of the agreement will cease for all other *Länder* as well—taking into account a one-year period of notification. Thus the blackmail-potential of the individual *Länder* was born, and could be observed for the first time in October 2004, when the government of Lower Saxony decided to terminate the agreement (Kropp, 2010). It was undoubtedly no coincidence that this decision fell into a time when the negotiations of the Federal Commission I were in a critical phase, mainly because of educational policy issues. Between the ministers of education and culture, as well as the prime ministers of the *Länder*, the decision of Lower Saxony led to a fierce dispute. The majority of the ministers defended the KMK's lasting existence as a necessary instrument of the states' self-coordination. However, the KMK has been criticized for decades as the core of cooperative executive federalism. In this federation type, the *Länder* governments have considerably more scope for action and decision-making at federal and state level than their parliaments. These weak parliaments are often seen as the losers in German federalism (Kilper & Lhotta, 2013; Laufer & Münch, 2010).

As a result of the 2004 KMK crisis, the Prime Ministers Conference (*Ministerpräsidentenkonferenz* [MPK]) commissioned the ministers of education to develop a reform concept. This concept was decided in December 2004 and subsequently implemented. Even after the reform, the unanimity principle has still been applied to key questions in the KMK plenum, such as the creation of necessary unity and mobility in the education system. At the same time, KMK decisions formally represent only common political expressions of intention. The negotiation logic of the KMK will thus continue to be decisively influenced by a mode of mutual exchange and adjustment by the *Länder*, which often is time consuming. This does not diminish party policy conflicts about topics that are ideologically controversial. However, decisions are usually adopted with the lowest common denominator. The KMK reform demonstrates that such an institution is apparently indispensable with regard to the mutual self-coordination of the *Länder* in terms of education policies. This seems to be especially relevant with regard to international benchmarking studies, the mobility between the education systems in Europe as well as in Germany itself, and integration and inclusion issues, which pertain to social justice issues.

Over three decades the *Bund-Länder*-Commission for Educational Planning and Research Promotion (BLK) was another forum for exchange and negotiations between the federal partners. The BLK was established in 1970 to coordinate the planning and implementation efforts of the newly institutionalized joint task (Art. 91 b GG). In the course of the 2006 federalism reform, the commission was transformed into a Joint Science Conference (GWK). The tasks of the GWK are aimed at a closely coordination of question of "common interest in the field of national, European and international science and research policy with the aim of strengthening Germany's position as a location for science and research in the international competition" (GEK, 2007, p. 1). It also "shall act jointly in cases of supraregional importance in promoting" (GEK, 2007, p. 1). A third objective of the GWK is to inform each other "of major plans and decisions which are not the objects of joint funding" (GWK, 2007, p. 1, own translation). The responsibilities of the individual *Länder* for education policy should be respected.

The Federal Constitutional Court (*Bundesverfassungsgericht*) has always played an important role in education policies. Already in the founding period of the Federal Republic, the court's jurisprudence made a decisive contribution to the definition of the cultural sovereignty as a constitutive element of the *Länder*'s own statehood and their parliamentary reserve (BVerfGE 6, 309 (354) and BVerfGE 12, 205 (229)). The Constitutional Court has often taken the role of a "policy broker" in educational policy conflicts (Sabatier & Jenkins-Smith, 1993, p. 129). Thereby, it introduced own ideas into the political debate. Examples from the recent past are the court decisions on the junior professorship and the ban on study fees (BVerfGE, 2 BvF 2/02; BVerfGE, 2 BvF 1/03). Both judgements fell into a critical negotiation phase of the Federalism Reform I, in which the division of competencies in educational matters was the main issue under dispute. Thus, the *Bund* was forbidden to enact both the new staff category of junior professor and a general ban on study fees. With both decisions, the Court clearly indicated its preference for the states' autonomy in terms of higher education. Only these should have the right to decide about the introduction of junior professorships and university fees. Nevertheless, after the implementation of study fees by different *Länder*, the topic became a subject of party political discussions. Above all, the Social Democrats (SPD) profiled themselves in various election campaigns with the demand for an abolition of study fees. In the end, Bavaria was the last German state to abolish the fees after six years in 2013.

The non-governmental research organizations, such as the German Research Foundation (*Deutsche Forschungsgemeinschaft*—DFG), the German Council of Science and Humanities (*Wissenschaftsrat*—WR), the German Rectors' Conference (*Hochschulrektorenkonferenz*—HRK), the German Academic Exchange Service (*Deutsche Akademischer Auslandsdienst*—DAAD), the German National Association for Student Affairs (*Deutsches Studentenwerk* e. V.) and the German Academic Scholarship Foundation (*Studienstiftung des deutschen Volkes*) also play important roles in the higher education policy network of the Federal Republic (Thieme, 2004). In some of the supervisory committees of these organizations, the federal government and the states are represented on a parity basis, since, for example, the DFG and the DAAD spend public money. The DFG is the central self-administration institution of science for the promotion of research at universities and publicly funded research institutes in Germany. The German Council of Science and Humanities was founded in 1957 and has an advisory function for *Bund* and *Länder* because it is tasked with regularly drawing up recommendations on the development of science, research and higher education, thus helping to ensure that German science and humanities remain competitive at national, European, and international levels. This includes considerations concerning quantitative and financial effects and the implementation of such considerations, always taking into account the demands of societal, cultural and economic life. The work of both institutions is achieved by separated administrative substructures. Additionally, many of their decision-making processes are based on the peer review principle, involving representatives of universities and independent research institutes.

FUNDING RESPONSIBILITIES

The most important principle of the financial constitution is the so-called apportionment of expenditures principle (*Konnexitätsprinzip*) which says: "The Federation and the *Länder* shall separately finance the expenditures resulting from the discharge of their respective responsibilities insofar as this Basic Law does not otherwise provide" (Article 104 para 1 BL). This means that the *Länder* have to bear the expenditures of their education policy autonomously, due to their cultural sovereignty. In reality, however, there exist countless exceptions. In recent years, the federal government has launched numerous expensive programs to support the states in various education sectors. The redistribution of all these funds between the states usually follows the so-called *Königsteiner Schlüssel*—an allocation formula, on which *Bund* and *Länder* agreed in 1949 and is recalculated annually. In concreto, two thirds of the money is distributed according to the *Länder*'s tax revenues and one third to their population. Particular needs or specific costs for pupils and students in the single states are in most cases disregarded.

Due to the constitutional distribution of responsibilities as well as the distinction between formal and non-formal education, the statistical surveys on the educational budget in the Federal Republic show certain weaknesses as data from different sources must be brought together and harmonized. As a result, the statistics show a lag time of three to four years, similar to the OECD. In 2013, the public and private sector spent a total of 257.4 billion euros on education, research and science in the Federal Republic. These were 9.1 percent of its GDP (Statistisches Bundesamt, 2016, p. 18). Nevertheless, international comparisons show that Germany spent only 4.3 percent of its GDP on formal education institutions from the primary to the tertiary sector in 2013, which is below the OECD average of 5.2 percent (Busemeyer, 2015; OECD, 2016). The German educational budget alone amounts to 186.5 billion euros in 2013 and 190.7 billion euros in 2014. From this amount, 143.9 billion euros were spent on cribs, kindergartens, schools, vocational training and universities—and the proportion is growing. Around four-fifths of the expenditure on education is funded by the public sector. In 2013, the *Länder* accounted for 71.6 percent, the municipalities for 21.5 percent and the *Bund* for only 6.9 percent. Expenditures by the federal government, the *Länder* and municipalities have risen steadily in recent years—by around 42.6 percent from 2005 (86.7 billion euro) to 2015 (123.7 billion euro) (Statistisches Bundesamt, 2016). The highest growth was recorded in early childhood education (77.6 percent), followed by higher education institutions (34 percent) and schools (17.2 percent). These growth rates clearly show the focus of the special programs of the *Bund.*

The investment rates of the *Länder* per pupil display considerable differences. One reason for this is that the financial power of the states has developed distinctively over the past years, despite a strong financial equalization scheme

(Lenk & Glinka, 2016; Scheller, 2015). This is also an expression of the regions' different socioeconomic strengths. In addition, all sixteen states have committed themselves by the Federalism Reform II from 2009 to anchor a so-called debt brake (*Schuldenbremse*) in their constitutions by 2020. These new instruments require far-reaching consolidation efforts and are restricting their fiscal scope—also in education policy (Hildebrandt & Wolf, 2016; Statistisches Bundesamt 2015, p. 52). This is especially true for the financially weak *Länder* of Berlin, Bremen, Saarland, Rhineland-Palatinate, North Rhine-Westphalia, Lower Saxony and some of the East German *Länder*, which have had high per capita debt rates and a low financial power for years. These disparities in the financial power of the *Länder* explain why, for example, Saxony and Bavaria were able to invest an average of 5,500 and 5,400 euros per pupil during the period from 2005 to 2012. Berlin and North Rhine-Westphalia, on the other hand, were only able to spent 1,400 and 1,600 euros, while the total average of all sixteen *Länder* was around 3,200 euros (Brand & Steinbrecher, 2016; Statistisches Bundesamt, 2015). Additionally, the municipalities estimated that in 2015 there was an investment backlog in the school sector only of around 34 billion euros (Scheller & Schneider, 2016). For good reasons regular media outcries problematize the desolate situation of German school buildings. Since there is a significant correlation between the structural condition of school buildings and individual educational success (Reidenbach et al., 2008), German federalism establishes a deficit of justice, since it depends where pupils and students live. These growing disparities in quality between the education systems of the *Länder* are perceived as s significant problem by the public.

The poor results of the first PISA study in 2001 also had impacts on the educational funding system in the Federal Republic. An immediate response was the all-day school program *Zukunft, Bildung und Betreuung*, initiated by the former chancellor Gerhard Schröder (SPD), which is still being evaluated by an accompanying research project. To date it is regarded as a successful project and a prime example of a federal educational program. The *Bund* had provided 4 billion euro for a period from 2003 to 2007. Since the *Länder* were incapable of retrieving the funds in time, the program was extended until 2009 through a cost-neutral approach. A basic difficulty of this program—as with all other federal transfer programs—was that the funds were only available for structural investments. Additional teachers or further qualification of the existing staff as well as any follow-up-costs arising from the maintenance of new buildings and conversions could not be explicitly covered by this program.

The *Bund*'s three funding programs for childcare in the *Länder* are similar examples of federal programs. Early childhood promotion had been neglected in the Federal Republic for decades. However, as a result of PISA and other comparative assessment studies, it became more and more apparent that social disadvantages of children and adolescents can best be countered by early childhood programs (Drieschner, 2011; Liegle, 2006). In April 2007, the federal government, the states, and the municipalities decided on the so-called crib summit (*Krippengipfel*) to launch the investment program *Kinderbetreuungsfinanzierung*. The program created a special fund from which the states and municipalities were able to call up around 4 billion euro (2.15 billion Euros for investments and 1.85 billion euro for operating costs) between 2008 and 2013 to increase the institutional facilities for children under three years old in 750,000 locations (von der Leyen, 2007).

The program, however, contradicted the so-called cooperation ban (*Kooperationsverbot*), which had been anchored in the Basic Law with the Federalism Reform I two years in advance (Welsh, 2014). The purpose of this ban was to strengthen the autonomy of the *Länder* and municipalities, especially in the field of education. Article 104 b para. 1 BL in the version that came into force on 1 September 2006 states: "To the extent that this Basic Law confers on it the power to legislate, the Federation may grant the *Länder* financial assistance for particularly important investments by the *Länder* and municipalities (associations of municipalities) which are necessary to: 1. avert a disturbance of the overall economic equilibrium; 2. equalize differing economic capacities within the federal territory; or 3. promote economic growth." The childcare program did not meet any of these conditions. In addition, the new Art. 84 para. 1 BL stipulates that no more tasks can be transferred to the municipalities by means of federal laws. This example illustrates the conflict of goals that exist in German educational federalism: from a family and educational policy point of view, there was a broad consensus around the need for a crib development program, both in the political and in the public sphere. Even the tight financial situation of the *Länder* and municipalities in the Federal Republic, which have little leeway in imposing taxes, spoke in favor of such a program. It was, above all, a normative and dogmatic theory of federalism that almost prevented this pragmatic solution. Not only since the negotiations about the Federalism Reform I, the (academic) federalism discourse in the Federal Republic has strongly been geared to the model of a dual federalism (Benz, 2008; Behnke & Kropp, 2016; Scheller, 2016), although constitutional practice is shaped through many cooperation necessities. In the end this dilemma was ultimately solved by a legal gimmick: for the transfer of the federal funds, a special property fund was chosen. In addition, the *Länder* and municipalities had to co-finance the funds in an amount of 10 percent of the total investment volume (Statistisches Bundesamt, 2015).

In the meantime, the Federal Government has launched two further investment programs to expand the overall child care facilities in Germany. Through these programs, 30,000 additional preschools were to be be created between 2013 and 2014. A third program for the years 2015 to 2018 was adopted with the *Act for the further relief of the Länder and municipalities from 2015 onwards and the quantitative and qualitative expansion of childcare support* (Gesetz zur weiteren Entlastung von Ländern und Kommunen ab 2015 und zum quantitativen und qualitativen Ausbau der Kindertagesbetreuung—LKEG 2015). Overall, the *Bund* will thus assume investment costs of around 5.3 billion euros for children's day care facilities by 2018 plus 1.7 billion euros of operating costs annually. The federal government and the *Länder* have not only defined the attainment of a target of 780,000 childcare places by 2018, but the program is envisaged to take qualitative requirements into account as well. For this reason, "investments should be eligible to meet the increased demand for all-day care, to further strengthen the quality of day-care and childcare facilities" (Parliamentary printed matter 18/2586, p. 13). In addition, "such investments should be eligible, which are strengthening health care, inclusion measures and full-day care" (Parliamentary printed matter 18/2586, p. 13). This list of criteria shows that the *Bund* is trying to use its funding programs—at least indirectly—to influence the education policies of the *Länder* also in pedagogical and conceptual terms.

In recent years, the Federal Government has launched comprehensive financial programs for the tertiary education sector, too. This includes the so-called Excellence Initiative (*Exzellenzinitiative*), which covers a financing volume of a total of 4.6 billion euros from 2005 to 2017. The funds were used to finance 45 graduate schools, 43 Clusters of Excellence and 11 Future Concepts (DFG, 2013) within the framework of two competition procedures. The *Bund* assumed 75 percent of the costs while the *Länder* covered 25 percent. After a comprehensive evaluation by an independent expert committee, *Bund* and *Länder* agreed to continue the program in summer 2016 ((Internationale Expertenkommission Exzellenzinitiative, 2016). The new funding period of the Excellence Strategy will begin in 2018. One criticism regarding the Excellence Initiative highlights the fact that primary universities and colleges in the financially stronger *Länder* of Bavaria, Baden-Wuerttemberg and Hesse were selected by the competition procedure (Lenzen, 2015). In the East German *Länder*, in contrast, only three universities in Saxony were supported. Another exception is Berlin with two Excellence Universities over the funding period. The educational north-south-divide between the *Länder*, which existed previously, was further strengthened through the funding allocations. The strongly differing quotas of university graduates are another example for these regional divergences (Autorengruppe Bildungsbericht, 2016).

In order to increase the number of study places at universities and colleges, the federal government and the states have launched by now three "University Pacts" (*Hochschulpakte*) (Welsh, 2014, p. 409). Over the period from 2007 to 2023, the *Bund* will provide a total of 20.2 billion euros and the *Länder* 18.3 billion euros additionally. The money shall help to increase the number of first-year students from 37 to about 50 percent. The university pacts are flanked by a Pact for Teaching Quality (*Qualitätspakt Lehre*). For the period from 2011 to 2020, the *Bund* will provide 2 billion euros. By 2016, 186 universities from all 16 *Länder* have been supported. A Professors Program, which is used to support female professors in the period from 2008 to 2017, is markedly smaller. The federal government and the *Länder* provide 300 million euros (150 million euro per phase). In order to strengthen non-university research, the federal government and the *Länder* have launched the Pact for Research and Innovation, which now includes the third funding period (2005–2010, 2011–2015, 2016–2020). In the recent period solely, the federal government's share amounts to 3.9 billion euros. In addition, the *Bund* and the *Länder* have agreed that the institutional funding base in the third phase should be increased by three percent per year. An annual monitoring is planned as well.

The historical genesis of these programs makes it clear that mixed funding programs by the federal government and the *Länder* in the field of education are indispensable—at least as long as a fundamental reform of the financial relations between the jurisdictional layers of government is postponed. Since such a reform seems unlikely in the future, *Länder* and municipalities will continue to rely on financial allocations by the *Bund.*

ACADEMIC STANDARDS AND QUALITY ASSURANCE

The course for a comprehensive quality assurance in the German education system was already set in 1997 by the *Länder*'s Standing Conference of the Ministers of Education and Cultural Affairs. The so-called Constance Resolution (*Konstanzer Beschluss*) therefore states: "With regard to the equivalence of school education, the comparability of school degrees and the transmittance of the education system in the Federal Republic of Germany the Standing Conference sees an important task in the development of measures to ensure the quality of school education" (KMK, 1997, p. 1, author translation). The instruments for quality assurance have already been described in this decision: "Carrying out regular cross-*Länder* comparisons about the learning- and performance-level of pupils of selected grades is an important supplementation of the *Länder*-specific quality assurance measures and is allowing each Land to draw conclusions with regard to the selected methods and quality assurance measures" (KMK, 1997, p. 1, author translation). This decision reveals that the *Länder* agreed long before the PISA surveys of the OECD about the need for regular education monitoring and benchmarking.

The PISA shock of 2001/2002 therefore was only a further catalyst, which led to a massive expansion of educational science research in Germany. Since 2004, a large number of new research institutes, networks and university professorships have been established. These include the Institute for Educational Quality Improvement (IQB) and its Research Data Centre (FDZ) (founded in 2004), the Institute for Research Information and Quality Assurance (iFQ) (founded in 2005), the German Institute for International Educational Research (founded in 2006), the National Educational Panel Study (NEPS) (founded in 2009), the Centre for International Student Assessment (ZIB) (founded in 2010), the German Centre for Higher Education Research and Science Studies (DZHW) (founded in 2013) and the Leibniz Institute for Educational Trajectories. The majority of these institutions are funded jointly by the federal government and the states. The large number of institutes leads to the question how far they can be distinguished from one another with regard to their research foci. This new network structure has contributed significantly to a kind of "scientification" of the political and public debate and has promoted a "governing by numbers" in education policy (Heintz, 2008, p. 120).

With a large number of surveys, new data-based findings are gained, which are in certain competition with one another—especially with regard to the multitude of educational science actors and institutions (Heinz, 2015). In public and political debates, which are regularly dominated by a media logic of shortening and scandalization, it is often difficult to comprehend on which indicators and assumptions the various research approaches and results are based. Nevertheless, many educational reforms are now justified by reference to the results of comparative evaluation studies and the supposedly relevant findings of educational science research. This is true even though the results measured in comparative studies such as PISA, TIMMS, ICILS, DESI, KESS and IGLU, are influenced by political reforms only in limited fashion and over long periods of time. Regardless, the various comparative studies have led to a heightened focus on education. Because a feedback and evaluation culture in the German education system had previously existed only to a basic degree, the resistance to conduct comparative studies in schools and universities has still been great—especially since the findings so far have not been used systematically for concrete improvements of the teaching and learning quality.

Nonetheless, for the first time the Federalism Reform I included a clear commitment to new educational governance mechanisms, such as benchmarking, monitoring and peer reviews. The new Article 91b para 2 BL provides: "The Federation and the *Länder* may mutually agree to cooperate for the assessment of the performance of educational systems in international comparison and in drafting relevant reports and recommendations." Even if this is an optional provision (*Kann-Bestimmung*) with self-commitment character, the pressure on the *Länder* for the harmonization and standardization of learning contents, audit tasks and even educational institutions has increased significantly over the last fifteen years. The alleged best practice examples of such comparative studies are usually used as a model for appropriate adaptation by the other *Länder*.

OUTLOOK

Germany's educational federalism is characterized by some vital tensions. On the one hand, the *Länder* insist on their power for education matters, which is legally derived from their cultural sovereignty. On the other hand, there are policy-based and institutional requirements in Germany's educational practice, which are promoted by an internationalization and economization of this policy field. The intersections between these special policy needs and the ideals of the normatively charged federalism discourse are small and therefore require a creative balancing by the political actors. In addition, the financial and budgetary autonomy of the *Länder* is subject to increasing restrictions, which make the implementation of such far-reaching governance reforms more difficult. The federal implications that unfold processes such as the Bologna reform for higher education or the participation in international benchmarking studies in the school system become recognizable in their entire scope only slowly. Among the participants in the different areas of the education system, the resistance against the complexity and the lack of transparency, growing bureaucratic burdens, the perceived under-financing of the individual institutions, as well as the ever-shorter sequencing of reforms are growing. The reform efforts to strengthen the individual educational institutions—particularly the universities and schools—have meanwhile enabled them to decide largely independently about their educational programs and their budgets as well as the choice of staff and students. However, the governments of the *Länder* have, in turn, obtained new control powers. This governance change in the German educational federalism is so decisive that it is still in a critical transition phase. With regard to the partly still weak acceptance on the side of the educational actors, it is by all means possible that individual reforms of the recent past are re-adjusted on a selective basis.

REFERENCES

Abromeit, H. (1993). *Der verkappte Einheitsstaat* [The disguised unitary state]. Berlin, Germany: Leske + Budrich.

Altrichter, H., et al. (2007). *Educational Governance: Handlungskoordination und Steuerung im Bildungssystem* [Coordination and management in the education system]. Wiesbaden, Germany: Vs Verlag für Sozialwissenschaften.

Anweiler, O., Fuchs, H. J., Dorner, M., & Petermann, E. (Eds.). (1992). *Bildungspolitik in Deutschland 1945–1990. Ein historisch vergleichender Quellenband* [Education policy in Germany 1945-1990: A historically comparative source volume]. Wiesbaden, Germany: Springer.

Association for Canadian Studies. (2010). *Survey*. Montréal (Québec), unpublished data set.

Autorengruppe Bildungsberichterstattung (Ed.). (2016). *Bildung in Deutschland 2016—Ein indikatorengestützter Bericht mit einer Analyse zu Bildung und Migration* [Education in Germany 2016—An indicator-based report with an analysis of education and migration]. Bielefeld, Germany: Bertelsmann Verlag.

Behnke, N., & Kropp, S. (2016). Ten years of federalism reform in Germany, *Regional and Federal Studies, 26*(5, Special Issue).

Benz, A. (1985). *Föderalismus als dynamisches System* [Federalism as a dynamic system]. Baden-Baden, Germany: Nomos Verlagsgesellschaft.

Benz, A. (2008). Föderalismusreform in der Entflechtungsfalle [Federalism reform in the unbundling trap]. In Europäisches Zentrum für Föderalismus-Forschung (Ed.), *Jahrbuch des Föderalismus 2007* [Yearbook of federalism 2007] (pp. 180–190). Baden-Baden, Germany: Nomos Verlagsgesellschaft.

Benz, A., & Broschek, J. (Eds.). (2013). *Federal dynamics. Continuity, change, and the varieties of federalism*. Oxford, UK: Oxford University Press.

Benz, A., Detemple, J., & Heinz, D. (2015). *Varianten und Dynamiken der Politikverflechtung im deutschen Bundesstaat* [Variants and dynamics of joint decision making in the German federal state]. Baden-Baden, Germany: Nomos Verlagsgesellschaft.

Bertelsmann Stiftung (Ed.). (2008). *Bürger und Föderalismus. Eine Umfrage zur Rolle der BundesLänder* [Citizens and federalism. A survey on the role of the federal states]. Gütersloh, Germany: Bertelsmann Stiftung.

Bertelsmann Stiftung (Ed.). (2009). *Was unzureichende Bildung kostet. Eine Berechnung der Folgekosten durch entgangenes Wirtschaftswachstum* [What insufficient education costs. A calculation of the consequential costs resulting from lost economic grow]. Gütersloh, Germany: Bertelsmann Stiftung.

Bertelsmann Stiftung, Institut für Schulentwicklungsforschung Dortmund, Institut für Erziehungswissenschaft Jena (Ed.). (2014). *Chancenspiegel 2014, Regionale Dis-*

paritäten in der Chancengerechtigkeit und Leistungsfähigkeit der deutschen Schulsysteme [Chancenspiegel 2014, Regional disparities in equal opportunities and performance of German school systems]. Gütersloh, Germany: Bertelsmann Stiftung.

Bologna Declaration. (1999). *The Bologna Declaration of 19 June 1999. Joint Declaration of the European Ministers of Education.* Bologna, Italy: European Higher Education Area.

Brand, S., & Steinbrecher, J. (2016). Kommunaler Investitionsrückstand bei Schulgebäuden erschwert Bildungserfolge [Municipal investment backlog in school buildings complicates educational achievements]. In *KfW Research Fokus Volkswirtschaft, 143.* Retrieved from https://www.kfw.de/PDF/Download-Center/Konzernthemen/Research/PDF-Dokumente-Fokus-Volkswirtschaft/Fokus-Nr.-143-September-2016-Investitionsr%C3%BCckstand-bei-Schulgeb%C3%A4uden.pdf

Bude, H. (2011). *Bildungspanik: Was unsere Gesellschaft spaltet* [Educational panic: What divides our society]. Munich, Germany: Carl Hanser Verlag.

Bundesministerium für Bildung und Forschung (Ed.). (2007). *Zur Entwicklung nationaler Bildungsstandards* [The development of national educational standards]. Berlin, Germany: Bundesministerium für Bildung und Forschung (BMBF).

Busemeyer, M. (2015). Bildungspolitik [Education policy]. In G. Wenzelburger & R. Zohlnhöfer (Eds.), *Handbuch Policy-Forschung, Wiesbaden, VS Verlag für Sozialwissenschaften* [Policy research guide] (pp. 615–640). Wiesbaden, Germany: VS Verlag für Sozialwissenschaften.

Christlich Demokratische Union Deutschlands (CDU), Christlich-Soziale Union in Bayern (CSU), & Sozialdemokratische Partei Deutschlands (SPD). (2005). *Gemeinsam für Deutschland. Mit Mut und Menschlichkeit. Koalitionsvertrag von CDU, CSU und SPD* [Together for Germany. With courage and humanity. Coalition agreement between CDU, CSU and SPD]. Berlin, Germany.

Cortina, K. S., Baumert, J., Leschinsky, A., Mayer, K. U., & Trommer, L., (Eds.). (1997). *Das Bildunswesen in der Bundesrepublik Deutschland* [Education in the Federal Republic of Germany]. Hamburg, Germany: Rowohlt Taschenbuch Verlag.

Deutsche Forschungsgemeinschaft (DFG). (2013). *Exzellenzinitiative auf einen Blick, Der Wettbewerb des Bundes und der Länder zur Stärkung der universitären Spitzenforschung, Die zweite Förderphase 2012 bis 2017, Graduiertenschulen—Exzellenzcluster—Zukunftskonzepte, Bonn.* [The Excellence Initiative at a glance: The competition of the federal government and the federal states to strengthen top-class university research, the second funding phase 2012 to 2017, graduate schools—Excellence cluster—concepts for the future]. Bonn, Germany: Deutsche Forschungsgemeinschaft (DFG), Bundesministerium für Bildung und Forschung (BMBF), Ministerien, Senatsverwaltungen und Behörden für Wissenschaft und Forschung der Länder.

Drieschner, E. (2011). Frühkindliche Erziehung oder Bildung? Zur bindungstheoretischen Begründung von Frühpädagogik [Early or later childhood education? On the foundation of binding theory in early childhood education]. In V. Bank et al. (Eds.), *Pädagogische Rundschau* [Pedagogic review] (pp. 285–304). Koblenz, Germany: Peter Lang.

Edelstein, B., & Allmendinger, J. (2012). Bildungsföderalismus—Déjà-vu mit Happy End? [Education federalism—Déjà-vu with happy-end?]. In T. Schultz & K. Hurrelmann (Eds.), *Bildung und Kleinstaaterei—Brauchen wir mehr Zentralismus? Päda-*

gogische Streitschriften [Education and state fragmentation—Do we need more centralism? Pedagogic Arguments] (pp. 16–18). Weinheim and Basel, Germany and Switzerland: Beltz Juvente.

Elm, R. (Ed.). (2002). *Universität zwischen Bildung und Business: Mit einem Anhang zur Europäischen Bildungspolitik* [University between education and business: With an appendix on European education policy]. Bochum, Germany: Projekt-Verlag.

Freitag, M., & Schlicht, R. (2009). Educational Federalism in Germany: Foundations of social inequality in education. *Governance: an International Journal of Policy, Administration and Institutions Volume, 22*, 47–72.

Füssel, H. P. (1989). Kooperativer Föderalismus im Bildungswesen: über die Arbeit von Kultusministerkonferenz und *Bund-Länder*-Kommission für Bildungsplanung und Forschungsförderung [Cooperative federalism in education: On the work of the conference of the ministers of education and cultural affairs and the Bund-Länder commission for educational planning and research promotion]. *Recht der Jugend und des Bildungswesens, 37*(4), 430–442.

Füssel, H.P., & Leschinsky, A. (2008). Der institutionelle Rahmen des Bildungswesens [The institutional frame of the education system]. In K. S. Cortina, J. Baumert, A. Leschinsky, K. U. Mayer, & L. Trommer (Eds.), *Das Bildungswesen in der Bundesrepublik Deutschland* [The education system in the Federal Republic of Germany] (pp. 131–203). Hamburg, Germany: Rowohlt Taschenbuch Verlag.

Gemeinsame Wissenschaftskonferenz (GWK). (2007). *Verwaltungsabkommen zwischen Bund und Ländern über die Errichtung einer Gemeinsamen Wissenschaftskonferenz (GWK-Abkommen) vom 11. September 2007* [Administrative agreement between the federal government and the federal states on the establishment of a Joint Science Conference (GWK Convention) of 11 September 2007]. Retrieved from: http://www.gwk-bonn.de/fileadmin/Papers/gwk-abkommen.pdf

Graßl, H. (2014). Keine Chancengleichheit auf dem Bildungsmarkt. Zur Ökonomisierung des konservativen Bildungsstaates [No equality on the education market. On the economization of the conservative educational state]. In G. S. Schaal et al. (Eds.), *Die Ökonomisierung der Politik in Deutschland. Kritische Studien zur Demokratie* [The economization of politics in Germany. Critical studies on democracy] (pp. 217–237). Wiesbaden, Germany: Springer.

Hadjar, A., & Becker, R. (2006). *Erwartete und unerwartete Folgen der Bildungsexpansion in Deutschland* [Expected and unexpected consequences of educational expansion in Germany.]. Wiesbaden, Germany: Springer.

Heintz, B. (2008). Governance by numbers. Zum Zusammenhang von Quantifizierung und Globalisierung am Beispiel der Hochschulpolitik [On the connection between quantification and globalisation using the example of higher education policy]. In G. F. Schuppert & A. Voßkuhle (Eds.), *Governance von und durch Wissen* [Governance of and by knowledge] (pp. 110–128). Baden-Baden: Germany: Nomos-Verlag.

Heinz, D. (2015). Politikverflechtung in der Schulpolitik: Koordination im Wandel [Joint decision-making in school policy: Coordination in change]. *Politische Vierteljahresschrift, 56*(4), 626–647.

Hepp, G. F. (2011). *Bildungspolitik in Deutschland. Eine Einführung* [Education policy in Germany. An introduction]. Wiesbaden, Germany: VS Verlag.

Herzog, W. (2013). *Bildungsstandards. Eine kritische Einführung* [Education standards. A critical introduction]. Stuttgart, Germany: Kohlhammer Verlag.

Hesse, K. (1962). *Der unitarische Bundesstaat* [The unitary federal state]. Karlsruhe, Germany: C. F. Müller.

Hildebrandt, A., & Wolf, F. (2016). How much of a sea-change? Land Policies after the reforms of federalism. *German Politics, 25*(2), 227–242.

Hopf, W. (2003). Soziale Ungleichheit und Bildungskompetenz-Erklärung und Exploration in den PISA-Studien [Social inequality and education competence—Explanations and explorations in the PISA-studies. Social inequality and education competence—Explanations and explorations in the PISA-studies]. *Zeitschrift für Soziologie der Erziehung und Sozialisation*, 10–23.

Hoymann, T. (2005). *Umdenken nach dem PISA-Schock* [Rethinking after the PISA-shock]. Marburg, Germany: Tectum-Verlag.

Humboldt, W. (1903). Über die innere und äußere Organisation der höheren wissenschaftlichen Anstalten in Berlin (1809 o. 1810) [About the internal and external organization of the higher scientific institutions in Berlin (1809/1819)]. In W. von Humboldt, Gesammelte Schriften, hrsg. v. d. Preußischen Akademie der Wissenschaften, Bd. 10, Berlin 1903, S. 250 ff. In W. von Humboldt (Ed.), *Preußische Akademie der Wissenschaften, Gesammelte Schriften Band 10* [W. von Humboldt, collected writings, Vol. 10]. Berlin, Germany: B.Behr's Verlag.

Immerfall, S. (2010). Der deutsche Bildungsföderalismus zwischen Aufbruch und Verflechtungsfalle—Macht sich die "Griechische Landschildkröte" auf den Weg? [The German educational federalism between break-up and joint decision making trap—Is the "Greek tortoise" on its way?] In J. von Blumenthal & S. Bröchler (Eds.), *Föderalismusreform in Deutschland* [Federalism reform in Germany] (pp. 197–215). Wiesbaden, Germany: Publisher: Springer Verlag für Sozialwissenschaften.

Institut für Demoskopie Allenbach (Ed.). (2012). *Schul- und Bildungspolitik in Deutschland 2011, Ein aktuelles Stimmungsbild der Bevölkerung und der Lehrer* [School and education policy in Germany 2011, A current picture of the mood of the population and teachers]. Retrieved from http://www.ifd-allensbach.de/uploads/tx_studies/7625_Bildungspolitik.pdf

Internationale Expertenkommission Exzellenzinitiative (Ed). (2016). *Internationale Expertenkommission zur Evaluation der Exzellenzinitiative, Endbericht* [International Commission of Experts on the Evaluation of the Excellence Initiative, final report]. Retrieved from http://www.gwk-bonn.de/fileadmin/Papers/Imboden-Bericht-2016.pdf

Jeffery, C., & Pamphilis, N. (2016). The myth and the paradox of 'Uniform Living Conditions' in the German Federal System. *German Politics, 25*(2), 2–17.

Kaiser, A., & Vogel, S. (2016). *Dynamic de/centralization in Germany*. Paper for the 24th World Congress of the International Political Science Association 2016. Poznan, Poland.

Kamm, R., & Köller, M. (2010). Hochschulsteuerung im deutschen Bildungsföderalismus [University management in German education federalism]. *Swiss Political Science Review, 16*(4), 649–686. doi: 10.1002/j.1662-6370.2010.tb00444.x

Kilper, H., & Lhotta, R. (2013). *Föderalismus in der Bundesrepublik Deutschland: Eine Einführung* [Federalism in the Federal Republic of Germany: An introduction].Wiesbaden, Germany: Springer Verlag.

Kisker, G. (1971). *Kooperation im Bundesstaat: eine Untersuchung zum kooperativen Föderalismus in der Bundesrepublik Deutschland* [Cooperation in the federal state:

An investigation of federalism in the Federal Republic of Germany]. Tübingen, Germany: J.C.B. Mohr.

Klemm, K. (2015). *Inklusion in Deutschland—Daten und Fakten. Gutachten im Auftrag der Bertelsmann Stiftung.* Gütersloh. [Inclusion in Germany—Data and facts. Expertise for the Bertelsmann Foundation]. Gütersloh, Germany: Bertelsmann Stiftung.

Klieme, E. (2009). *Pisa 2009: Bilanz nach einem Jahrzehnt* [Pisa 2009: Review after a decade]. Münster, Germany: Waxmann.

Kropp, S. (2010). *Kooperativer Föderalismus und Politikverflechtung* [Cooperative federalism and policy integration]. Wiesbaden, Germany: VS Verlag für Sozialwissenschaften.

Kuhlmann, C. (2012). *Bildungspolitik und Leistungsvergleichsstudien* [Education policy and benchmarking studies]. Wiesbaden, Germany: VS Verlag für Sozialwissenschaften.

Kultusministerkonferenz (KMK). (1955). *Geschäftsordnung der KMK vom 19. November 1955 i. d. F. vom 2. Juni 2005* [Rules of procedure of the Kultusministerkonferenz from 19 November 1955, in the version of 2 June 2005]. Retrieved from https://www.kmk.org/fileadmin/Dateien/pdf/gogr.pdf

Kultusministerkonferenz (KMK). (1997). *Grundsätzliche Überlegungen zu Leistungsvergleichen innerhalb der Bundesrepublik Deutschland—Konstanzer Beschluss—(Beschluss der Kultusministerkonferenz vom 24.10.1997)* [Fundamental considerations regarding performance comparisons within the Federal Republic of Germany-Konstanzer Resolution (Resolution of the Conference of Ministers of Education and Cultural Affairs of the Federal Republic of Germany) of 24.10.1997)]. Retrieved from http://www.kmk.org/fileadmin/Dateien/veroeffentlichungen_beschluesse/1997/1997_10_24-Konstanzer-Beschluss.pdf

Kultusministerkonferenz (KMK). (2009). *Gemeinsame Leitlinien der Länder zur Deckung des Lehrkräftebedarfs(Beschluss der Kultusministerkonferenz vom 18.06.2009)* [Common guidelines of the federal states to cover the teacher demand (resolution of the Conference of Ministers of Education and Cultural Affairs of 18.06.2009)]. Retrieved from http://www.kmk.org/fileadmin/Dateien/veroeffentlichungen_beschluesse/2009/2009_06_18-Deckung-Lehrkraeftebedarf.pdf

Kultusministerkonferenz (KMK). (2015). *Lehrerbildung für eine Schule der Vielfalt Gemeinsame Empfehlung von Hochschulrektorenkonferenz und Kultusministerkonferenz (Beschluss der Kultusministerkonferenz vom 12.03.2015/Beschluss der Hochschulrektorenkonferenz vom 18.03.2015)* [Teacher education for a school of diversity. Joint recommendation of the Rectors' Conference and the Conference of Ministers of Education and Cultural Affairs (resolution of the Conference of Ministers of Education and Cultural Affairs of 12 March 2015/resolution of the Rectors' Conference of 18 March 2015)]. Retrieved from http://www.kmk.org/fileadmin/Dateien/veroeffentlichungen_beschluesse/2015/2015_03_12-Schule-der-Vielfalt.pdf

Kultusministerkonferenz (KMK). (2016). *Erklärung der Kultusministerkonferenz zur Integration von jungen Geflüchteten durch Bildung (Beschluss der Kultusministerkonferenz vom 06.10.2016)* [Declaration by the Conference of Ministers of Education and Cultural Affairs on the integration of young refugees through education (resolution of the Conference of Ministers of Education and Cultural Affairs of 06.10.2016)]. Retrieved from https://www.kmk.org/fileadmin/Dateien/pdf/PresseUndAktuelles/2016/RS2016-377_355-KMK_TOP4-Fluechtlinge-KMK-Erklaerung-A2_-_Internet.pdf

Lanzendorf, U., & Pasternack, P. (2008). Landeshochschulpolitiken [Higher education policies of the federal states]. In A. Hildebrandt & F. Wolf (Eds.), *Die Politik der BundesLänder, Staatstätigkeit im Vergleich* [Policies of the federal states in comparison] (pp. 43–66). Wiesbaden, Germany: VS-Verlag.

Laufer, H., & Münch, U. (2010). *Das föderale System der Bundesrepublik Deutschland.* [The federal system of the federal republic of Germany]. Munich, Germany: Springer Verlag für Sozialwissenschaften.

Lehmbruch, G. (1976). *Parteienwettbewerb im Bundesstaat.* [Party competition in the federal state]. Stuttgart, Germany: Opladen.

Lehmbruch, G. (2001). Der unitarische *Bund*esstaat in Deutschland: Pfadabhängigkeiten und Wandel [The unitary federal state in Germany: Path dependencies and change]. In A. Benz & G. Lehmbruch (Eds.), *Föderalismus—Analysen in entwicklungsgeschichtlicher und vergleichender Perspektive* [Analyses of federalism in developmental and comparative perspective] (pp. 53–110). Wiesbaden, Germany: Sonderheft Politische Vierteljahresschrift 32, 2001.

Lenk, T., & Glinka, P. (2016). Interessenausgleich unter den *Länder*n?—Einefinanzwissenschaftliche Bewertung des MPK-Beschlusses [Balancing of interests among countries? A financial assessment of the MPK decision]. In M. Junkernheinrich, S. Korioth, T. Lenk, H., Scheller, M., & Woisin (Eds.), *2016: Jahrbuch für öffentliche Finanzen 1–2016—Verhandlungen zum Finanzausgleich, in: Schriften zur öffentlichen Verwaltung und öffentlichen Wirtschaft, Band 233* [Yearbook on public finances series: Public administration and public economy publications, Volume 233] (pp. 131–146). Berlin, Germany: Berliner Wissenschaftsverlag.

Lenzen, D. (2015). *Die Exzellenzinitiative. Deutungsmacht und Wandel im Wissenschaftssystem* [The Excellence Initiative. The power of interpretation and change in the scientific system]. Wiesbaden, Germany: Springer.

Liegle, L. (2006). *Bildung und Erziehung in früher Kindheit* [Education in early childhood]. Stuttgart, Germany: Kohlhammer.

Lörz, M., & Schindler, S. (2011). Bildungsexperten und soziale Ungleichheit: Zunahme, Abnahme und Persitenz ungleicher Chancenverhältnisse—Eine Frage der Perspektive? [Education experts and social inequality: increase, decrease and persistence of unequal chances—A question of perspective?] *Zeitschrift für Soziologie, 40*(6), 458–477.

Münch, R. (2010). *Globale Eliten, lokale Autoritäten: Bildung und Wissenschaft unter dem Regime von Pisa, McKinsey & Co.* [Global elites, local authorities: Education and science under the regime of Pisa, McKinsey & Co.]. Munich, Germany: Suhrkamp.

Münch, U. (2007). Materielles Abweichungsrecht der *Länder* und föderative Asymmetrien in der *Bund*esdeutschen Bildungspolitik [Substantial deviation law of the federal states and federal asymmetries in federal German education policy]. In Europäisches Zentrum für Föderalismus-Forschung Tübingen (Ed.), *Jahrbuch des Föderalismus 2007* [Yearbook of federalism 2007] (pp. 224–278). Baden-Baden, Germany: Nomos Verlagsgesellschaft.

Münch, U. (2009). Von Leuchttürmen, Bildungsgipfeln und Konjunkturtälern. Zur Topographie des deutschen Bildungsföderalismus [From lighthouses, educational summits and economic valleys. On the topography of German education federalism]. In Europäisches Zentrum für Föderalismus-Forschung Tübingen (Ed.), *Jahrbuch des*

Föderalismus 2009 [Yearbook of federalism 2009] (pp. 225–235). Baden-Baden, Germany: Nomos Verlagsgesellschaft.

Münch, U. (2010). Föderale und parteipolitische Interdependenzen bei schulpolitischen Innovationsprozessen [Federal and party political interdependencies in school politics innovation processes]. In Europäisches Zentrum für Föderalismus-Forschung Tübingen (Ed.), *Jahrbuch des Föderalismus 2010* [Yearbook of federalism 2010] (pp. 188–199). Baden-Baden, Germany: Nomos Verlagsgesellschaft.

Neumann, A. (2014). Mehr Wettbewerb, weniger Humboldt? Ökonomisierung in der Wissenschaftspolitik [More competition, less Humboldt? Economization in science policy]. In G. S. Schaal et al. (Eds.), *Die Ökonomisierung der Politik in Deutschland. Kritische Studien zur Demokratie* [The economization of politics in Germany. Critical studies on democracy] (pp. 239–258). Wiesbaden, Germany: Springer.

Organisation for Economic Co-operation and Development (OECD) (Ed.). (2016). *Bildung auf einen Blick 2016* [Education at a glance 2016]. Retrieved from https://www.bmbf.de/files/Education_at_a_Glance_2016.pdf

Picht, G. (1964). *Die deutsche Bildungskatastrophe, Analyse und Dokumentation* [The German educational catastrophe: analysis and documentation]. Freiburg im Breisgau, Germany: Olten.

Poeppelt, K. S. (1978). *Zum Bildungsgesamtplan der Bund-Länder-Kommission. Einfügung des Art. 91 a/b GG und der Prozess der Bildungsplanung für den Elementar-, Primar- und Sekundarbereich in der Bund-Länder-Kommission für Bildungsplanung* [The overall education plan of the Bund-Länder Commission. Insertion of Art. 91 a/b GG and the process of educational planning for elementary, primary and secondary education in the Bund-Länder Commission for Educational Planning]. Weinheim, Germany: Verlag Beltz,.

Reidenbach, M., Bracher, T., Grabow, B., Schneider, S., & Seidel-Schulze, A. (2008). *Investitionsrückstand und Investitionsbedarf der Kommunen. Ausmaß, Ursachen, Folgen, Strategien* [Investment backlog and investment needs of the municipalities. Extent, causes, consequences, strategies]. Berlin, Germany: DIFU.

Reinberg, A. (Ed.). (2001). *Arbeitsmarktrelevante Aspekte der Bildungspolitik* [Labour market-relevant aspects of education policy]. Nürnberg, Germany: Institut für Arbeitsmarkt- und Berufsforschung der *Bund*esanstalt für Arbeit.

Reiter-Meyer, P. (2005). Die Ständige Konferenz der Kultusminister im föderalen System: Zur Rollenfindung und Reformfähigkeit [The instiutionalized Conference of Ministers of Culture in the Federal System: On role finding and reform capability]. In Europäisches Zentrum für Föderalismus-Forschung Tübingen (Ed.), *Jahrbuch des Föderalismus 2005* [Yearbook of federalism 2005]. (pp. 163–173). Baden-Baden, Germany: Nomos Verlagsgesellschaft.

Reuter, L. R., & Linde, A. (1999). *Die Aufgaben der UNESCO im Bereich der Bildung, Erziehung und Weiterbildung.* [UNESCO's tasks in the field of education and training. Hamburg, Germany: Universität der Bundeswehr]. Universität der Bundeswehr, Hamburg, Germany.

Sabatier, P. A., & Jenkins-Smith, H. C. (1993). Policy change and learning: An advocacy coalition approach. *Journal of Policy Analysis and Management, 15*(1), 110–121.

Sandberger, G. (2008). Die Umsetzung der Föderalismusreform im Hochschulbereich [Implementation of the reform of federalism in higher education]. In Europäisches Zentrum für Föderalismus-Forschung Tübingen (Ed.), *Jahrbuch des Föderalismus*

2008 [Yearbook of federalism 2008] (pp. 160–171). Baden-Baden, Germany: Nomos Verlagsgesellschaft.

Scharpf, F. W. (1985). Die Politikverflechtungs-Falle: Europäische Integration und deutscher Föderalismus im Vergleich [The joint decision making trap: European integration and German federalism in comparison]. *Politische Vierteljahresschrift, 26*(4), 323–356.

Scharpf, F. W., Benz, A., & Zintl, R. (1992). *Horizontale Politikverflechtung: Zur Theorie von Verhandlungssystemen* [Horizontal joint-decision making: on the theory of negotiation systems]. Frankfurt a.M., Germany: Schriften des Max-Planck-Instituts für Gesellschaftsforschung.

Scharpf, F. W., Reissert, B., & Schnabel, F. (1976). *Politikverflechtung: Theorie und Empirie des kooperativen Föderalismus in der Bundesrepublik* [Political integration: Theory and empiricism of cooperative federalism in the Federal Republic of Germany]. Kronberg, Germany: Cornelsen Verlag.

Scheller, H. (2007). Die Bildungspolitik der EU—politischer Gestaltungsanspruch in einer kompetenzrechtlichen Grauzone? [The educational policy of the EU - political agency in a legal competence grey area]. In G. G. Sander & R. Vetter (Eds.), *Regelungswut in der EU—Wahrheit oder Mythos?* [Regulatory frenzy in the EU—Truth or myth?] (pp. 109–130). Berlin, Germany: Kovacs Verlag.

Scheller, H. (2010). Der deutsche Bildungsföderalismus im Spannungsfeld zwischen föderalem Kompetenzstreit und europäischer Harmonisierung [German educational federalism in the conflict between the conflict of federal competences and European harmonisation]. In K. Detterbeck, W. Renzsch, & S. Schieren (Eds.), *Föderalismus in Deutschland* [Federalism in Germany] (pp. 225–256). Munich, Germany: Oldenbourg.

Scheller, H. (2015). Der "erschöpfte" Föderalstaat. Diskrepanzen zwischen Reformdebatte und Verfassungsrealität im deutschen *Bund*esstaat [The "exhausted" federal state. Discrepancies between reform debates and constitutional reality in the German federal state]. *Aus Politik und Zeitgeschichte (APuZ), 28*(30).

Scheller, H. (2016). Der föderalismustheoretische Diskurs in der Bundesrepublik—Zwischen Pfadabhängigkeit und normativer Verselbständigung? [The theoretical discourse on federalism in the Federal Republic of Germany—Between path dependency and normative independence?]. In Hausteiner, E.M. (Ed.). *Föderalismen. Traditionen und Modelle jenseits des Bundesstates* [Federalism. traditions and models beyond the state]. Baden-Baden, Germany, Nomos Verlagsgesellschaft.

Scheller, H., & Schneider, S. (2016). *KfW-Kommunalpanel 2016* [Reconstruction Credit Institute—Municipal Panel Study]. Berlin, Germany: KfW-Bank.

Schemmann, M. (2007). Internationale Weiterbildungspolitik und Globalisierung: Orientierungen und Aktivitäten von OECD, EU, UNESCO und Weltbank [International continuing education policy and globalisation: orientation and activities of OECD, EU, UNESCO and World Bank]. In Das Deutsche Institut für Erwachsenenbildung (Ed.), *Theorie und Praxis der Erwachsenenbildung* [Theory and practice of adult education]. Bielefeld, Germany: Bertelsmann Verlag.

Schwager, R. (2005). PISA-Schock und Hochschulmisere—Hat der deutsche Bildungsföderalismus versagt? [PISA shock and university misery—Has German educational federalism failed?] *Perspektiven der Wirtschaftspolitik 2005*, *6*(2), 189–205.

Statistisches Bundesamt (Ed.). (2015). *Bildungsfinanzbericht 2015* [Financial education report 2015]. Wiesbaden, Germany. Retrieved from https://www.destatis.de/DE/Publikationen/Thematisch/BildungForschungKultur/BildungKulturFinanzen/Bildungsfinanzbericht1023206157004.pdf?__blob=publicationFile

Statistisches Bundesamt (Ed.). (2016). *Bildungsfinanzbericht 2016* [Financial education report 2016]. Wiesbaden, Germany. Retrieved from https://www.destatis.de/DE/Publikationen/Thematisch/BildungForschungKultur/BildungKulturFinanzen/Bildungsfinanzbericht1023206167004.pdf?__blob=publicationFile [03.03.17].

Thieme, W. (2004). *Deutsches Hochschulrecht. Das Recht der Universitäten sowie der künstlerischen und Fachhochschulen in der Bundesrepublik Deutschland* [German higher education law. The law of the universities and colleges of arts and crafts in the Federal Republic of Germany]. Köln, Germany: Heymanns.

Tillmann, K. J., et al. (2008). *Pisa als bildungspolitisches Ereignis: Fallstudien in vier BundesLändern* [PISA as an education policy event: Case studies in four federal states]. Wiesbaden, Germany: VS Verlag für Sozialwissenschaften.

von der Leyen, U. (2007). Rede der *Bund*esministerin für Familie, Senioren, Frauen und Jugend zur Haltung der *Bund*esregierung zur Finanzierung des geplanten Ausbaus von Kinderkrippen vor dem *Bund*estag am 11. Mai 2007 in Berlin [Speech by the Federal Minister for Family Affairs, Senior Citizens, Women and Youth on the Federal Government's position on financing the planned expansion of day nurseries before the Bundestag on 11 May 2007 in Berlin]. *Bulletin der Bundesregierung, 53–3.*

Welsh, H. (2014). Education, federalism and the 2013 *Bund*estag elections. *German Politics. Journal of the Association for the Study of German Politics, 23*(4), 400–414.

Wernstedt, R. (2005). Die KMK ist besser als ihr Ruf! Ein skeptischer Rückblick mit zuversichtlicher Perspektive [The Standing Conference of the Ministers of Education and Cultural Affairs (Kultusministerkonferenz) is better than its reputation! A sceptical glance back with a confident perspective]. *Die deutsche Schule*, *97*(2), 148–158]

Weymann, A., & Martens, K. (2005). Bildungspolitik durch internationale Organisationen, Entwicklung, Strategien und Bedeutung der OECD [Education policy through international organisations: development, strategies and importance of the OECD]. *Österreichische Zeitschrift für Soziologie, 30*(4), 68–86.

Wixforth, J. (2011). Qualifizierungsinitiative für Deutschland und der Streit um die Höhe der öffentlichen Bildungsausgaben [Qualification initiative for Germany and the dispute over the level of public expenditure on education]. In *Jahrbuch für öffentliche Finanzen 2011* [Yearbook of public finances 2011] (pp. 437–458). Berlin, Germany, Berliner Wissenschafts-Verlag.

Wolf, F. (2006). Bildungspolitik: Föderale Vielfalt und gesamtstaatliche Vermittlung [Education policy: Federal diversity and national mediation]. In M. G. Schmidt & R. Zohlnhöfer (Eds.), *Regieren in der Bundesrepublik Deutschland. Innen- und Außenpolitik seit 1949* [Governing in the Federal Republic of Germany. Domestic and foreign policy since 1949] (pp. 221–241). Wiesenbaden, Germany: VS-Verlag.

Wößmann, L. (2011). Die Bedeutung der Bildung für die marktwirtschaftliche Ordnung [The importance of education for the market economy order]. In *Jahrbuch für die Ordnung von Wirtschaft und Gesellschaft Band 62* [Yearbook for the Order of Economy and SocietyVolume 62] (pp. 146–175). Stuttgart, Germany: Lucius & Lucius Verlag.

CHAPTER 7

THE ITALIAN EDUCATION SYSTEM

Constitutional Design, Organization and Policy-Making

Elisabeth Alber and Martina Trettel[1]

1. INTRODUCTION

No univocal pattern can be found when it comes to dealing with the distribution of competencies in the field of education in federal and regional countries. On the one side, there are States like the US and Canada in which centripetal wind is blowing (McGuinn, 2012): competencies in education as well as the implementation of education policies are re-allocated to the central level in order to guarantee efficiency and unity within the State-wide education system. On the other side, there are States in which the need is exactly the opposite: governance schemes

[1] During the common elaboration of this paper, Parts 2, 3, 4, 7, 8, 9 were written by Elisabeth Alber, Part 5 by Martina Trettel and Part 1, 6 by both. Both authors are researchers at the Institute for Studies on Federalism and Regionalism at the European Academy of Bolzano/Bozen (EURAC Research) and can respectively be reached at elisabeth.alber@eurac.edu and martina.trettel@eurac.edu.

Federalism and Education: Ongoing Challenges and Policy Strategies in Ten Countries, pages 131–161.

in education are legislatively, administratively and financially ever more decentralized due to structural reforms and in response of claims by constituent units within a State. This is the case in Italy.

With regard to Italy's State structure, it is important to recall that in 1948, the Italian Constitution (ItConst) altogether foresaw twenty regions (art. 131 ItConst) with fifteen regions[2] relying on an ordinary mechanism of power-sharing and five regions[3] on a special mechanism of power-sharing (art. 116 ItConst). Such a constitutional design translated into a highly asymmetric system combining moderate regionalism in most areas of the Italian State with peaks of advanced federal traits in some peripheral special regions. However, the regionalist two-track constitutional design did not properly dismantle Italy's unitary tradition and its centralist political governance,[4] because ordinary regions were only created in the beginning of the 1970s. Moreover, after the creation of ordinary regions, many attempts at devolution of powers from the central to the regional level initially failed. It took multiple decades to devolve legislative competencies from the central State level to the regional one.

Today, the gap between ordinary and special regions is still present with regard to both autonomy arrangements and policy-making (Palermo, 2008). As a general rule, Northern regions are calling for more autonomy while Southern regions are reluctant to do so because of fears of worsening cleavages over economic and living standards. Following the gradual process of regional emancipation in the 1990s, the constitutional reform of 2001 introduced a main element of a federal State design: wide ranging legislative powers for all regions. Since 2001, regions have been entitled to legislate in all areas not expressly reserved to the exclusive power of the State nor to the concurrent legislation. However, in absence of genuine federal political culture both at the central and regional level and with the 2008–2009 financial crisis straining the political system, there has been an increase of judicial litigation and an extensive use of concurrent powers by the central State. The Constitutional Court (ConstCourt) became a key player in resolving numerous conflicts on competence sharing between the State and both

[2] Out of the 15 ordinary regions, eight are in the North (Piedmont, Emilia-Romagna, Liguria, Lombardy, Marche, Tuscany, Veneto and Umbria); two are considered to be in central Italy (Lazio and Abruzzo), while five are located in the South (Apulia, Basilicata, Calabria, Campania and Molise).

[3] The Northern regions Trentino-Alto Adige/Südtirol, Friuli-Venezia Giulia and Valle d'Aosta as well as the island regions Sicily and Sardinia were vested with special powers due to, respectively, the presence of linguistic minorities and socio-economic specificities.

[4] Asymmetric regionalism as a new form of political decentralization was the compromise between federalists and supporters of administrative regionalism. Within the constituent assembly the governing Christian Democrats (DC) were in favor of regional decentralization in order to guarantee uniformity of services throughout the whole Italian territory. The Italian Communist Party (PCI) favored a strong centralist State, while the supporters of a federal State were in a clear minority position. After the elections in 1948, the attitude towards regional decentralization changed: both DC (who won and formed a government with the liberals) as well as the PCI followed partisan advantages (respectively in Rome and in central Italy) in order not to lose their power and were thus against real decentralization.

ordinary and special regions, and it has increasingly decided to the detriment of the regions' autonomy.

Keeping this in mind, the paper in Part 2 discusses relevant constitutional provisions, basic facts and the evolution of the Italian education system. Part 3 elucidates details as to the design and the operation of early childhood education and care systems (ECEC), compulsory education and higher education. It also highlights key actors and their role in education governance. An analysis of the most recent national reform strategy on education, the "Good School Reform," is undertaken in Part 4, while Part 5 focuses on the distribution of legislative and administrative competencies in the field of education by analyzing provisions applying to ordinary regions. Part 6 provides an overview on how education is financed and Part 7 describes how education is dealt with in special regions having linguistic minorities. Part 8 focuses on the case study of the Autonomous Province of Bolzano/Bozen, a constituent part of the Autonomous Region Trentino-Alto Adige/Südtirol (South Tyrol), in the northernmost Italian province where both monolingual school systems based on the right to enjoy mother tongue education and a plurilingual one are in place. In Part 9, concluding remarks and an outlook on the Italian education system are advanced.

2. BASICS AS TO THE STATUS QUO AND THE EVOLUTION OF THE ITALIAN EDUCATION SYSTEM

The ItConst of 1948, in its articles 33 and 34, enunciates basic principles of education referring to the freedom of education (mentioning in particular the free teaching of arts and sciences) and the State's responsibility to provide schooling and schools at various branches and grades for all individuals regardless of their background. Accordingly, schooling is compulsory, free of tuition and provided through a system of public schools. Additionally, the establishment and parity of non-State schools is foreseen; law n. 62/2000 sets non-State schools on a par with State schools by recognizing them as *scuole paritarie* if they—among other criteria—offer a plan of educational objectives in accordance with State-wide standards, have qualified teaching staff and are accessible to all qualified pupils.[5] *Scuole paritarie*—which are mostly catholic schools—are financed both directly (e.g. school buildings) and indirectly by the State (e.g. grants to pupils and tax relief for families) (Alber & Wisthaler 2015.

In terms of educational policy-making, improving inequality of educational opportunities *(i.e.* accessibility and quality of education) is a constant concern,

[5] In the school year 2015/2016 out of more than 8 million of pupils, 7.861.925 were enrolled in State schools (2.583.514 in primary, 1.649.408 in lower secondary and 2.628.648 in upper secondary school) and 960.000 in private schools having equal status. Pupils were subdivided in 369.902 classes and in 8.384 schools. The regions with most pupils were Lombardy (1.185.662), Campania (920.964) and Sicily (763.529) (Ministero dell'Istruzione e della Ricerca, MIUR, 2015). In the school year 2014/2015 slightly less pupils were enrolled (MIUR, 2014), but there are no significant numerical differences.

not only due to recent challenges deriving from (im)migration but also due to the North-South divide, with Southern regions performing worse than Northern ones (Agasisti & Longobardi, 2014; Braga & Checchi, 2010). Moreover, when it comes to educational facilities and schools as well as the performances of pupils, imbalances are significant not only across regions but also within regions. Over the last decades, the Italian education system was subject to a series of reforms; however, those reforms never really managed to properly address the issue of unequal access to education and training due to political instability and the scarce perception of education as a common good enhancing the development of both individual and collective capacities. During the 1960s, the gap between North and South in educational infrastructures was reduced and the participation in compulsory schooling began to increase due to key State interventions.[6] These were years of dramatic economic boom, which turned Italy from an agricultural country to an industrial one. However, the economic gap persisted because the Southern regions continued to be predominantly rural (Putnam, 1993). This resulted in advantages for the North in terms of both school expansion and access to education (Ballarino, Panichella, & Triventi 2014). In the 1970s, several Italian scholars were successful in calling for the improvement of early school failure and new pedagogy concepts defining the school as a promoter of democracy and participation (Calonghi, 1976; Vertecchi, 1976). This informed the creation of innovative evaluation forms meant to be a means of facilitating the communication between the school and the parents. It also translated into provisions regulating both the presence of parents' as well as pupils' representatives in schools and the employment of support teachers assisting pupils with disabilities. The Bassanini-reform introduced in 1997 (see Part 5: Constitutional Distribution of Powers between the State and Ordinary Regions) granted more autonomy to schools. However, this autonomy was mostly limited to organizational aspects and to didactics (Höllrigl et al., 2005).

Originally, education in Italy was viewed as a key means for the creation of a unified Italian society. Accordingly, the Italian State Education System dates back to 1859 when the Casati law n. 3725 mandated educational responsibilities for the upcoming Italian State unification in 1861 (Inzerillo, 1974).[7] In short, the Casati law made two out of four years of primary education compulsory, pursued the goal of increasing literacy and foresaw that the municipalities controlled primary education, the provincial government secondary education and the State tertiary education. However, especially in Southern Italy, the implementation of the law encountered difficulties primarily because, unlike in the Northern territories, lit-

[6] For instance, law n. 105/1955 and law n. 555/1959 concerning the improvement of school facilities in the Southern Italian regions.

[7] The Casati law—promulgated by Vittorio Emanuele II on 13 November 1859—in its five titles and 379 articles focused on administration of the education system (46 articles), higher education (141 articles), secondary education (84 articles), secondary vocational education (43 articles) and primary education and normal schools (for elementary teacher preparation).

eracy and schooling was viewed skeptically by the governing elites in large parts of the South. To counteract such difficulties, the Coppino law n. 3961/1877 increased primary education to five years, and, most importantly, the Orlando law n. 407/1904 raised the compulsory age of schooling to twelve years and foresaw financial aids to municipalities that were not able to provide for primary schooling. As a further step, in 1911, with the Daneo-Credaro law n. 487, control over primary education was centralized with the aim of augmenting literacy in economically disadvantaged rural areas. However, its implementation was hindered by the advent of fascism. In 1923, with the Gentile reform[8], the compulsory age of education was raised to 14 years and after the cycle of primary schooling (five years), a twofold system was introduced in secondary education, giving access either to the *liceo* and higher education or to work training (*avviamento al lavoro*). In 1962, law n. 1859 abolished the work training track and lower secondary schools were unified under the name of *middle school* (*scuola media*, now called *scuola secondaria di primo grado*). Moreover, work including traineeship was made illegal for children under the age of 15, and, in 1968, the State pre-primary school (*scuola materna*) was established. Apart from regulations regarding gender and class, the introduction of further school types and issues related to administration, from 1962 onwards, no major changes occurred with regard to schooling cycles.

In order words, the Italian education system continues, by and large, to be informed by rationales that date back to its very origins and comprise the central position of the teacher as the most prominent source of knowledge, a prevalently deductive kind of teaching and an uncoordinated approach between educational facilities and the labor market. Innumerable legislative interventions over education after 2001 (reform of school cycles, secondary schooling and higher education) accentuated the complexity of the Italian education system, but did not resolve major issues at stake. This led to the broad national education reform strategy, the Good School Reform (see Part 4: The National Education Reform Strategy: the Good School Reform).

3. GOVERNANCE SCHEMES: STRUCTURES, ACTORS, MANAGEMENT

The Italian education system includes pre-primary (*scuola materna*), primary (*scuola elementare*), lower and upper secondary (*scuola secondaria di primo e secondo grado*), post-secondary and higher education (Eurydice/Indire, 2014). In the field of pre-primary education, early childhood education and care systems (ECEC) for children aged less than 3 years is organized at the local level and not yet part of the education system, while ECEC for children aged from 3–6 years is part of the education system but not compulsory. At present, compulsory education lasts for ten years from 6 to 16 years of age (law n. 296/2006

---

[8] Royal legislative decrees of 31 December 1922, n. 1679, 16 July 1923, n. 1753, 6 May 1923, n. 1054, 30 September 1923, n. 2102 and 1 October 1923, n. 2185.

and ministerial decree n. 139/2007) and comprises, as a general rule, five years of primary school, three years of lower secondary school and, at least, two years of either upper secondary school or vocational training courses provided for by the regional education systems (law n. 133/2008). Once compulsory education has been accomplished, students receive a certification attesting the competencies acquired. Access to tertiary education is reserved to those students who passed the State exam at the end of the upper secondary level (a five years cycle that students exiting, as a general rule, at the age of 18/19 years). According to law n. 53/2003, everybody has a right and a duty to profit from education and training for at least twelve years or until he or she has obtained a three-year vocational qualification by the age of 18. Moreover, a 14/15-year-old can decide to spend his or her last phase of schooling on apprenticeship (law n. 183/2010).

Higher education is offered by universities and institutes of the higher education in art and music mostly according to the Bologna structure (Bologna Follow-up Group Secretariat, 2015), higher technical institutes or higher specialized institutions. With regard to higher education, in December 2010 a comprehensive reform (law n. 240/2010) overhauled its governance, which, until then, was characterized by very detailed State regulations and only limited academic self-governance (Rebora & Turri, 2008).[9] The Gelmini Reform was passed to grant higher education institutions more autonomy and make them less path dependent. However, instead of following a *steering from distance* approach as other European countries did in the governance of tertiary education, the Gelmini Reform mainly aimed to solve previous inefficiencies and only marginally provided for structural and organizational innovation. The bureaucratic fulfilment in being a part of public services remains the dominant approach and the Gelmini Reform did not have any substantial impact on power distribution.

With regard to administration, at the national level, the Ministry of Education, University and Research (MIUR) and its several agencies are responsible for both the general administration and policy-making, while each school is administered and run at a decentralized level through regional school authorities and local offices. In practice, the MIUR lays down a general framework for school autonomy to ensure uniformity within the Italian educational system by setting the general and specific objectives of the educational process (pupils' skills, subjects in the national curricula, annual number of teaching hours dedicated to the subjects, the annual compulsory timetable, standards for a quality education, assessment criteria). The regional and local level are responsible for organizing the school network, defining the school calendar and managing school buildings. In sum, MIUR is charged with the definition of limits and contents of school autonomy, the definition of school regulations, the definition of evaluation of learning, the

[9] This led to a situation "where the Academic Senate and Administrative Board, who officially held power, simply satisfied the requirements of the most important internal interests, to a situation in which the rector prevailed, despite having little official power" (Donina, Meolia, & Palearia, 2015, p. 28).

definition of basics as to the compulsory school cycle, the definition of public exams, rules as well as procedures for issuing school certificates and diplomas, the definition of evaluation and monitoring criteria, the creation of criteria for the training as well as for the selection and recruitment of school personnel, the definition and recognition of rights and duties of private schools and schools having equal status. The regional and local level is in charge of regional programming as well as allocating staff and personnel over the territory with the local level being also responsible for pre-primary and primary school buildings. In regions vested with special statutes, the regulations on the organization of the regional authorities differ because the powers of the State authorities are limited (see Part 7: Constitutional Distribution of Powers between the State and Special Regions). For example, in the Autonomous Region Trentino-South Tyrol, there are no regional school offices; education is, in conformity with national principles, under the responsibility of its two constituent units, the Autonomous Province of Bolzano/Bozen (South Tyrol) and the Autonomous Province of Trento (Trentino). Both autonomous provinces have set up their own school systems, which differ in terms of content and didactics because of the presence of linguistic minorities (see Part 8: Case Study: The Autonomous Province of Bolzano/Bozen [South Tyrol]).

As a general rule, with regard to the contents and didactics, each Italian school draws up its own educational offer plan (POF) in conformity with the general and specific objectives of the educational process sets forth by the MIUR. The teachers' council draws up a three-year educational offer plan together in accordance with the objectives set forth by the school principal, who is the legal representative of the educational institution and responsible for the quality in the school as well as the overall management of the school. The district council (primary schools) or school council (comprehensive institutes and secondary schools) then approves the POF. If in conformity with the general framework set forth by the MIUR, the POF can also take into account local needs. It can foresee flexible timetables, create special training programs and activate personalized courses to answer to special needs of the territory. For example, special training programs can be set forth for pupils with disabilities. (It is worth mentioning that, in Italy, disabled pupils are an integral part of ordinary classes and support teachers facilitate them; unlike in other systems, they are not singled out in different classes, which is widely considered a very positive element of the school system (Rossi-Doria, 2009).).

With regard to day-to-day school management, the school principal is assisted by a director of administrative services alongside the teachers' council and so-called intersection or interclass councils (depending on the type of school and on its size). Worth noting is the fact that according to the most recent reform in 2015 (see Part 4: The National Education Reform Strategy: the Good School Reform), school principals are enabled to directly offer the available teaching posts in their schools to qualified persons included in the respective local recruitment lists starting from 2016/2017.

In tertiary education, the rector is responsible for the fulfilment of the university's quality objectives and for guaranteeing the principles of efficacy, efficiency, transparency and merit. An elected academic senate gives mandatory instructions on teaching and research issues and approves the university regulations, while a board of directors is, together with the rector, responsible for the overall management of the university and its staff.

When it comes to evaluation, the National Institute for the Evaluation of the Education System (*Istituto nazionale per la valutazione del Sistema di istruzione,* short: INVALSI) together with the National Institute of Documentation, Innovation and Educational Research (*L'Istituto Nazionale di Documentazione, Innovazione e Ricerca Educativa,* short: INDIRE) and the Inspectorate of the Ministry of Education make up the national evaluation system next to other bodies at both national and regional level in the field of tertiary and vocational education and training. The creation of a national service for the evaluation of the education system in Italy was a long and difficult birth. The task of INVALSI is to prepare tests for the external evaluation of pupils' learning outcomes; moreover, INVALSI works on the improvement of professional development of teachers. INDIRE supports schools in their improvement and innovation process; among other goals, it facilitates in the use of new technologies for in-service training of teachers, of the administrative, technical and auxiliary staff and school managers. The inspectorate focuses on the evaluation of schools and school principals. As a general rule, school evaluation processes start from self-evaluation and external evaluation is carried out in its piloting phase (European Commission/EACEA/ Eurydice, 2015).[10] The implementation of the National System for Evaluation of schools started in 2014/2015 and follows a three-year cycle: self-assessment reports, public reporting and, from the school year 2015/2016 onwards, evaluation by external teams who visit up to 10% of all schools per year (European Commission/DG EAC, 2015).

4. THE NATIONAL EDUCATION REFORM STRATEGY: THE GOOD SCHOOL REFORM

On July 9th, 2015, a very ambitious attempt to overhaul the Italian education system took place. Despite protests from both stakeholders and students, the "Good School Reform" was passed in parliament (227 votes in favor, 173 against and four abstentions). Interestingly, as a part of the legislation's development, from September 15th to November 15th 2014, the Renzi Government had made the

[10] In Europe, external evaluation of schools is currently carried out in 31 education systems located in 26 countries. External evaluation focuses on the school as an entity and essentially aims to monitor and improve its quality by a three step approach: preliminary analysis, site visits and reporting.

document "The good school—let's make the country grow" available for public consultation. All interested parties could participate in the debate on the website.[11]

In sum, law n. 107/2015 gives full implementation to school autonomy aiming at improving the quality of education, reducing early leaving from school (Ballarino & Schadee, 2010; European Commission/EACEA/Eurydice/Cedefop, 2014), increasing both general and practical students' competences and guaranteeing all persons the right to study and receive an appropriate training. It includes an extraordinary plan to finally recruit temporary teachers on a permanent basis (over 100,000), highlights the importance of the three-year educational offer plans (POF) and introduces a yearly merit-based bonus for teachers that is assigned by the school principals. The school principals will identify the best-performing teacher using criteria established by the school's teacher evaluation committee composed of the school principal, three teachers, an external evaluator, two parent representatives (primary school and lower secondary school) or one parent representative and one student representative (upper secondary class). Based on a three-year assessment of the merit-based components for teacher salaries, the MIUR will elaborate national guidelines to evaluate the teachers' performances. Law n. 107/2015 also increases the powers of school principals in recruiting teachers from the regional registers; so far teachers have been allocated to schools by the MIUR through a system of lists ranking teachers according to a set of criteria. To what extent the measure of augmenting the margin of discretion for school principals to manage human, technological and financial resources will render the school system more flexible and responsive to current challenges largely depends on the proper implementation of both the concrete teachers' evaluation and, in general, the translation from theory into practice of all rules concerning the accountability of the system.

In order to better serve the labor market and thus to reduce unemployment among young peoples, law n. 107/2015 foresees an improved and increased alternance of study and work programs and highlights the importance of improving both the digital competence of pupils as well as their skills in mathematical-logical and scientific subjects. The law also stresses the importance of a stronger focus on subjects such as language (by, among others, the introduction of the Content and Language Integrated Learning Method), music, art, law, economy and active citizenship. The law puts a particular focus on economics in hopes of counteracting the deficiencies Italian students have in financial literacy compared to international standards (Organisation for Economic Co-operation and Development, OECD, 2014a). Moreover, law n. 107/2015 mandates more clarity in the field of education both by the creation of a single school data website and by delegating to the central government the task of working on a consolidated act of all provisions on education. Special attention is given to the revision of the

[11] 1.800.000 actors participated online and offline. A detailed analysis of the consultation process is available at https://labuonascuola.gov.it/i-numeri-della-partecipazione/ (24.05.2016).

system of teacher education and recruitment, to the promotion of school inclusion of students with special educational needs, to the revision and coordination of vocational trainings and to the reorganization of the early childhood education and care systems (ECEC).

With regard to ECEC, law n. 107/2015 gives the central government the power to create within 2017 an integrated system of early childhood education and care for children below 6 years. The main innovation is the integration of ECEC for children up to 3 years within the responsibility of the MIUR, and the attempt to create ECEC structures at the premises of primary schools or comprehensive schools in order to make early education services more accessible.

Projections suggest that the school reform is likely to have the largest positive impact on GDP in the long-term (Ministero dell'Economia e delle Finanze, 2015). However, for the time being, the reform has been criticized for allegedly paving the way for an ever more asymmetric system that can easily widen the gap between richer and poorer territories, and for not having paid enough attention to issues such as quality and equity when training future generations. Principal objections to the reform can be summarized as follows: Firstly, the intention to give stability to teachers who have not yet a permanent contract or resulted successful in the last general competition does counteract the phenomena of precarious employment that characterizes Italy's primary, lower and upper secondary schools, but it lacks consistency because it leaves out technical institutes. Secondly, by conferring new powers to school principals in the field of teachers' evaluation, the reform does also disproportionately augment the principals' powers in choosing and poaching teachers from other schools, and arguably may risk concentrating too much power in one official and his or her managerial abilities. Thirdly, in addition to public financing, public schools from now on may seek funding from voluntary tax donations by parents and private donations and this measure could easily contribute to widening the gap between public schools in affluent neighborhoods and those in low-income districts. Fourthly, by fostering internships, work-study programs and closer links between schools and the private sector, the reform might undermine the general educational aspect of the school system. Concretely, in the school system a number of work-study hours (200 hours for high schools, 300 for professional and technical institutes) are introduced to be used during the final three years of studies, also in the afternoon, and, accordingly, students spend these hours on the workplace as well as at private and public institutions. Fifthly, the reform contains provisions that grant tax deductions to parents who send their children to private school on a per student per year basis. This indirect legal support of private education might have negative consequences on the public school system.

5. CONSTITUTIONAL DISTRIBUTION OF POWERS BETWEEN THE STATE AND ORDINARY REGIONS

Articles 117 and 118 of the ItConst (as modified by constitutional law n. 3/2001) lay down the overall distribution of legislative and administrative competencies between the State and the 15 ordinary regions. The articles also stipulate competencies in the field of education. From the legal perspective, one can differentiate four time periods with regard to the distribution of competencies in education: the first prior to the 2001 constitutional reform (const. law n. 3/2001); the second right after 2001; the third between 2004–2009, 2004 being the year in which the ConstCourt adopted its first ruling on the distribution of competencies; and the last one, from 2009 until today.

The Period prior to the 2001 Constitutional Reform

Until 2001, competence in the field of education was strictly a matter of the central State, with the only exception being that of professional training and school support, the latter being shared competencies between the State and the regions. Through the Bassanini reform (law n. 59/1997 and its enactment decree n. 112/98) (Vipiana Perpetua, 2011), the regions and the local entities were vested with administrative functions regarding specific aspects of the school organization (e.g. the distribution of economic resources between schools). Moreover, the Bassanini reform devolved considerable organizational and didactic autonomy in education to the schools themselves. Therefore, the schools started to be seen as key players involved in the decision-making process for the allocation of competencies in education (Bibee, 2007; Cocconi, 2003; Troilo, 2013).

The Period after the 2001 Constitutional Reform

The 2001 constitutional reform (const. law n. 3/2001) changed the whole second part of Title V of the ItConst, which deals with the division of legislative and administrative competencies defined in art. 117. It foresaw a competence catalogue with exclusive central government competencies and concurrent competencies between the State and the regions. The reform dictated that all areas not explicitly mentioned in the ItConst were to be assigned to the regional level of government (e.g. professional training). In the field of education, art. 117 laid down that the State is competent for the adoption of basic norms on education (general education standards—art. 117 para. 2 lit. n) and that aspects of education are a matter of shared competence. In practice, this meant that legislative power would be allocated to the regions, except for specific fundamental principles that would have to be set forth by the State (art. 117 para. 3 ItConst). Moreover, the State was granted exclusive competence in the field of "determination of minimal levels of essential services across national territory" (art. 117 para. 2 lit. m ItConst). It horizontally crosscut all the other competencies, including education, by identifying purposes and setting goals that have to be reached in each specific policy field (Sacco, 2014).[12] As stated by the ConstCourt in ruling n. 282/2002 (section 3), this competence may touch upon all those matters that imply the need of established legal provisions in order to assure the equal enjoyment of public services at a minimum standard level. All this caused a high degree of overlapping of legislative responsibilities in the field of education, mainly with regard to the distinction between *basic norms*, *fundamental principles* and *minimal levels of essential services* (Auriemma, 2005). Moreover, after the 2001 constitutional reform, administrative powers—in all policy fields—became subject to the subsidiarity principle (art. 118 ItConst). This meant that the school administration were to be primarily be organized by local entities (e.g. aspects in programming, monitoring and evaluating locally grounded educational needs) (Morzenti Pellegrini, 2004; Troilo, 2013). The State and the regions were to intervene only if specific services could not be effectively performed by local entities. However, 15 years later, it seems that the subsidiarity principle was never fully applied and the so-called *parallelism principle* is still in place: those entities holding legislative competences are also the ones who actually administer them (Bordignon & Fontana, 2010).

The Period from 2004 to 2009

This complex overlapping of legislative and administrative competences created many misunderstandings and conflicts between the different layers of government. In 2004, the ConstCourt began to clarify some aspects of the distribution of education-related competences (Castelli, 2004). The first ruling (n. 13/2004, section 3) concerned the administrative division of competences: the ConstCourt stated that the Bassanini reform (which gave localities competence for school administration) was still in force, even if the division of competences occurred prior to the 2001 constitutional reform. This ruling signified an effort to give full implementation to the subsidiarity principle. Notwithstanding this pivotal statement, these legal provisions remained *law in the books* and never turned into *law in action* (Pound, 1910). However, the ruling didn't shed light on the most blurry aspect: the interpretation of the relation between *basic norms, fundamental principles* and *minimal levels of essential services* (Mangiameli, 2003; Poggi, 2004; Sandulli, 2003).

With regard to this aspect, the ConstCourt first provided an interpretation in its ruling n. 279/2005 (section 2.1) and, afterwards, in ruling n. 200/2009. The former sketched a first-hand distinction between *basic norms* and *fundamental principles*. It explained that "basic norms" were to be considered rules whose content aimed to respond to unitary needs and therefore they had to be applied unconditionally all over the State territory and beyond a merely regional scope. *Fundamental principles*, on the other hand, even if aiming at setting equality standards,

[12] This argument applies even to the policy fields regarding the protection of the environment and competition.

were not to be translated in directly applicable norms. Hence, these were specific principles that needed to be implemented through regional legal provisions (Nicodemo, 2005). Ruling n. 200/2009 added another piece to this puzzling picture with the ConstCourt's more precise definition of what was to be considered a *basic norm on education.* These are the national legal provisions that define the basic structure of the national educational system and that have to be equally applied to all the national territory in order to ensure the following elements: a homogenous educational offer, parity of treatment between all the subjects involved in the education system and the freedom of establishing (public and private) schools. These norms were directly applicable, meaning that they didn't need any regional legal measure to be effective. Moreover, they outlined the basics of national schooling by providing univocal curricula and qualified personnel aiming at both protecting the national cultural identity and preserving the *freedom of teaching* as stated in art. 33 ItConst (section 24). Furthermore, in this pivotal ruling the ConstCourt provided a definition of "fundamental principles" by describing them as those legal rules that fix criteria, objectives and disciplines with regard to the way in which the education-service has to be provided. The *fundamental principles* differ from the general norms because they wait for regional laws to be fully implemented (section 25). The regional legislation, therefore, needs to comply with the *fundamental principles,* the *basic norms* and—of course—the constitutional principles. Moreover, the ConstCourt pronounced itself on an aspect that, up to that point, had not been completely clear: that the connection between the *fundamental principles* included in the national *framework legislation* and the related regional *implementing legislation.* The *framework legislation* worked only as a junction between *basic norms* and regional *implementing legislation.* In fact, it fell to the regional legislatures to implement the "fundamental principles" by means of concrete tools and instruments (ConstCourt ruling n. 34/2005, ConstCourt ruling n. 309/2010). Finally, regarding the *minimal levels of essential services,* the Court stated that these are supposed to be national laws that define the minimum quality and quantity standards of the State services in education (e.g. the age requirements for pupils to access public schools, the schooling evaluation system, the exams' regulation, the quantitative parameters for the formation of school classes and the legal value of qualifications) (D'Aloia, 2004).[13]

The Period from 2009 to 2016

The stratification between the analyzed pieces of legislation and the rulings offered a bit more clarity with regard to the distribution of competencies in the field of education. However, after the pivotal ruling in 2009, the conflicts between the State and the regions in front of the ConstCourt didn't diminish; on the contrary,

[13] Moreover, it is important to notice that the Court included the employment of teachers in the State exclusive competence catalogue regarding the administrative organization of the State and national public entities (art. 117 para.2 lit. g).

a conspicuous number of rulings were adopted in the last past seven years. The ConstCourt followed the reasoning stated in the above mentioned rulings. For example, in the rulings n. 92/2011 and 147/2012, the ConstCourt tried to safeguard the margin of discretion afforded to regions by both emphasizing the importance of the subnational *implementing legislation* allowing regions to concretely apply fundamental principles and basic norms, and by highlighting the importance of the regional layer of government in acknowledging regional socio-cultural and economic specificities (Fagnani, 2013). In essence, the Court has pushed decentralization in education policies so as to better manage highly diverse regionalist and local needs.

In 2015, the Italian government adopted the extensive reform of the school system, the Good School Reform (law n. 107/2015). While the contents of this new piece of legislation were scrutinized in Part 4, it is also important to notice that this reform has already led to conflicts between the State and the regions. Two ordinary regions (Puglia and Veneto) appealed to the ConstCourt, claiming a new breach of the regional legislative and administrative responsibilities in the field of education (appeals n. 85/2015 and 88/2015).

6. FUNDING RESPONSIBILITIES AND EDUCATION: WHO PAYS FOR WHAT?

Broadly speaking, Italian regions are afforded a very low degree of revenue autonomy. Their spending autonomy, however, which is linked to their legislative and administrative powers as described in art. 117 ItConst, is significantly more substantial. Notwithstanding the fact that the fiscal federalism framework law n. 42/2009 does not present any clear and sound strategy for a territorially comprehensive reform in federal terms, its entry into force was considered one of the crucial steps of Italy's federalizing process (Alber, 2014a; Frosini, 2010).

Fiscal Federalism in the Italian Context

The fiscal federalism law n. 42/2009 intended to finally implement financial autonomy for subnational territories according to art. 119 of the ItConst. By doing so, it intended to adapt the Italian institutional order and intergovernmental financial relations to the 2001 constitutional reform of Title V of the ItConst. In 2001, subnational entities were provided with a myriad of new functions. As a consequence they also required financial means to properly perform the functions. To this end, art. 119 of the ItConst provided for a new arrangement of financial relations as well as the introduction of partial fiscal autonomy at the subnational level. It guaranteed all territorial entities financial autonomy with regard to revenues and expenditure. The implementation of art. 119 of the ItConst was repeatedly urged by the ConstCourt [Const Court ruling n. 370/2003 (section 7) and Const Court ruling no. 37/2004 (section 5)], which stated that the different areas of competencies configured by the new constitutional provisions would be contradicted in absence of its implementation. But it took until 2009 for art. 119 to obtain organic implementation by the central State legislator: the path towards fiscal federalism was finally paved by the law n. 42/2009.

The tremendous delay had further worsened the asymmetry between the expenditure and the revenue accountability as far as territorial autonomies are concerned. While the ordinary regions and local entities were entitled to 50% of the total public spending, they were responsible for only 18% of the revenue. Put simply, the balance of 32% translated into a vertical fiscal gap, highlighting the lack of accountability within the system. Law n. 42/2009 was given the task of reducing this inconsistency (Antonini, 2009) and rests on five pillars: financial and partially also fiscal autonomy[14], tax territoriality, equalization mechanism[15], the criterion of standard costs[16] and transparent as well as accountable performance budgeting[17]. The last pillar, budgeting performance *via* a carrot and stick system, is based on a rather simple idea: at the end of their mandate, regional and local authorities themselves have to answer to their electorate for the manner in which they managed tax resources procured from the territory by drawing up an inventory (such an inventory does not, however, have to be drawn up at the beginning of each mandate). Even if such electorate accountability is a noble aim, such a carrot and stick system can only properly work if subnational entities are assigned true spending and revenue autonomy, which is not the case. Moreover, the body that shall be entrusted with the task of controlling the whole budgeting performance

[14] The right of subnational entities to partially introduce own taxes as well as to modify tax rates, deductions and allowances must respect the principle of tax territoriality (taxing power restricted to the territory of competence) as well as the principles of correlation (taxes and benefits must be correlated) and the one of moderation (taking power limited to the area of spending competencies). The overall tax system, however, still remains mostly centralized as far as the legislative power is concerned (in line with the European trend, with the sole exception of the Swiss Federation). This to guarantee tax pressure uniformity within the whole Italian territory. In general, subnational entities will finance their functions through own taxes (including tax rates on national tax rates), shares of national tax revenues and redistributive transfers. For a comparative analysis as to European case studies see chapter three in Alber and Valdesalici, 2012.

[15] A large equalization fund is foreseen in fundamental services for areas having less fiscal capacity per inhabitant. It refers to standard needs and costs as to the expenditure in connection with essential levels of service and for fundamental functions of local authorities, which are to be guaranteed throughout the whole national territory.

[16] This is the most innovative and critical issue. With the introduction of a standard cost model, the historical expense criteria shall be gradually eliminated. Financing resources shall be assigned to subnational entities on the basis of a standards costs model valid all over Italy. This cost model is calculated against established efficiency norms or benchmarks, both defined in legislative decrees. Financial needs of subnational entities are thus no longer assessed on the bases of spending patterns of the previous year.

[17] The enactment decree no. 149/2011 introduced a carrot and stick system. More precisely, subnational governments get rewards if they perform in a virtuous and efficient manner in the exercise of tax power and financial and economic management in general. Those who fail to conform to the in practice top-down defined benchmarks of economic and financial equilibria get sanctions (for example, disqualifications from office).

system is itself permeable to political logic as it is composed of representatives of the different institutional levels of government (Piperno, 2012). A further critique is that the law n. 42/2009 is only a framework law, containing principles and directive criteria that need further translation into implementing measures. The executive gets a *maxi-delegation* and is in charge of deciding the methods according to which the financial autonomy of the territorial units will be implemented. The parliament is thus to a large extent an external spectator.

In such a decentralized financial structure, regions become *coordinators* of the entire public finance system. However, the most important and most unclear aspect of the whole system, the equalization mechanism, has neither been implemented nor fully designed yet. This is partly due to the impact of the financial crisis and the top-down austerity measures that hindered the implementation of law n. 42/2009. In fact, the issue of fiscal decentralization and fiscal federalism has nearly disappeared from the political agenda in the last years. However, on paper the system designed in law n. 42/2009 saw regions receiving a share of indirect taxes and income tax levied at the central level, and powers to propose new taxes in the fields not covered by existing taxes. Moreover, transfers from central governments, which are largely based on historic expenditures, would be replaced by transfers granted on a standard cost calculation, privileging more efficient and responsible financial management. Until now, nine legislative decrees have been adopted (Portale Federalismo Fiscale, 2016). However, the laws are far from being turned fully into practice (Antonini, 2014; Piperno, 2015). Therefore, one can undoubtedly affirm that, in the field of education, the blurriness characterizing the distribution of legislative and administrative competencies applies even to a greater extent to the division of spending responsibilities between the State and the regions.

The Multiplicity of Actors and the Blurriness of Regional Budgets in the Field of Education

If one attempts to put together a picture of the division of financial responsibilities, it has to be underlined that the information regarding the spending efforts in education of both State and regions is scarce and incomplete. In fact, neither ISTAT (Italian National Institute of Statistics) nor the State administration provide periodical analysis specifically on education spending. The data used here refers to a report elaborated in 2010 by Massimo Bordignon and Alessandro Fontana, where the authors tried to sketch out an estimate of how the financial responsibilities are divided between regions and the State. The major difficulty in elaborating such data is given by the fact that the structure of regional budgets is blurry. In fact, each region has its own structure; thus, it is very difficult to correctly compare the data across regions. This unclearness is attributable mostly to the high number of actors involved in financing education: the minister of education, the other ministers with peripheral responsibilities in education financing (e.g. the minister of foreign affairs who provides funds for Italian schools abroad), the local entities and—of course—the regions that, as already highlighted, enjoy significant legislative and administrative responsibilities. Taking 2007 as the year of analysis, the total expenses in the field of education was 52.386 billion euros. Of that sum, 82% was paid by the State (of which only 1.7% cannot be attributed to national expenditure referred to regions). 11.5% of the total expenses were paid by municipalities, 2.9% by provinces and only 3.4% by regions. This simple information shows the small amount of spending responsibilities ordinary regions are vested with regarding the field of education, in contrast with what is actually foreseen in the laws that regulate spending powers and responsibilities.

However, it is easier to obtain regional data and information regarding the *per capita* amount of expenditure linked to education and the related percentage on the internal regional GDP (see Table 7.1). In a horizontal comparison, the data illustrate that spending for education policies in the Italian regions corresponds to differing behaviors among them: the Southern regions invest relatively more in this area, whereas in the other parts of Italy, spending on education and train-

TABLE 7.1. Public Administration's Education Expenditure.

Region	Expenditure per Capita (€)	Percentage of GDP
Piemonte	907	3.1%
Valle d'Aosta	1,784	5.0%
Lombardia	848	3.0%
Liguria	842	2.5%
Trentino- Alto Adige/Südtirol (Autonomous Provinces of Trento and Bolzano/Bozen)	1,626	4.8%
Veneto	816	2.7%
Friuli Venezia Giulia	871	2.9%
Emilia Romagna	868	2.6%
Tuscany	940	3.2%
Umbria	989	4.1%
Marche	978	3.7%
Lazio	1,041	3.3%
Abruzzo	1,009	4.4%
Molise	1,045	5.1%
Campania	1,155	6.9%
Puglia	1,073	6.1%
Basilicata	1,241	6.8%
Calabria	1,234	7.2%
Sicily	1,193	7.0%
Sardegna	1,087	5.4%

Table created based on 2011 ISTAT data. Data available at: http://noi-italia2015.istat.it/index.php?id=7&user_100ind_pi1%5Bid_pagina%5D=33&cHash=5db14c10c7c783d93a1a82b1cc4c62f4 (24.05.2016) and in the report "La spesa pubblica regionale, Ufficio Studi Confcommercio,"[Regional spending] 2014, available at: http://www.confcommercio.it/documents/10180/3599445/La+spesa+pubblica+regionale/f2e5335b-c8a1-4cc8-a299-9977da3abd2f.

ing in relation to GDP is much lower; data in Central and Northern regions stand still just below 3%. By comparison, in Calabria, Sicily, Campania, Basilicata and Puglia, the incidence of public spending in education and training was higher (between 6.1 and 7.2% of the GDP in 2011). Among the areas of the Centre-North, the Autonomous Region Valle d'Aosta and the Autonomous Region Trentino-Alto Adige/Südtirol (South Tyrol) show higher values than the other regions of the same area. The latter can be attributed to the fact that these regions, for their special status, enjoy a broader amount of administrative competencies in the education field and therefore need to spend more resources in order to finance them. In fact, it is important to notice that the legislative picture and the data set out above, do not affect the autonomy of special regions, which—in general terms—enjoy greater financial autonomy as well as more legislative and administrative competencies. (On these last two aspects see Part 7: Constitutional Distribution of Powers between the State and Special Regions and Part 8: Case Study: The Autonomous Province of Bolzano/Bozen [South Tyrol].)

7. CONSTITUTIONAL DISTRIBUTION OF POWERS BETWEEN THE STATE AND SPECIAL REGIONS

As already elucidated in the Part 1, in 1948 the ItConst foresaw the creation of five special regions (art. 116 ItConst). The special regions Trentino-Alto Adige/Südtirol (South Tyrol), Valle d'Aosta/Vallée D'Aoste (Aosta Valley) and Friuli Venezia Giulia were created because of the presence of linguistic minorities. Especially in the two northernmost regions, Trentino-South Tyrol and Aosta Valley, the introduction of special mechanisms of power-sharing was of fundamental importance for the peaceful living-together of its language groups (German-Italian- and Ladin-speakers in South Tyrol and French-speakers in Aosta Valley). As in other subnational contexts with territorially concentrated ethnic minority groups, in these two regions (and especially in South Tyrol), the design of the school system was important with regard to the settlement of conflict and the establishment of a multilingual administration.

In such minority contexts, one can identify five patterns within school models: 1) monolingual mother tongue education based on separation (e.g. schooling in South Tyrol having German or Italian as the language of instruction, see Part 8: Case Study: The Autonomous Province of Bolzano/Bozen [South Tyrol]), 2) bilingual education based on parity with regard to the two (or even more) languages of instruction (e.g. Aosta Valley), 3) the language parity model, in which none of the language of instruction is the pupils' mother tongue (the Ladin model in South Tyrol to a certain extent is an example of such a design, see Part 8.3: The Plurilingual Parity Model of Ladin Schooling), 4) mixed education models with the (partly limited) right for parents to choose the school (e.g. Brussels area), and 5) monolingual majority education with some instruction in minority languages (e.g. the instruction in Ladin in some mountainous municipalities in the almost entirely Italian-speaking Autonomous Province of Trentino) (Palermo & Woelk,

2008). Overall, the monolingual majority school model is the prevailing one, even though bilingual education is increasingly discussed as an ideal model (Abello-Contesse, 2014) and new didactics such as CLIL are being increasingly adopted in ethnically divided societies (Alber, 2016).

Before turning to the case study of South Tyrol, it is important to briefly refer to the relevant regulations on language use in the Italian regions that have a special statute. This is to facilitate the overall understanding of both the differentiated linguistic minority regime set forth by the Italian State and the regulations of the case study South Tyrol, which, in comparison to those of other special regions having linguistic minorities, differ substantially. While in South Tyrol, all public acts are written both in German and Italian (and some even in Ladin), in Aosta Valley, they can be written either in French or Italian, with the exception of judicial provisions (art. 38 of the statute of the Aosta Valley). Education is guaranteed in both languages in all grades and all types of schools. Furthermore, the same number of hours is guaranteed for teaching the French and the Italian language, and French may also be used as a vehicular language to teach other subjects (Gaggero, 2013). The special statute of the region Friuli-Venezia Giulia in its art. 3 states that all citizens are equal and have equal rights regardless of their linguistic origin. This concrete protection of the Slovene minority in Friuli-Venezia Giulia derives from a complex pattern of international agreements (for instance, the Treaty of Osimo in 1975) and from various legislative acts regarding administration and schooling in the provinces of Trieste and Gorizia as well as from regional legislation related to the media sector (Gaggero, 2013). A comprehensive law was passed only in 2001. Essentially, the law granted rights that were already in force: the use of Slovene names, bilingual toponomy, schools with Slovene as the teaching language and the use of Slovene in dealing with the public administration. The passage of the regional law was facilitated by the approval of the State law n. 482/1999 that finally implemented art. 6 of the ItConst ("The Republic takes appropriate measures to safeguard linguistic minorities"). Law n. 482/1999 *inter alia* acknowledged the principle of territoriality and recognized twelve linguistic minorities in its art. 2 (among many others, Albanians, Catalans, Greeks, Friulan, Occitan). Financial means for a full implementation of the law to allow for activities such as mother tongue education or the use of the mother tongue in media and public offices were and still are missing. Law n. 482/1999, as a general rule, does not concern linguistic minorities in the Northern special regions, which favor a special competence catalogue and financial regime due to international obligations set forth in art. 116 of the ItConst.

International obligations were of key importance for the establishment of the power-sharing system between the main language groups living in South Tyrol, German- and Italian-speakers. The Gruber—De Gasperi Agreement of 1946 (Annex IV of the Paris Peace Treaty) calls for equal rights for German-speaking Italian citizens, and the creation of special provisions that safeguard the ethnic and cultural character of German-speakers (i.e. the parification of the German and

Italian languages in the public sphere, mother tongue education in the compulsory education cycle and equality of rights with regard to the employment in the public sphere, *ergo*: an ethnic quota system). Today, art. 99 of the statute of the special region Trentino-South Tyrol sets the use of the German language on par with the territory of the Autonomous Province of Bolzano/Bozen, while art. 19 articulates the mother-tongue principle in education. Accordingly, in the schools having Italian as the language of instruction, all subjects are taught in Italian, and, conversely, in schools having German as the language of instruction, all subjects are taught in German. Teaching of the "second language" (this is the official name of Italian in German schools and of German in Italian schools) is compulsory. As to the administration in education, each language group runs its own schools, from the nursery to secondary schools. Teachers must also prove their mother tongue to be entitled to teach in the school of the respective group. A plurilingual model is in place only in the Ladin valleys, and for tertiary education (where it translates in an extensive use of English in addition to German and Italian).

8. CASE STUDY: THE AUTONOMOUS PROVINCE OF BOLZANO/BOZEN (SOUTH TYROL)

The development and the implementation of the educational regime in South Tyrol has to be considered through the lens of history: South Tyrol's annexation to Italy in 1919, the fascist occupation that dismantled the German-language school system by means of its Italianization measures, the regulations enshrined in the First Autonomy Statute of 1948 and the regulations enshrined in the Second Autonomy Statute of 1972 (Vidoni, 2006).

South Tyrol is the northernmost Italian entity bordering Austria and Switzerland. Throughout its whole territory (7.400 km^2), a power-sharing system based on the strict separation between the two major groups, German- and Italian speakers, comprehensively regulates the living-together of its 520,023 inhabitants[18] in politics, administration, education and even in the judiciary (Second Autonomy Statute of 1972, presidential decree n. 670 of 31 August 1972). South Tyrol managed to successfully accommodate its language groups (69.41% German, 26.06% Italian and 4.53% Ladin speakers)[19] by establishing a political system based on consociationalism (Pallaver, 2008; Wolff, 2008). All provisions and stipulations on the use of language are assisted by strict legal guarantees and remedies (Alber & Palermo, 2012).

[18] Data as of 30.09.2015. Source: http://www.provinz.bz.it/astat/de/bevoelkerung/442.asp.

[19] Data refers to the linguistic declaration at the last census in 2011. 453,272 valid linguistic declarations or affiliations were handed in. Important to note is that the different language groups are distributed heterogeneously throughout the territory of South Tyrol (with the exception of the Ladins). However, German-speakers mainly populate rural areas, and Italian-speakers mainly urban areas as well as the Southern part of the province.

The Period from 1948 to 1972

In 1948, the Italian Parliament issued the First Autonomy Statute, which ensured far-reaching autonomy, though essentially at a regional level. Taking the whole region into consideration, Italians were the majority and German-speakers were very easily outnumbered in decision-making. With regard to education, the Province of Bolzano enjoyed primary legislative powers only in relation to specialized courses in agriculture and commerce. For primary, secondary and upper-secondary education, the Province of Bolzano was only granted secondary legislative powers within the limits of a national framework law. Teaching in mother tongue and 'mother tongue teaching' in the second language was provided even though its organization was extremely difficult due to both the absence of qualified teachers and the little autonomy in the field of education. Teachers whose mother tongue was German generally did not have an appropriate educational background. Therefore, in cooperation with the Italian University of Padua, the Austrian University of Innsbruck provided a series of specialization courses. In German-language schools, teaching of Italian (being the official language) was obligatory. On the contrary, Italian-language schools did not have to provide German language classes. The teaching and administrative staff were an integral part of the Italian national educational system, and, back then, the provincial school system had little financial means.

Such frameworks were dissatisfactory and negotiations at local, national and international level led to the so-called "package" of legislative measures, which became the 1972 Second Autonomy Statute (ASt). The most relevant legislative and administrative powers were subsequently transferred from the Autonomous Region Trentino-South Tyrol to the two "Autonomous Provinces" of South Tyrol and Trentino. Today, South Tyrol enjoys the most extensive self-government within Italy (nearly all competencies except the army, the police and a few minor issues (Alber & Zwilling, 2014)). The ASt applies generally to both autonomous provinces in the same way, but South Tyrol in addition has special provisions regarding, among others, the use of mother tongue in the school system.

The Period from 1972 to 2016

According to the ASt and the respective enactment decrees, the three-tier school system is subject to an administration referable to the provincial institutional regime and responds to the principle of monolingualism. According to art. 8 ASt, South Tyrol enjoys exclusive legislative power on nursery schools, school welfare, school buildings and vocational training. Furthermore, the Province is entitled to issue laws on primary and secondary education (and teacher training) in conformity with the principles established by State legislation. Art. 19 of the ASt provides for mother tongue instruction and the compulsory teaching of the second language German or Italian. Further, it provides for special measures in the schooling contents, the structure and the administration of the provincial school system in derogation of the principles established by State law and functional to the needs of South Tyrol.

As to the didactics and contents, South Tyrol is granted the right to adapt syllabi to local necessities, notwithstanding their conformity with the fundamental principles at national level. As to diplomas obtained in German-language secondary schools, they are equivalent to those of schools having Italian as the instruction language. In order to guarantee this equivalence, the MIUR must be consulted for teaching programs and examinations.

With regard to the administration of South Tyrol's school system, since 1996 the Provincial Government has had the power to appoint both the superintendent (in agreement with the MIUR) as well as the German and Ladin school inspectors (prior consultation with the MIUR). As already pointed out in earlier parts, in the rest of Italy, the regional level together with the local level are responsible for implementing the overall national education and schooling offer.

The principle of free choice in enrolling either in German-, Italian- or Ladin-language schools applies in South Tyrol (art. 19 para. 3 ASt). Parents have the right to enroll their children in any school they choose. This right cannot be abused to influence in any manner the language of instruction of the respective school. The school authority has the right to contest and refuse inscriptions if the pupil's language skills are considered to be too weak. The case is submitted to a joint commission with equal representation appointed by the respective school inspector and the superintendent. Provided that the respective school authority confirms its decision to refuse the enrollment, the parents have the option of challenging the decision in front of the Autonomous Section of the Bolzano/Bozen Regional Court of Administrative Justice. As to the enrollment of foreign students, art. 19 ASt also finds application *vis-à-vis* foreign pupils. Accordingly, the parents of foreign pupils can choose to send their child to either German- or Italian-language nursery, primary and secondary schools. Schools, however, are differently confronted with the need of integrating foreign children. In line with the trend in the rest of Italy, the number of enrolled South Tyrolean pupils (Italian citizens) is decreasing in some school grades (Italian-language nursery schools, German-language primary schools and Ladin primary schools, German-language secondary schools), while the number of enrolled foreign pupils increases in all schools (Medda-Windischer & Girardi, 2010). In contrast with the autochthonous population, for immigrants, the apprehension of Italian and German language is not a matter of identity-building, but first and foremost a tool for a successful integration in the local labour market.[20]

[20] For the time being, there is no data on how immigrants educated in South Tyrol integrate in the local labour market. Too few immigrants have concluded their schooling in South Tyrol and there is not yet a second and even third generation of migrants.

The training of teachers is offered by the Free University of Bolzano/Bozen and its Faculty of Education.[21] German and Italian experts in education sciences cooperate to create the contents of teacher training programs. This makes the programs unique in the German-speaking area. In fact, programs had to be created whose contents did not resemble degree courses offered in Germany or degree courses offered in Austria (being the South Tyrolean education system in any case bound to Italian national framework legislation). Considering the principle of separation in education in South Tyrol, the degree course in primary education is divided into three sections: training of teachers who will work in German-language schools, training of those who will be employed in the Italian-language schools and training of teachers who will be part of the Parity Model of Ladin Schools. Students have to enroll in one section even though they may take additional classes in the other section as well (optional multilingualism). For tertiary education, in 1979 German and Ladin speakers were set on a par with Austrian citizens for the sake of access to higher education in Austria (*Gleichstellungsgesetz, Bundesgesetz* 25.01.1979, BGBl. N. 57). In concrete terms, this implied that diplomas of secondary education were equated with those of Austrian high schools and that South Tyroleans were entitled to the same treatment with regard to study fees. In 1982, Austria and Italy agreed on the manner and extent to which a cooperation of universities should become reality. The Agreement between the Republic of Austria and the Republic of Italy that came into force on October 1st, 1983 paved the way for the *integrated curriculum on Italian law* of the University of Innsbruck in Austria.

The Plurilingual Parity Model of Ladin Schooling

In South Tyrol, Ladin speakers are granted the right to use their language in public offices in the Ladin municipalities,[22] but also in offices located outside of those valleys, if the offices represent Ladin interests. This means that Ladin can also be used in contact with regional and provincial authorities (for example, with the Ladin Education Authority established in 1975 and the Ladin Pedagogical Institute created in 1987).

Ladin schools are informed by the principle of teaching language parity with the same number of hours given in German and Italian language. Ladin itself is also taught, used as a back-up language, and, in the lowest grade, also used as a language of instruction.[23] The right to Ladin-language schools is enshrined in art. 19 para. 2 of the ASt. Interestingly, the Ladin population has always fought for the creation of a trilingual primary school system. The debate remained heated even

[21] The Free University of Bolzano/Bozen was established in 1997. For the Faculty of Education see https://www.unibz.it/en/faculties/education/ (24.05.2016).

[22] Unlike German speakers, who are present throughout the whole territory of South Tyrol, Italian-speakers are mostly concentrated in the cities and larger towns, and Ladin speakers are in the valleys of Gherdëina and Badia.

[23] Two forms of 'Ladin' are in use, the "Badia Ladin" and the "Gherdëina Ladin."

with the entry into force of the ASt in 1972. Because of its calls for full autonomy in the school system, the South Tyrolean People's Party (SVP) was demanding either a German or Italian school in the Ladin valleys (in conformity with the right of mother tongue instruction throughout all subjects during obligatory education). The dispute culminated in an appeal against art. 7 of the enactment decree n. 116/1973, which concerns the principle of teaching language parity and the use of Ladin as an assistant language. The ConstCourt dismissed the appeal (ruling n. 101/1976) and the Parity Model of Ladin schools became the official one in the Ladin municipalities (Runggaldier, 2010). The ruling excludes the possibility of choosing between a school having Italian or German as language of instruction and confirms the *de facto* discrimination of German- or Italian-speaking children with regard to mother-tongue instruction. According to the ConstCourt, the right to attend German or Italian language schools is precluded in the Ladin municipalities under the terms of art. 19 of the ASt because of the trilingualism of the Ladin schools (Rautz, 2008).

Today, the Ladin school model arouses public interest, because of the high success rate of Ladin-speakers in the bi(tri)lingualism exam on provincial level. Already in nursery school, children are confronted with three languages. Moreover, English is introduced as foreign language already in primary school. As to enrollment, the same principle as in German- and Italian-language schools is in force: free choice of the parents. Everybody can enroll in the Ladin parity schools. Teachers have to know all three languages to be employed in Ladin-language schools and with regard to nursery and primary schools, employment is preconditioned on teachers declaring themselves affiliated to the Ladin language group.

9. CONCLUDING REMARKS AND OUTLOOK

The evidence presented in this paper shows how the Italian education system is caught between the two poles of centralization and decentralization aiming at guaranteeing both a certain degree of homogenization in schooling throughout Italy, and the recognition and valorization of territorial specificities for the common wealth of the State. Overall, Italy's governance schemes in education allow for regional diversifications in a system that is progressing at different rates in different locations (Bordignon & Fontana, 2010) and continuously looks for an ever more coordinated approach between its key stakeholders. The introduction of school autonomy certainly augmented the chances of renewing the education system bottom up; however, it comes in a centralized context in which economic and human resources are still scarce and poorly coordinated.

The 2001 constitutional reform has vested regions with broad autonomy, but, in absence of a genuine federal political culture, it did not manage to create a well-functioning system of intergovernmental relations between the governmental levels. It, rather, resulted in governance schemes with conflicting competencies and political instability. Such dynamics had strong impacts on the policy field of education. The implementation of constitutional provisions on education has, thus, until today been very blurred, and, as a general rule, the education system remains centralized, not least because of the fact that the control over three important issues in education—the definition of general rules, the recruitment of the personnel and the allocation and management of finances—is in the hands of the central State.

Overall, the education system continues to operate on a centralistic imprint that responds to the following constitutional principles: the right and duty of parents to provide education for their children, the duty of the State to support persons in getting free education at all grades; the freedom of teaching, the duty of the State to provide education open to everyone, the right of universities and higher institutions to lay down their own regulations, and the right of private individuals to establish school at no cost for the State.

With regard to the distribution of competencies, general issues on education aimed at guaranteeing minimum standards throughout the whole territory are of exclusive legislative State competence (e.g. school staff, quality assurance, State financial resources and foreign schools). The regions have some concurrent powers, as they are, for example, solely responsible for the field of vocational education and training. However, the distribution of powers in the field of education differs in a few Northern regions that have special statutes. There, different school models are in place due to the presence of linguistic minorities and innovative practices are increasingly experimented. For example, South Tyrol serves as an example to this regard since its education model in the field of vocational training is considered to be a best practice within Italy.

Generally speaking, Italian educational policies are still scarcely integrated with social and work policies. This explains why there are marked differences in basic skills proficiency across the Italian regions and why the early school leaving rate—even though it is decreasing since 2008—remains well above the EU average (European Commission/DG EAC, 2015). Compared to the EU average, the higher education attainment rate for young people is also low in Italy.

Another challenge Italy's education system is facing is the fact that work-based learning is not sufficiently well-developed and the move from education to employment is anything but seamless, even though some regions have developed innovative strategies to respond to the transition from education to employment thanks to their own institutional autonomy. The development of such strategies is, however, often left to the whims of local or regional initiatives and the scarce and uncoordinated use of financial resources in times of crisis does not appear to leave much space for the regional and local level to continuously work on innovative practices in education. It also should be noted that, in Italy, general central government expenditure on education as a proportion of GDP is among the lowest in the EU, particularly in higher education (European Commission/DG EAC, 2015).

A relatively recent challenge is the development of integration policies in schooling with regard to pupils having immigrant background. The proportion of pupils and students not having Italian citizenship has been increasing significantly in recent years (Fondazione ISMU, 2015) and demands a modernization of teaching practices and didactic concepts both in terms of digitalized teaching and learning as well as in the field of teacher career systems and teachers' salaries (European Commission/DG EAC, 2015. The status of the teaching profession is perceived to be rather low because of the limited career perspective and the relative low salaries. This explains why the teaching profession has difficulties in attracting best-qualified graduates. The creation of the merit-based component for teachers' salaries in the 2015 Good School Reform is a positive step as it introduces the principle of assessing teachers' work and rewarding good performance, but it might only be a drop in the ocean as the reform does not modify the teacher career system.

Overall, Italy is making some progress in improving and modernizing its education system in terms of pedagogic practice and organizational policy as well as practice (OECD, 2014b), but there is still a long way to go to properly develop policies that efficiently address inequalities across the Italian territory.

REFERENCES

Abello-Contesse, C. (2014). Bilingual and multilingual education: An overview of the field. In C. Abello-Contesse et al. (Eds.), *Bilingual and multilingual education in the 21st Century* (pp. 3–23.). Bristol, UK, Buffalo, NY, & Toronto, Canada: Multilingual Matters.

Alber, E. (2014a). Italy's Piecemeal Path Towards Fiscal federalism: One Step Forward, Two Steps Back? In S. Lütgenau (Ed.), *Fiscal Federalism and Fiscal decentralization in Europe. Comparative Case Studies in Spain, Austria, the United Kingdom and Italy* (pp. 139–171). Innsbruck & Wien, Austria, and Bozen, Italy: Studienverlag.

Alber, E. (2014b). Haut-Adige/Tyrol du Sud: Un système éducatif divisé dans les Alpes [South Tyrol: A divided education system in the Alps]. *Revue Internationale de Politique Comparée, 21*(4), 59–82.

Alber, E., & Palermo, F. (2012). South Tyrol: Lost in Interpretation? In X. Arzoz (Ed.), *Bilingual Higher Education in the Legal Context* (pp. 287–309). Leiden, The Netherlands & Boston, MA: Martinus Nijhoff Publishers.

Alber, E., & Valdesalici, A. (2012). Reforming fiscal federalism in Europe: Where does the pendulum swing? *L'Europe en Formation, 363*, 325–366.

Alber, E., & Wisthaler, V. (2015). Kommentar zu Art. 13 [Commentary to Art. 13]. In R. Hofmann et al. (Eds.), *Rahmenübereinkommen zum Schutz nationaler Minderheiten, Handkommentar* [Framework convention for the protection of national minorities, commentary] (pp. 411–413). Baden-Baden, Germany: Nomos.

Alber, E., & Zwilling, C. (2014). Continuity and Change in South Tyrol's Ethnic Governance. In L. Salat et al. (eds.), *Autonomy Arrangements Around the World, Romanian Institute for Research on National Minorities* (pp. 33–66). ECMI, Flensburg, Germany: University Babes-Bolyai, EURAC Research, Bozen, Italy.

Agasisti, T., & Longobardi, . (2014). Inequality in education: Can Italian disadvantaged students close the gap? *Journal of Behavioral and Experimental Economics, 52*, 8–20.

Antonini, L. (2009). La rivincita della responsabilità. A proposito della nuova legge sul federalismo fiscale [The re-match of reponsibility. The new fiscal federalism law]. In *I quaderni della sussidiarietà, No. 7.* Milano, Italy: Fondazione per la sussidiarietà.

Antonini, L. (2014). L'autonomia finanziaria delle regioni tra riforme tentate, crisi economica e prospettive [The financial autonomy of regions caught between reform attempts, economic crisis and prospects]. *Rivista dell'Associazione Italiana dei Costituzionalisti, 4*, 1–17.

ASTAT, South Tyrolean Provincial Statistics Office (2016). *South Tyrolean population data as of 30.09.2015.* Retrieved from http://www.provinz.bz.it/astat/de/bevoelkerung/442.asp

Auriemma, S. (2005). *Istruzione e scuola nell'assetto costituzionale delle competenze* [Education and school: Constitutional design of competence distribution]. Napoli, Italy: Tecnodid.

Ballarino, G., Bison, I., & Schadee, H. (2010). *So far so good? Early school leaving and social stratification in Italy.* DSLW Working Paper, 7/2010, Dipartimento di Studi del Lavoro e del Welfare. Milano, Italy: Universita degli Studidi Milano.

Ballarino, G., Panichella, N., & Triventi, M. (2014). School expansion and uneven modernization. Comparing educational inequality in Northern and Southern Italy. *Research in Social Stratification and Mobility, 36*, 69–86.

Bibbee, A. (2007). *Making federalism work in Italy*. Economics department working paper no. 590, *OECD Papers*, 2007, 17. Retrieved from http://www.oecd.org/officialdocuments/publicdisplaydocumentpdf/?doclanguage=en&cote=eco/wkp(2007)50

Bologna Follow-up Group Secretariat/Secrétariat du processus de Bologne. (2015). *The European higher education area in 2015: Bologna process implementation report 2015*. Retrieved from www.ehea.info/

Bordignon, M., & Fontana, A. (2010). *Federalismo e istruzione. La scuola italiana nell'ambito del processo di decentramento istituzionale* [Federalism and education. Institutional decentralization of the Italian school]. Working Paper n. 34. Turin, Italy: Fondazione Gianni Agnelli, 2010.

Braga, M., & Checchi, D. (2010). Sistemi regionali e capacità di sviluppo delle competenze. I divari dalle indagini Pirsl e Pisa [Regional systems and competencies. Differences of PIRSL and PISA analyses]. *Rivista delle Politiche Sociali/Italian Journal of Social Policy, 3*, 1–25.

Calonghi, L. (1976). *Valutazione* [Evaluation]. Brescia, Italy: La Scuola.

Castelli, L. (2004). Istruzione e Regioni: La legislazione regionale dopo il titolo V [Education and regions: Regional legislation after Title V]. *Giornale di diritto amministrativo* (pp. 839–842).

Cocconi, M. (2003). L'autonomia funzionale delle istituzioni scolastiche fra riforma del Titolo V, riordino del sistema formativo e coordinamento comunitario [The autonomy of school caught between reform and TItle V. The re-arrangement of the education system and the coordination with EU law]. *Amministrazione in Cammino* (pp. 8–15).

D'Aloia, A. (2004). I livelli essenziali delle prestazioni in materia di istruzione e formazione professionale alla luce della riforma del titolo V della Costituzione [Essential services in education and vocational training after the reform of Title V of the contitution]. *Autonomie locali e servizi sociali*, 367 ff.

Donina, D., Meolia, M., & Palearia, S. (2015). Higher education reform in Italy: Tightening regulation instead of steering at a distance. *Higher Education Policy, 28*, 215–234. doi:10.1057/hep.2014.6

European Commission/DG EAC, (2015). *Education and training monitor*. Italy, Luxembourg: Publications Office of the European Union, Retrieved from http://ec.europa.eu/education/tools/et-monitor_en.htm.

European Commission/EACEA/Eurydice. (2015). *Assuring quality in education: Policies and approaches to school evaluation in Europe*. Eurydice Report. Luxembourg: Publications Office of the European Union. Retrieved from http://eacea.ec.europa.eu/education/eurydice/eurypedia_en.php

European Commission/EACEA/Eurydice/Cedefop. (2014). *Tackling early leaving from education and training, in Europe: Strategies, policies and measures*. Eurydice and Cedefop Report. Luxembourg: Publications Office of the European Union. Retrieved from http://eacea.ec.europa.eu/education/Eurydice/thematic_reports_en.php

Eurydice/Indire. (2014). The Italian education system. *I Quaderni di Eurydice, 30*. Retrieved from www.indire.it/eurydice/eurypedia

Fagnani, E. (2013). La Corte si pronuncia nuovamente sul riparto di competenze in materia di istruzione e boccia l'assunzione diretta dei docenti in Lombardia [The constitutional court on the distribution of competencies in education: No direct hiring of teachers in Lombardy]. *Le Regioni*, 844–850.

Fondazione ISMU/MIUR. (2016). *Alunni con cittadinanza non italiana. La scuola multiculturale nei contesti locali, rapporto nazionale A.S. 2014/2015* [Pupils with foreign citizenship. The multicultural school in local context. National report]. Quaderni ISMU 1/2016, Milano, Italy. Retrieved from http://www.istruzione.it/allegati/2016/Rapporto-Miur-Ismu-2014_15.pdf

Frosini, T. E. (2010). The gamble of fiscal federalism in Italy. *Italian Journal of Public Law, 1*, 124–146. Retrieved from http://www.ijpl.eu/archive/2010/issues-11/the-gamble-of-fiscal-federalism-in-italy

Gaggero, M. (2012). Minoranze linguistiche ed Istruzione nelle regioni ad autonomia differenziata [Linguistic minorities and eduation in special regions]. In E. Ceccherini & M. Cosulich (Eds.), *Tutela delle identità culturali, diritti linguistici e istruzione* [Protection of cultural identities, linguistic rights and education] (pp. 87–114). Padova, Italy: CEDAM.

Höllrigl, P., Meraner, R., & Promberger, K. (Eds.) (2005). *Schulreformen in Italien und ihre Umsetzung in Südtirol* [School reforms in Italy and their implementation in South Tyrol]. Innsbruck and Wien, Austria, and Bozen, Italy: Studienverlag.

Inzerillo, G. (1974). *Storia della politica scolastica in Italia. Da Casati a Gentile* [The history of education policies in Italy: From Casati to Gentile]. Roma, Italy: Editori Riuniti.

Istituto Nazionale di Documentazione, Innovazione e Ricerca Educativa (INDIRE). (n.d.) Retrieved on June 28, 2016, from www.indire.it

Istituto nazionale per la valutazione del sistema educativo di istruzione e di formazione (INVALSI). (n.d.). Retrieved on June 28, 2016, from www.invalsi.it/invalsi/index.php

Mangiameli, S. (2003). Prime considerazioni sulla tecnica di riparto delle competenze legislative nel nuovo disegno di legge costituzionale di revisione del titolo V [First insights into the distribution of legislative competencies in the constitutional draft law for the revision of Title V.]. *Forum di quaderni costituzionali*. Retrieved from www.forumcostituzionale.it/wordpress/wp-content/uploads/pre_2006/142.pdf

McGuinn, P. (2012). Introduction to the Publius Virtual Issue: Federalism and educational policy. *Publius: The Journal of Federalism*, 1–5.

Medda-Windischer, R., & Girardi, R. (2010). Jahresbericht über Einwanderung in Südtirol 2010 [Annual report on immigration in South Tyrol, 2010]. EURAC research, Bolzano/Bozen, Italy.

Ministero dell'Economia e delle Finanze. (2015). *Documento di economia e finanza. Sezione III Programma Nazionale di Riforma* [Document on economy and finances. Section III—National program of reform]. Rome, Italy.

Ministero dell'Istruzione e della Ricerca (MIUR)—Servizio Statistico, Focus. (2014). Anticipazione sui principali dati della scuola statale [Statistical office: Focus on facts and data on the public school]. A.S. 2014/2015, settembre 2014. Retrieved from http://www.istruzione.it/allegati/2014/Avvio_Anno_Scolastico2014_2015_3.pdf (28/06/2016).

Ministero dell'Istruzione e della Ricerca (MIUR). (2015). *Anno scolastico al via per oltre 8 milioni di studenti* [School year: More than 8 million students]. Ufficio Stampa, Roma, Italy. Retrieved from http://hubmiur.pubblica.istruzione.it/web/ministero/cs130915 (28/06/2016).

Morzenti Pellegrini, R. (2004). *Istruzione e formazione nella nuova amministrazione decentrata della Repubblica. Analisi ricostruttiva e prospettive* [Education and vocational training and decentralized and administration. Analyses and prospects]. Milan Italy: Giuffrek Editor.

Nicodemo, S. (2005). Livelli di legislazione e "livelli di principi" in materia di istruzione [Multilevel legislation in education]. *Forum di quaderni costituzionali 2005*. Retrieved from http://www.forumcostituzionale.it/wordpress/wp-content/uploads/pre_2006/331.pdf

Organisation for Economic Co-operation and Development (OECD). (2014a). *PISA 2010 results: Students and money. Financial literacy skills for the 21st Century*. Volume VI, 2014a. Retrieved from http://www.oecd.org/pisa/keyfindings/PISA-2010-results-volume-vi.pdf

Organisation for Economic Co-operation and Development (OECD). (2014b). *Measuring innovation in education: A new perspective, educational research and innovation*. OECD Publishing. Retrived from http://dx.doi.org/10.1787/9789264215696-en

Palermo, F. (2003). Il regionalismo differenziato [Asymmetric regionalism]. In T. Groppi & M. Olivetti (Eds.), *La Repubblica delle autonomie. Regioni ed enti locali nel nuovo titolo V* [The autonomies. Regions and local entities in the new Title V] (pp. 55–62). Torino, Italy: Giappichelli.

Palermo, F. (2008). South Tyrol's special status within the Italian Constitution. In J. Woelk, F. Palermo, & J. Marko (Eds.), *Tolerance through law—Self governance and group rights in South Tyrol* (pp. 33–49). Leiden, The Netherlands and Boston, MA: Martinus Nijhoff Publishers.

Palermo, F., & Woelk, J. (2008). *Diritto costituzionale comparato dei gruppi e delle minoranze istruzione*. [Comparative constitutional law and of groups of minorities] Padova, Italy: Cedam.

Pallaver, G. (2008). South Tyrol's consociational democracy: Between political claim and social reality. In J. Woelk, F. Palermo, & J. Marko (Eds.), *Tolerance through law—*

Self governance and group rights in South Tyrol (pp. 303–327). Leiden, The Netherlands and Boston, MA: Martinus Nijhoff.

Parolari, S., & Palermo, F. (Eds.) (2015). *Riforma costituzionale e Regioni. Riflessioni a prima lettura sul nuovo Titolo V della Costituzione* [Constitutional reform and regions. Considerations on the new Title V of the constitution]. Istruzione. Bolzano, Italy: Eurac Book No. 55.

Piperno, S. (2012). Implementing fiscal decentralization in Italy between crisis and austerity: Challenges ahead. *Perspectives on federalism, 4*(3), 98–124.

Piperno, S. (2015). Il federalismo fiscale in mezzo al guado [What is the matter with fiscal federalism?]. *Rivista Centro Studi sul Federalismo, 56*, 1–2.

Poggi, A. (2004). *Un altro pezzo del ''mosaico'': Una sentenza importante per la definizione del contenuto della competenza legislativa concorrente delle regioni in materia di istruzione* [Another piece of teh mosaic: The constitutional court on the distribution of legislative concurrent competencies of the region in education]. Federalismi.it. Retrieved from http://aperto.unito.it/bitstream/2318/45508/1/28012004040522.pdf

Portale federalismo fiscale. (n.d.). Retrieved from https://www.portalefederalismofiscale.gov.it/portale/web/guest/ap_Pound, R. (1910). Law in the books and law in action. *American Law Review, 44,* 12–36.

Putnam, R. D. (1993). *Making democracy work. Civic traditions in modern Italy*. Princeton, NJ: Princeton University Press.

Rautz, G. (2008). A minority within a minority: The special status of the Ladin valleys. In J. Woelk, F. Palermo, & J. Marko (Eds.), *Tolerance through law—Self governance and group rights in South Tyrol* (pp. 279–290). Leiden, The Netherlands and Boston, MA: Martinus Nijhoff.

Rebora, G., & Turri, M. (2008). La governance del sistema universitario in Italia: 1989–2008 [The governance of the Italian university system]. Liuc Papers n. 221, *Serie Economia Aziendale 32*.

Rossi-Doria, M. (2009). *Di mestiere faccio il maestro* [My job is being a teacher]. Napoli, Italy: L'Ancora del Mediterraneo.

Runggaldier, J. (2010). Die paritätische Schule der Ladiner in Südtirol [The teaching parity school of the ladins in South Tyrol]. In G. Pallaver (Ed.), *Politika10, Jahrbuch für Politik, Südtiroler Gesellschaft für Politikwissenschaft* [Politica10. Yearbook of teh South Tyrolean political science association] (pp. 477–493). Bozen, Italy: Edition Raetia.

Sacco, F. (2004). *Competenze statali trasversali e potestà legislativa regionale: Un tentativo di razionalizzazione (a proposito della "tutela della concorrenza") della Corte costituzionale* [State competencies and regional legislative competencies: An attempt of rationalization]. Associazione Italiana dei Costituzionalisti 2004. Retrieved from http://archivio.rivistaaic.it/cronache/archivio/competenze_statali/index.html

Sandulli, A. (2003). *Il sistema nazionale di istruzione* [The national system of education]. Bologna, Italy: Il Mulino.

Troilo, S. (2013). Titolo V e nuova governance del sistema scolastico tra Stato, Regioni e autonomia locali. Il ruolo delle Istituzioni scolastiche autonome [Title V and teh new governance of the school system between the state, the regions and the local entities. The role of the school institutions]. *Forum di quaderni costituzionali, 2,*

1. Retrieved from www.forumcostituzionale.it/wordpress/images/stories/pdf/documenti_forum/paper/0419_troilo.pdf

Valdesalici, A. (2014). Features and trajectories of fiscal federalism in Italy. In S. Lütgenau (Ed.), *Fiscal federalism and fiscal decentralization in Europe. Comparative case studies in Spain, Austria, the United Kingdom and Italy* (pp. 73–101). Innsbruck and Wien, Austria, and Bozen, Italy: Studienverlag.

Vertecchi, B. (1976). *L'archivio decimologico per l'autovalutazione delle scuola* [Self-evaluation of the school]. Milano, Italy: FrancoAngeli.

Vidoni, C. (2006). *La scuola dell'autonomia provinciale* [The provincial autonomy and its school]. Roma, Italy: Armando Editore.

Vipiana, P. P. M. (2011). Osservazioni sul cosiddetto federalismo amministrativo nella sua evoluzione e nei suoi sviluppi [Observation of the so-called administrative federalism]. *Le Istituzioni del Federalismo, 2*, 395–421.

Wolff, S. (2008). Complex power sharing as conflict resolution: South Tyrol in Comparative perspective. In J. Woelk, F. Palermo, & J. Marko (Eds.), *Tolerance through law. Self-Governance and group rights in South Tyrol* (pp. 329-370). Leiden, The Netherlands and Boston, MA: Martinus Nijhoff Publishers.

CHAPTER 8

FEDERALISM AND EDUCATION

Governance, Standards, and Innovation for the 21st Century in Spain

Mario Kölling and Xavier Rambla

INTRODUCTION

The Kingdom of Spain is one of the most decentralized countries in the world. The decentralization process started after the end of the Franco dictatorship and in parallel to the transition to democracy during the second half of the 1970s. The Spanish education system in this context has undergone several changes. The most relevant has been the off and on, asymmetric transfer of competencies and resources from the central administration to the 17 Autonomous Communities (ACs). Some ACs, Catalonia and the Basque Country, for example, received control over their educational systems in the early 1980s, developing their own bilingual education programs and distinctive curricula. In the ensuing two decades, the transfer process expanded to the whole country, setting a new educational system in which, except for small differences, all ACs have the same power to develop their own educational models within the framework defined by the national government.

Federalism and Education: Ongoing Challenges and Policy Strategies in Ten Countries, pages 163–186.

Historically, the socio-economic development of Southern and North Western Spain has been quite disparate. A number of urban and industrial areas such as the Basque Country, Catalonia, and more recently, Madrid as well as some tourist regions such as the Balearic Islands have attained higher levels of income per capita than more rural Southern regions such as Andalusia or Extremadura. In the context of the Spanish decentralized education system, there have been many efforts to ensure equal educational opportunities for schoolchildren in the whole country and for decades, experts and policy-makers have been concerned with regional disparities in education. Yet despite this attention, according to international PISA tests, the ACs still have vastly different educational outcomes. These disparities stem both from the variety of regional social structures (e.g., instruction level of the adult population) and from the significant structural cleavages (e.g. based on historical legacy, or regional preferences for school models) existing within the education system and affecting outcomes. Nevertheless, in general terms, the decentralization process in education has been an important opportunity for successful policy change in the past decades.

In this text, the education system has been analyzed from different points of view and academic disciplines, both regarding the driving forces of school system development (e.g. political dynamics or external factors) and regarding the school system outcomes and the impact of different geographical, historical and sociocultural variables.

Based on these contributions, we will apply a broader focus in our analysis on the evolution and current challenges of the Spanish model. First to allow a comparative perspective with other case studies in this publication, and, second, in order to concentrate on policy lessons that might be learned from the case in a wider context. In this sense, we will study the evolution of the decentralization process and the education model underpinning the crucial reform steps, both of which determined the current design of the model and explain the dynamics between convergence and diversity in the Spanish educational model.

Generally speaking, the creation of regional governments or 'autonomous communities' (AC) in Spain shows how a former highly centralized country can be very successful in accommodating multilingual and cultural demands by decentralising competencies in education. However, the Spanish case also unveils some institutional shortcomings, not least the difficulty in aligning legal harmonization with efficient policymaking and a continuous dialogue among the levels of government.

The first section will also show that the model has been shaped by socio-economic struggles over distribution as well as by conflicts over religious, linguistic-cultural and national identity issues. Furthermore, we will analyze the political factors that have been important driving forces in the evolution of education policy in the ACs.

In our second section, we will concentrate on the constitutional distribution of competencies in the Spanish education model between the Central State and the

ACs, underlining some central characteristics of the model. For instance, the Constitution has seldom been changed during the past decades. In addition, the current concept of ACs deals with the linguistic and cultural heterogeneity of Spain.

The third section explores the financing of the Spanish model. The findings support our argument of the differing impact of the financial crisis on the education policies of the ACs, both regarding the performance of Spanish students, and regarding the reduction in public resources devoted to education.

In our section on intergovernmental relations, we will highlight some political and institutional factors that hinder the cooperation between ACs and the central government. Similar to other policy fields, the institutional design seems to yield some deficits in intergovernmental relations. Finally, we will concentrate on key policy outcomes of the model. Thus, we underline the legacy of a dual and deeply unequal educational system, but also point to recent improvements.

Our text also gives some insight on the background of the ongoing discussion in Spain related to recent educational reform, which, according to several political parties and ACs threatens the quality of the Spanish educational system, and seems to be a recentralization of the system.

EVOLUTION OF THE FEDERAL AND EDUCATION MODEL

Centralism, together with authoritarianism, has been a traditional feature in the recent history of Spain, but there have also been attempts towards decentralization, especially in the First Republic (1873) and the Second Republic (1931–1936). These efforts had important consequences for the development of the current educational system.

The Public Instruction Act of 1857 was the first comprehensive framework regulation of the Spanish educational system, introducing obligatory schooling for children between the ages of six and nine throughout the whole territory. The Act specified the role of the Catholic Church in schools and provided a legal framework for private education. Both elements remain important determinants of the educational model today. Although brief, the Second Spanish Republic is of great importance to understanding the decentralization of Spanish education. From 1931–1936, decentralization and education became major issues within the political debates. While the Constitution established basic standards such as a unified system of schools, cost-free and compulsory primary education and academic freedom, it also considered the possibility of teaching in the mother tongue (in regions where there was another co-official language different from Spanish). Moreover, during the Second Republic, Catalonia and the Basque Country were formally recognized, this distinction also having been a reason for their special status during the decentralization process which started in the second part of the seventies. The Statutes of Catalonia and the Basque Country considered for the first time the possibility of assuming competencies in education. In addition, other regions were starting during the Second Republic projects for their own statutes in order to assume responsibilities for self-government. However, most could not approve their Statutes because of the outbreak of the Spanish Civil war in 1936. During the Franco regime, the Catholic Church gained a strong influence within the education system. The Franco regime deconstructed the liberalized educational system of the Second Republic and constructed a system that was oriented around Spanish nationalism, reinforcing the unity of the state (Maravall, 1996).

While transitioning to democracy during the second half of the 1970s, democratising and modernising the education model was a main goal of the constituent process. However, the distribution of powers between the Central state and the AC was not directly defined in the Constitution. This is not only a specific feature of the educational system, but also a general feature of the open-ended character of the territorial distribution of power in Spain. At the beginning of the Spanish democratization process, it was uncertain whether all of Spain would be decentralized or whether only a few territories, in particular the *historic Autonomous Communities* (Catalonia, the Basque Country and Galicia), would receive a Statute of Autonomy[1]. In this sense, the Constitutions offered the possibility of a very asymmetrical decentralization, during which the territories could have taken paths towards autonomy or not. Indeed, article 149.3 offered the possibility that most powers in the field of education could be transferred to the Autonomous Communities within the framework legislation, on which the Central state had not passed specific framework laws. Within this constitutional design, the education system has undergone a decentralization process in several phases in which the Central Government gradually transferred functions, services, and resources to the ACs. The motivations for assuming responsibilities in education were different among the ACs. Education was a specific issue for Autonomous Communities with their own languages and a high level of regional identity. ACs with governments composed of nationalist parties could gain greater powers and responsibilities in education at the very beginning of the decentralization process. In this sense, the *historic Autonomous Communities* Catalonia and the Basque Country assumed the competencies in education (excluding university education) at the beginning of the eighties. In addition, Andalusia, the Canary Islands, Valencia, Galicia and Navarra started the process of assuming competencies in education (again, excluding university education) in the later eighties and completed this process towards the beginning of the nineties. All other ACs expanded their Autonomy Statutes to include education during the nineties. Among the ACs that were not governed by nationalist parties, the demands for more power in education policy were not based on the rational of a better provision of programs and resources, but usually had more to do with the different political colours of both governments. The decentralization process has not been free of conflict, but the Constitutional Court has generally allowed considerable space to the ACs, especially in languages mat-

[1] The Statutes of Autonomy constitute the basic institutional law of the Autonomous Communities. They are approved by absolute majority in a final voting in Congress. The Statutes regulate essential aspects, such as each Autonomous Community's identity symbols, organization, functioning and competencies.

TABLE 8.1. Main Steps of the Decentralization Process in Education.

First phase 1979–1980	Catalonia and the Basque Country
Second phase 1981–1992	Andalucía, Canarias, Comunidad Valenciana, Galicia and Navarra
Third phase 1992– 2000	Aragón, Asturias, Baleares, Cantabria, Castilla-La Mancha, Castilla y León, Extremadura, La Rioja, Madrid, Murcia

ters. Furthermore, the transfer of competencies in educational and linguistic matters to the AC has smoothed political problems without attacking the core of the Central state power in education (Cotino, 2013).

The model, which at the beginning of the nineties might have been considered asymmetric, has become increasingly symmetric. Between 1981 and 2000, the responsibilities, functions, services and resources of both university and non-university education have been assumed by all ACs. Today only the Spanish Autonomous Cities Ceuta and Melilla have not assumed responsibilities in education. Remarkably, in little more than two decades, Spain was transformed from the most centralized nation in Europe to one of the most decentralized in education and government. During the process, there have not been excessive variations in the distribution of competencies and the Central state has maintained as much oversight power in education as was possible in the ACs. Although there are not major differences in the competencies between ACs, each autonomous community has established its own educational model and there are important governance and administrative variations among them. In this sense, the challenge during recent years has been to ensure that Spain has one educational system made up of 17 integrated, semi-autonomous parts rather than 17 separate educational systems. These regional differences are the key to understanding the modern Spanish state (Heywood, 1995). Education also plays a different role among the Statutes of Autonomy. The new or amended Statutes of Autonomy since 2006 gave special attention to education. Thus, most included a specific reference to the right to education, the quality of education, the equity of access to education, the right to vocational training and lifelong learning, and the right to participation in teaching. However, most statutes included references to education without major consequences, and in most cases, these laws represent only a shift from regulatory standards to organic laws. Nevertheless, the 2006 Catalan Statute provoked a debate over its constitutionality, especially regarding the language issue. According to the Spanish Constitution, Spanish is the official language of Spain. Some ACs have a co-official language, namely Catalan, Valencian, Galician (all Romance languages deriving from Latin) and Basque, which is spoken in the Basque Country and in some areas of Navarre.

Along with the religious, linguistic-cultural and national identity issues pushing the decentralization process, political factors were also important driving forces for the evolution of the education systems. In the last 35 years, there have been different national education laws, which, on the one hand have responded to the evolution of the model, but on the other, have been strongly motivated by partisan preferences. Illustrating this latter point, not a single educational law has been passed with the two major parties in agreement and national education policy approaches have been modified whenever the parliamentary majority has changed. Similar to other policy fields, the lack of consensus and extreme politicization of educational issues have had major implications for the Courts (Holesch & Nagel, 2012). Consequently, the Constitutional Court played an outstanding role in the development of the system, generally allowing considerable space for the ACs. But the ruling of the Constitutional Court has changed over time and recent judgments seem to bolster the overall responsibilities of the Central State in the education model[2].

Conflicts over framework regulation have always contained disputes related to the balance of the Central State and the ACs, but also can include questions related to the cleavage of church vs. state or governing party vs. opposition parties. Particularly relevant for the purpose of this study is the cleavage of nation/linguistic minorities vs. the majority identity. The debate on the current framework legislation, the LOMCE, has seen especially high levels of conflict, but this comes as a reflection of such existing cleavages. The legislative proposal of the Popular Party government, which was supported by an absolute majority in parliament, received the opposition from all other political groups, educators, some regional authorities and a large part of society. One of the main arguments has been that the new law invaded the decision-making powers' of regional governments and fostered the recentralization of the education model.

AC with the Spanish Socialist Workers' Party (PSOE) governments have frequently used this argument, often regarding language and identity issues. The current law divides languages into three categories: core (Spanish and the first foreign language); specific (a second foreign language) and specialism (Catalan, Basque, and Galician). The first should occupy at least 50% of the time, the second a maximum of 50%, and the third does not have a minimum amount of time assigned. Furthermore, under the proposals, students may obtain their secondary school degree without having to prove their knowledge of the co-official language. According to the law, ACs with co-official languages must guarantee students the availability of a place at a school that teaches Spanish, even if this means attending a grant aided private school paid for by public-regional funds. However, three years and two elections after the adoption of the education law, with new majorities in parliament, the law will likely be amended.

CONSTITUTIONAL DISTRIBUTION OF POWER

The legislative framework of the Spanish education system is based on the 1978 Spanish Constitution and the Statute Laws for each AC, which implement the

[2] (FJ 3rd STC 184/2012, of 17 October)

principles and rights set out in the Constitution. Specifically, Article 27 of the Spanish Constitution addresses the basic principles of the education model and Article 149.1.xxx, regulates the conditions under which academic and professional titles are acquired, exhibited and recognized. It also makes the establishment of the basic norms, rights and freedoms mentioned in Article 27 a responsibility of the Central government. Article 149.1.i is also important to mention, which underlines that the Central government holds exclusive competence in regulating the basic conditions guaranteeing the equality of all Spaniards in the exercise of their rights and in the fulfilment of their constitutional duties, in which education is included.[3] The Constitution is silent about the distribution of competencies in education among the different levels of government. Nevertheless, the Constitutional Court affirmed in several judgments that the Central government is responsible for the design of the education model[4]. However, how far the design of the education model may go has been a constant dispute between the ACs and the Central government.

Since 1978, the design of the education model has been determined by different organic laws, passed in accordance with the Constitution and determined by endogenous political and cultural/linguistic dynamics, including:

- The 1985 Organic Act on the Right to Education (LODE) aimed at guaranteeing the right to education and academic freedom, encouraging society's involvement in education and rationalising the provision of publicly funded schools.
- The 2002 Organic Act on Qualifications and Vocational Training (LOCFP) had the objective of organising vocational training, qualifications and accreditation.
- The 2006 Organic Act on Education (LOE) reformed the basic regulation for the general organization of the Spanish non-university education system.
- Lastly, the Organic Act on Education Standards Improvement (LOMCE—Ley Org 8/2013) is the current legislative framework that expands upon Article 27 of the 1978 Spanish Constitution and specifies the distribution of powers between the Central state, the Autonomous Communities and the educational institutions (Ministerio de Educación, 2014).

According to the constitutional and legal framework, the central government designs the outline, which regulates the principles, objectives and organization of the different educational levels, as well as some of the contents. The Central State

[3] Additional key constitutional specifications for the organic laws are the equality of all Spanish people before the law (Article 14), freedom of religious and ideological denominations (Article 16), the freedom of teaching (Article 20.1), the guarantee of professional schooling (Article 40.2) and the capacity to transfer specific powers to international organizations or institutions (Article 93).

[4] (FJ 3rd STC 184/2012, of 17 October)

has retained exclusive powers in ensuring the unity, homogeneity and guarantee of the basic conditions of equality in the exercise of educational rights. For the most part, these are regulatory powers governing basic aspects of the system, although some are also executive in nature, mainly focusing on evaluation and quality. These powers include, among others, the general organization of the education system, the definition of minimum requirements for educational establishments, the formulation of the nation-wide general plan for education and the establishment of common educational standards. According to article 6.a of the LOMCE (the current legislative framework), the Central government is responsible for the design of the core curriculum in relation to the objectives, skills, content, evaluation criteria, standards and measurable learning outcomes. (Ministerio de Educación, 2013).

The Ministry of Education, Culture and Sport is the Central Government body responsible for proposing and implementing these guidelines and for carrying out the powers in education exclusive to the State. The Ministry implements government policy in pre-primary, primary, secondary education, and with higher education. In order to implement these competencies, the Ministry of Education has an Education Inspectorate in each AC who is charged with exercising government functions in the area to control education standards and compliance with Central state requirements. The Ministry acts as the education authority in Ceuta and Melilla and in governmental institutions located abroad.

According to the LOMCE, the ACs are responsible for complementing the contents of the core subjects, and establishing the contents of the subjects considered important by a specific Autonomous Community. Based on their respective Autonomy Statutes, the Autonomous Communities have the regulatory power to develop the basic state standards, regulate non-basic elements of the education system, and manage the resources for exercising these powers. In total, the ACs are responsible for the everyday routine of running the system, the administrative tenure of educational institutions, the founding, construction and management of public educational institutions, the teachers and other staff. They may also grant and administer scholarships and grants. The ACs are responsible for the licensing of private non-subsidized schools (*centros privados*) and for grant-aided private schools (known as *centros concertados*).[5] The ACs develop school curricula inside the framework provided by the Central government. This entails complying with the state's regulations on the different grades, stages, and modalities of the curriculum.

Local authorities do not have specific executive and legislative competence, but work with the Central government and the ACs on the planning and development of education policy. In this sense, education laws simply recognize the ability of local bodies to assist the Central government and the ACs in the field of

[5]According to summary data for the year 2015: 28.162 state schools, 19.093 grant aided private schools, and 9.069 purely private schools.

TABLE 8.2. Distribution of Responsibilities between Central State and ACs.

Responsibilities of Central State	Responsibilities of ACs
• The enactment of basic standards that specify the constitutional right to education, through the general organization of the education system and the laying down of minimum requirements for educational institutions. • International cooperation in educational matters. • The promotion and general coordination of research. • The formulation of the nation-wide general plan for education, the establishment of the core curricula and the regulation of academic and professional diplomas and nation-wide valid certificates. • The regulation of basic education required to guarantee the right and duty to have a command of the Spanish language. • The Senior Inspection of the education system, in order to supervise and enforce compliance with basic regulations. • General investment planning for education in accordance with the predictions of the Autonomous Communities. • The policy of educational grants charged to the State budget. • Educational statistics for State purposes.	• The Education Inspection Service. • The administrative tenure of educational institutions, the functions derived from it and the powers to create and/or authorize and operate public and private educational institutions. • The drawing up, passing and execution of reform projects, fitting out and construction. • The administration of personnel. • The design, development and approval of experimental and pedagogical research plans. • The development of State provision regarding educational curricula and the regulation of levels, modalities, grades and specializations. • The processing and granting, where appropriate, of private educational institutions. • The administration of scholarships and study grants. • The regulation of the composition and functions of the School Councils in each Autonomous Community with educational functions and services.

education. These local authorities participate in planning schools. They are also responsible for obtaining the land for building schools, for the conservation and the maintenance of public kindergartens and primary schools, as well as for the enforcement of compulsory education laws. With regard to primary schools, the municipalities are also responsible for covering additional costs including the provision of textbooks and other school materials. They provide the staff necessary to administer school facilities. One of the most controversial recent issues has been the question of school meals for needy pupils and students. Eventually, the ACs agreed to pay for this service, but local authorities deliver the meals.

FUNDING RESPONSIBILITIES

At approximately the time of Franco's death in 1975, Spain was spending only 1.78 percent of its GNP on education, the lowest percentage in Western Europe by a considerable margin. The European average (including the USSR) was 5.1

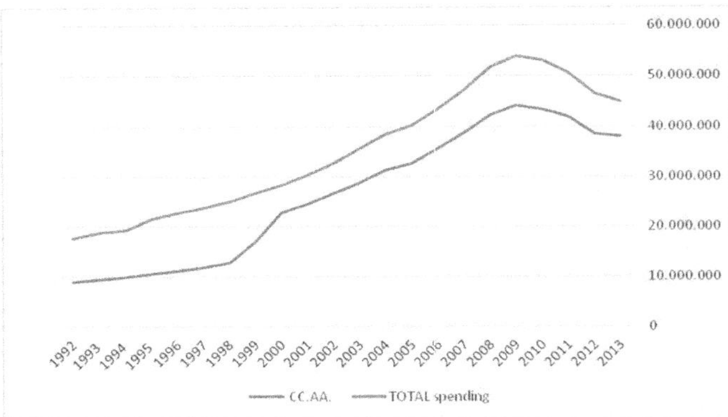

FIGURE 8.1. Evolution of Expenditure on Education by Autonomous Communities (CCAA) vs Total Spending

percent, and the African average was 4.1 percent.[6] Since the democratic transition, there have been important rises in spending levels, both in absolute terms and as a share of public budgets. The increasing level of spending in education can largely be explained by economic growth and increasing state spending and, thus, may not have been related to the decentralization process. Expenditure per student in primary, secondary and post-secondary non-tertiary education institutions has risen during the past decades. In 2011, annual expenditure per student by educational institutions for all services was near the OECD average from primary to tertiary education. However, there was also a decrease in percentage of GDP spent on education between 1995 and 2013, which can be explained mainly by the demographic changes that have occurred in Spain and the recent economic crisis.

Moreover, as a direct effect of decentralization, the relation of the spending between the public administrations changed. While, in 1980, the central state bore 95.5% of educational costs, over the course of decentralization, its contribution has sunk considerably. With the completion of the decentralization in 2000, the proportion of central state expenditure fell to under 15% of the total expenditure in education. In 2013, the ACs were responsible for 85% of public spending in education,7% of public spending in education corresponded to the Central government and 5.2% to the local government. The share carried by ACs significantly exceeded the share of constituent units in Belgium and Germany (Calero & Choi, 2013).

Education in Spain is both publicly and privately financed. With regard to the public financing, there are different funding and fiscal arrangements. Moreover,

[6] See: Centro de Investigacion y Documentacion Educativa, 1995; Engel, 2008; Moreno, Arriba, & Serrano 1998; UNESCO 1987.

it is necessary to differentiate between the general fiscal system and the charter system among ACs (*comunidades forales*). The charter ACs (the Basque Country and Navarre) have extensive fiscal powers, and regional authorities collect all the yield of nation-wide taxes (except for customs). In this sense, the charter ACs enjoy financial autonomy, since, unlike the rest of the ACs, they are not dependent upon vertical transfers from the central government.

The ACs of the general system receive state funds to finance their education systems. Such funding can come in two different ways: first, the Central state can transfer funds directly to the Department of Education and/or provide funds to the Department of Finance of each AC. These funds are not only allocated by the ACs to the public sector, but also earmarked for subsidizing non-grant-aided and grant-aided private schools. Secondly, the ACs also contribute from their own budgets to finance the cost of education within their territory. Among the ACs, there are different funding and fiscal arrangements, which, in many cases, translate into different levels of spending. This diversity is the result of the orientation of educational policies, the financial resources available and the number of private and grant aided private schools in each AC.

With regard to the percentage of each AC's GDP spent on education, we can see a range between 2.8% (Madrid) and 5.99% (Extremadura). This vast range is explained not only by the intensity of public education spending, but by the wealth of each community (the same amount of expenditure can represent a different percentage of the GDP). Moreover, the intensity of public education spending is different according to the number of grant-aided private schools, non-grant-aided

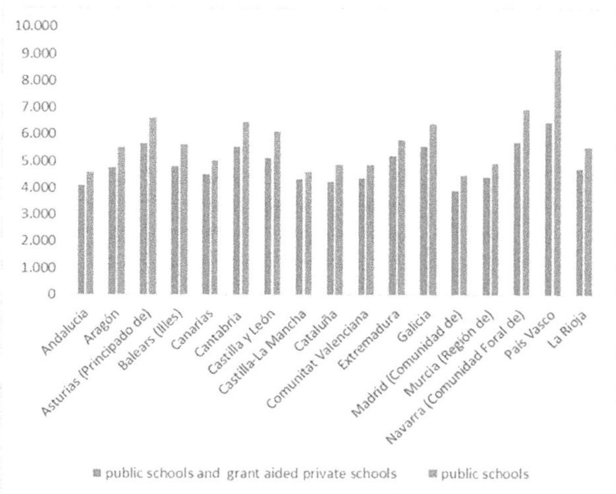

FIGURE 8.2. Public Expenditure in Public or Grant-Aided Private Schools per Student in 2013 (euros). Source: MECD (2016).

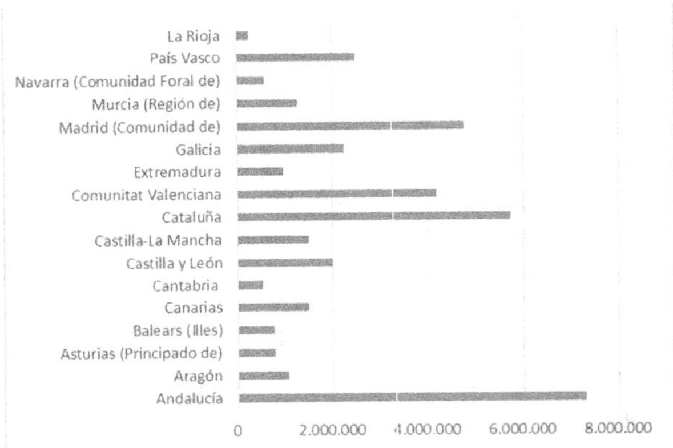

FIGURE 8.3. Total Expenditure on Education by AC in 2013 (euros). Source: MECD (2016).

private schools and public schools. In Madrid, La Rioja, Catalonia, the Balearic Islands and Navarre, where there are more grant-aided private schools, the GDP is higher than the average (Calero & Choi, 2013).

If we analyze public expenditure on education per capita, we can see a correlation with the data presented in Figure 8.1. There are important differences between ACs belonging to the general fiscal system and the charter ACs (the Basque

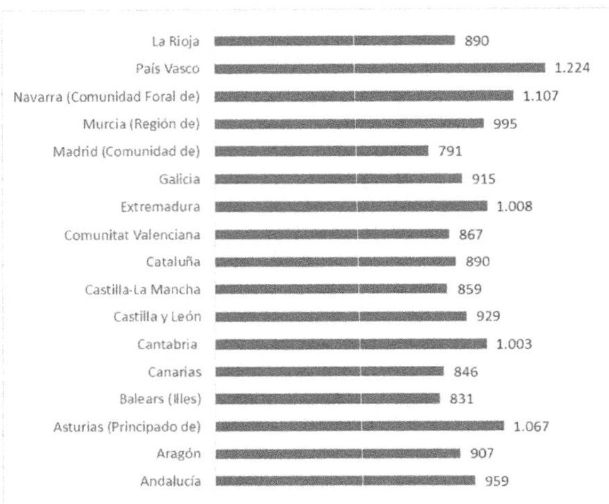

FIGURE 8.3. Public Expenditure on Education per Capita in 2013 (euros). Source: MECD (2016).

Country and Navarre). For example, Madrid spent 433 euros less per student than the Basque Country in 2013.

The Effect of the Fiscal Crisis on Education Spending

The education sector has not been spared the impact of the fiscal crisis, as evidenced by the dip in spending shown in Figure 8.5. However, the ACs adopted different strategies at a regional level to address budgetary constraints. After falling since 2010, general government expenditure on education as a share of GDP stood at 4% in 2013, below the EU average of 5%. As a share of total public expenditure, education spending has slightly decreased from 9.6% in 2011 to 9.1% in 2013. The total 2016 budget for education for all the Autonomous Communities (35,926.17 million euros) saw a 2.53% increase from 2015. But despite this increase, total education spending is still far from what was budgeted for education in 2012 (37,288.8 million euros). Analysing the period between 2012 and 2016, we can detect a reduction in spending on education in most of Autonomous Communities, with the exception of the Balearic Islands, Cantabria, Ceuta, the Basque Country, Extremadura and La Rioja. Asturias and Madrid are the Autonomous Communities with the most major cuts during this period (-9.60% and -8.61% respectively). The cuts on education spending have also been severe in Castilla-la Mancha (-7.63% extended) and the Canaries Islands, Andalusia, Valencia and Aragón with more than a 5% of decrease.

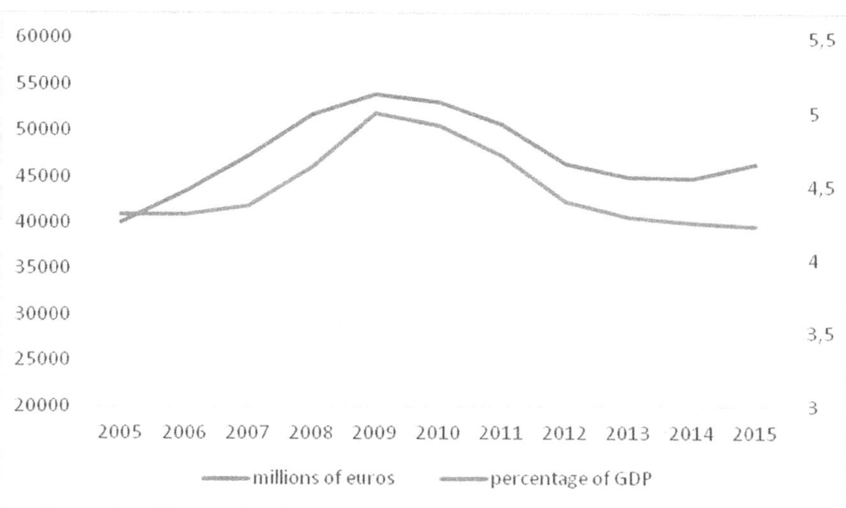

FIGURE 8.5. Public Expenditure on Education and Expenditure-to-GDP Ratio During the Economic Crisis (all public administration). Source: MECD (2016).

INTERGOVERNMENTAL RELATIONS

Vertical and horizontal cooperation among different tiers of government as well as technical coordination are always key challenges for education systems in decentralized countries. In Spain, since the late nineties, Sectoral Conferences (*Conferencias Sectoriales*) have become increasingly important in facilitating cooperation between the central government and the governments of the ACs. Sectoral Conferences are multilateral cooperation bodies among the central government and the ACs for specific policy sectors (e.g. health or environment). Recent studies on mechanisms of intergovernmental relations in Spain show how Sectoral Conferences have become decision-making bodies that reach common agreements on shared-cost programmes and coordinate policies in various sectors (Colino, 2012; Leon & Ferrín Pereira, 2011). Given the division of powers between different levels of government, particularly state and regional, coordination is required between educational authorities to ensure the proper performance of certain functions. Areas of exclusive legislation from these departments are rare in Spain. Similar to other policy areas, the central state is responsible for framework legislation, while the ACs are able to enact laws and are responsible for administration. Decisions on the different stages of the educational system (pre-primary, primary, secondary and tertiary) also often need the cooperation of both the state and AC level. The bodies responsible for administrative coordination are the Education Sector Conference and the General Conference for University Policy, composed of the education ministers of the Autonomous Communities and the Minister of Education, Culture and Sports. The two bodies are together called the Sectoral Conferences. This form of cooperation is typical in the Spanish State and reflects the absence of an upper chamber with territorial representation. The Education Sector Conference meets three times a year. There is also a preparatory body, the Education Sector Commission, which meets more frequently. At a lower level, the General Director Commissions are the permanent cooperation and coordination bodies among the ACs (e.g., the Commission on Statistics, University Issues, or International Relations in Education). These General Director Commissions meet on an ad hoc basis based on specific issues. In this sense, the Sectoral Conference maintains the day-to-day cooperation between the central state and the ACs in education policy. Compared with Sectoral Conferences working on other policy areas, the Sectoral Conference on Education meets with a very high frequency. Moreover, it has been, until recently, the unique Conference with a permanent cooperation and coordination body.

Public policy creation on topics of language, prevention of early school leaving, and vocational education and training has relied heavily on intergovernmental relations.[7] Language varies the most visibly across ACs in Spain, and has been

[7] Some research papers, seminars and official papers are available to sketch the current state of these policy areas. However, we lack enough evidence to discuss other ones where municipalities have played a greater role, such as early childhood education and care and school admission schemes.

a burning issue since the Catalan government undertook educational responsibilities in the early eighties. Prevention of early school leaving and vocational education and training formally respond to the recommendations of the Organization of Economic Cooperation and Development and the European Union. These two issues are very salient, and illustrate the relationships between the Government of Spain, the ACs and the European Union.

Although Spanish is the official language according to the 1978 Constitution, Basque is co-official in the Basque Country and Navarre, Catalan is co-official in Balearic Islands, Catalonia and the Valencian Community, and Galician is co-official in Galicia. Some of these languages have a minor status in Asturias, Aragon, Ceuta and Melilla.

As a rule, two approaches to language policy can be distinguished, with legislative underpinning and effective implementation depending on the region. Firstly, after some pilot programmes had been experimented previously, in Catalonia schools were required to teach by means of 'immersion in Catalan' in the early nineties. This arrangement was later enshrined by different autonomous laws and the 2006 Statute, so much so that the Constitutional Court ruling on the validity of such Statute required the Catalan Government to re-word the policy into 'immersion in Catalan and Spanish' (Branchadell, 2012). So far, the Balearic Islands and Galicia have retrieved some components of the 'immersion' approach. However, their regulation has not achieved the same legislative level. In addition, between 2011 and 2015, the incumbent Conservative governments attempted to introduce a new scheme by dividing instruction hours into three equivalent thirds of Spanish-medium, Catalan- and Galician-medium, and English-medium subjects.

Secondly, in the eighties, the Basque Government decided to distinguish Basque-medium and Spanish-medium schools, and the Valencian Community followed suit in the nineties, adopting a similar arrangement. Once again, the underlying philosophy was not necessarily translated into the same level of legislation if both communities are compared. Recently, a Conservative government also wanted to introduce the three-thirds (Spanish, Catalan and English) arrangement in Valencia.

It is hard to evaluate the educational impact of these modes of multilingualism because of the continuous change of design policy in many regions. Actually, the 'immersion' approach explicitly expects that all students become fluent in both the official and the co-official languages, but the general goal of the other approaches remains unclear (Branchadell, 2012).

In Catalonia, the students' fluency in both languages can be estimated by drawing on the data of the official school examinations. In 2014, approximately 75% of fifteen-year-old students scored either an average or a high level of Catalan and Spanish in the official test they take at the end of their compulsory education

---

When presenting a few data on regional disparities, we will adumbrate some suggestions on school admission policies, but certainly a general appraisal of the roles of the many local and the seventeen regional governments would be an overgeneralization on the grounds of the available evidence.

for statistical purposes (Consell d'Avaluació del Sistema Educatiu, 2014, p. 145). The 2010 edition of the General Diagnosis Evaluation, carried out by the Government of Spain, is helpful in comparing the scores estimating thirteen-year-old students' communicative skills in Spanish for both Catalonia and the average of Spain. This source indicates that the levels of mastery did not show a significant statistical difference between these two populations (Ministerio de Educación 2011, p. 75). Thus, an initial observation can state that the 'immersion' approach is not fully successful in promoting strong skills in both languages in Catalonia, since a quarter of students suffer from some shortcomings. However, the policy does not appear to affect students' Spanish language skills, since Catalan students learn both languages to a very similar degree and achieve the average communicative skills in Spanish. In sum, an explicit statement of the official educational objectives of the autonomous language policies is necessary if any further conclusion on the innovative potential of these schemes is to be suggested.

In contrast, it is much easier to discuss policies addressed to tackle early school leaving. This relative ease of comparison comes because all policies must respond to the template of the European Union 2020 Education and Training Strategy in some shape or form. These policies were also influenced by the Lisbon Process between 2001 and 2010.

When the Lisbon Process was enacted, most autonomous governments were already concerned with compensatory education. In the 1980s, the Ministry of Education had issued a decree creating a service of specialized teachers who attended to students with a vulnerable social background throughout Spain. Simultaneously, the government of the Basque Country added extra support by delivering a scholarship to low-income teenagers who enrolled in further education after the school leaving age of sixteen. Other ACs, however, were experimenting with immigrant reception programmes, affirmative action in favour of disadvantaged schools and districts, learning communities, distance education for rural areas, and participatory local planning of after-school activities. At that time, these initiatives were not effective in compensating for a long-term correlation between the average regional educational level of the adult population and the proportion of youth who did not obtain the Baccaleaureat graduate at eighteen (Rambla & Bonal, 2007).

In 2005, the Socialist government created a scheme of 'territorial coordination' based on intergovernmental relations that has been formally maintained by the successor Conservative government. In this vein, the Remedial, Guidance and Support Plan (Plan PROA) funded remedial courses in schools between 2005 and 2011. The central government called schools and autonomous governments to apply for grants, and the autonomous governments provided some technical support. The official evaluation focused mainly on the implementation of these measures, but one outcome of the policy was a shift in the prevailing professional culture, challenging the previous commonly-held confidence in content-centred pedagogies (Manzanares & Ulla, 2012). Afterwards, the fiscal consolidation programme implemented in 2011 severely curtailed these funds, although some of these initiatives were maintained in the most disadvantaged schools.

Despite intense ideological controversy, the 2005 (Socialist) Education Framework Act became the matrix of the 2013 (Conservative) Framework Act for Quality Education. The latter changed some articles of the former, yet it kept many others. At first sight, both governments, both parties, and both pieces of legislation disagree regarding the scale of single-ability grouping: the former aimed at tackling early school leaving by grouping low-performing fourteen- and fifteen-year-olds only in certain schools, while the latter transformed the measure into an almost compulsory requirement for twelve- and thirteen-year-olds. Nevertheless, both policies share a very similar confidence in the capacity of single-ability grouping to counteract the main risks of early school leaving.

In 2005, the Socialist government legislated 'attention to diversity.' The articles of that law emphasized school autonomy, allowing schools to cater to vulnerable students in a flexible way. Eventually, as the PROA plan showed, this approach virtually meant that schools would gather vulnerable students in remedial courses and initial vocational programmes that provided alternative learning arenas.

Compulsory secondary education must combine the principle of a common education with attention to the diversity of students, thus allowing schools to implement the organizational and curricular measures which are more appropriate for the characteristics of their intake. This has to be a flexible solution that schools are autonomous to use (Ministerio de Educación, 2006, pp. 17162–17163).

In 2013, the Conservative government argued that the system had to be flexibilized and thus, vocational tracking was introduced within the compulsory, comprehensive, lower secondary education programme (Ministerio de Educación, 2013) This requirement scaled up the former schemes, but eventually relied on the same causal belief that ability grouping was the crucial tool to tackle early leaving.

The rigidity of the educational system leads to the exclusion the students whose expectations do not fit with the established framework. However, the possibility to choose between different pathways guarantees them an easier permanence in the educational system, thus bigger possibilities for their personal and professional development. The flexibilization of pathways helps each student to develop all her potential. This flexibilization consists of learning and performance improvement programmes in the second and the third years of compulsory low secondary education, the introduction of basic Vocational Education and Training (within this compulsory low secondary education), and the advance of the choice between a propedeutic fourth year leading to *Bachillerato* and an alternative pathway leading to VET. In this way, students can receive individual support that guides them to the most suitable pathway for their needs and aspirations, thus favouring their progress within the educational system (Gobierno de España, Ministerio de Educación, 2013, p. 97864.

The adoption of this approach by means of framework acts has two important implications. Firstly, most ACs have deployed their own schemes to organize the corresponding remedial courses and the initial vocational schemes (Tarabini, 2015). To the extent that this is a common pattern acros the ideological spectrum of the regional governments, single-ability grouping has become a cornerstone of the 'territorial coordination' that was already enshrined in 2005. Secondly, this understanding narrows down the objectives of the European Commission Education and Training 2020 Strategy with regard to early leaving. Significantly, the European Commission stresses the importance of preventative action and intervention including such instruments as experimenting with a more encouraging curriculum, avoiding socio-economic segregation, institutionalising teacher mentors and building an integrated system of career guidance for all students (European Commission, 2013).

The third and final focus of this section has to do with vocational education and training (VET) and active labour market policies (ALMP). According to the 1978 constitution, both issues are areas of central responsibility that autonomous governments can develop in their own terms within a common and compulsory framework (Cueto & Suárez, 2015).

Vocational education mostly consists of medium-level programmes available to students who have obtained their secondary education certificate, and upper-level programmes, which require the *Bachillerato*. Over time, some courses have been created allowing graduates of medium-level programmes to take an entry exam for upper-level programmes. These programmes are coordinated mainly at the central government level. The central government convenes a council of VET with unions and employers' associations, though ACs can have their own consultative councils as well. Thus, international assessments have focused on the strengths and the challenges of the central VET legislation. The most remarkable international observations, which have been issued by the OECD, notice that the agenda is much wider in other European Union member states. This legislation has certainly adopted the general guidelines that advocate for establishing an official framework of qualifications and fostering the permeability of pathways. However, the same report points out that, in Spain, most school-based counsellors have never had a professional experience in other fields than education and psychology. This scope of professional expertise hinders the development of a multi-party system of working-place training, where different levels of government could play specific roles (Field, Kis, & Kuczera, 2012).

In addition, regional and local authorities have been drawing on vocational training to reduce unemployment in their territories. Since the eighties, the central government has allowed them to participate in the deliverance of these services, so long as they comply with central oversight. When the 2012 reform of labour legislation also allowed private, for-profit providers to enter this activity, both regional governments and private providers started to compete for central funds. To monitor this competition, a new system of evaluation has been introduced to detect the impacts and the possible dysfunctions of these programmes. But it is hard to conclude that the reform introduced significant policy innovation, as the system of evaluation mostly pays attention to the effective implementation of the courses regardless of the final outcomes and impacts (Cueto & Suárez, 2015).

In conclusion, even though the seventeen ACs are allowed to develop their own educational language policy, their policies have to fit within a clearly stated common legal framework. This understanding of 'territorial coordination' does not seem to underpin a larger approach extending to other areas of education policy. The extreme importance of legal definitions, for example, has been more important than the educational objectives of multilingual policies, which has not induced the borrowing of the multidimensional EU framework addressing early school leaving. Finally, the government of Spain has easily passed decrees and acts regulating qualifications and pathways for students, but has not been not so capable as to put in place a new VET system grounded on programmes of career guidance and working-place training.

ACADEMIC STANDARDS AND QUALITY

Both the central and some autonomous governments have created their own agencies for the evaluation of education policy. In 2006, the Socialist administration introduced diagnostic tests, which over time complemented similar tests in various ACs. In 2013, the Conservative government introduced a new system of compulsory, stricter examinations (Egido & Valle, 2015).

Table 8.3 maps out the average scores of most ACs in the last OECD Programme for International Student Assessment report and includes the lower secondary education completion and early school leaving rates of these regions. The table indicates that many more students suffer from academic difficulties in mathematics than in reading and science. The proportion of low-performing students in mathematics lays between five to eight percent points above the other subjects. This gap is a significant pattern in all cases, but is particularly remarkable in the communities whose average is the lowest.

Overall in the European Union, the share of low-performing students is higher than the early school leaving rate. However, in Spain, Table 8.3 does not reflect this pattern so clearly. Instead of recovering low-performing students, the devices intervening on school failure and compensating for its consequences after the official school leaving age do not seem to be very effective in Spain. Both proportions are relatively similar in a few autonomies, mostly in Asturias, the Basque Country and Cantabria. However, in most Autonomous Communities, the proportion of students who do not achieve their secondary education certificate is much higher than the proportion of low-performers in PISA (Pérez-Esparrells & Morales, 2012). Table 8.3 also shows that the R2 coefficient of correlation between the regional distribution of PISA scores and the early school leaving rates yields values below 0.5. The immediate conclusion these data suggest is that academic skills are not the only driver of students' pathways in many communities.

Although the correlation between the completion of lower secondary education and the early school leaving rate is relatively higher, Table 8.3 also singles

TABLE 8.3. Educational Outcomes and Regional Disparities

Autonomous Community	Students With PISA 2012 Reading Skills Below Level 2 (%)	Students With PISA 2012 Maths Skills Below Level 2 (%)	Students With PISA 2012 Science Skills Below Level 2 (%)	Gross Graduation Rate in Compulsory Secondary Education, 2012–3 (%)	ESL- Early School Leaving Rate, 2014 (%)
Andalusia	21	27	19	74.3	27.7
Aragon	17	21	16	76.7	18.4
Asturias	15	19	12	83.6	13.6
Balearic Islands	23	27	19	65.5	32.1
Basque Country	14	15	12	85.4	9.4
Canary Islands				74.2	23.8
Cantabria	19	22	15	82.9	9.7
Castile Leon	14	15	9	78.4	16.8
Castile La Mancha				71.2	22.2
Catalonia	15	20	16	80.6	22.2
Extremadura	30	33	21	75.9	22.9
Galicia	16	22	13	79.1	18.5
Navarre	13	14	11	80.1	11.8
Madrid	10	17	10	78.3	18.3
Murcia	28	31	21	72.4	24.1
La Rioja	18	20	13	69	21.1
Valencian Community				63.1	23.9
Average	18.04	21.64	14.79	75.92	19.79
Standard deviation	5.7	5.92	4	6.3	6.2
Coefficient of Variation (%)	31.56	27.34	27.08	8.2	31.33
SPAIN	18	24	16	75.4	21.9
EUROPEAN UNION	20	24	18		11.1
R2 with ESL	0.32	0.47	0.45	0.63	

Source: Ministry of Education (2015). *Sistema Estatal de Indicadores de la Educación. Madrid: MECD*. Available at www.mecd.gob.es (retrieved, Feb 2016).

out some interesting patterns that should inspire more research. For instance, the Balearic Islands is a well-known extreme case insofar as a high GDP per capita coincides with very poor educational outcomes. In this extreme case, completion is low and early leaving high. However, a look at Castile La Mancha and Catalonia shows that different completion rates can lead to similar early leaving rates. Once again, the policy mix that impinges on students' pathways should be carefully studied to make more precise observations.

Finally, a key variation among autonomous communities has to do with educational inequalities within their school systems. Different studies looking at performance in PISA and the social composition of school intakes have noticed that these internal inequalities are moderate in Castile Leon, Galicia, Navarre and La Rioja. However, disparities between public and private dependent schools seem to provoke important gaps in all the other cases (Ferrer, Valiente, & Castel, 2010; Mancebón & Ximenez-de-Embun, 2010).

To sum up, in Spain, some parties vindicate more power for regional education policies while others claim that devolution threatens to damage both legal harmonization and educational equality. However, this section reports on a very complex geographical distribution of educational outcomes, where quite complex and multifarious forces seem to play a role. The data hardly find any correlation between policy commonalities and differences, on the one hand, and regional educational disparities, on the other hand.

OUTLOOK AND CONCLUSIONS

The Spanish case shows how a formerly highly centralized country can be very successful in accommodating multilingual and cultural demands by decentralising competencies in education. The Constitution enabled an open-ended process where subnational units and the central government could negotiate the transfer of competencies in education according to the need and demands of cultural and linguistic minorities. This open-ended process also created intensive conflicts for competencies and has not been accompanied by the building of institutions for cooperation and coordination among the different tiers of government.

Our analysis has shown that the Spanish educational system has not been shaped solely by socio-economic struggles over distribution or conflicts over religious, linguistic-cultural and national identity issues, but that political factors have always been important driving forces for reforms.

The transfer of competencies to regional governments in the last two decades and the creation of separate spaces for political contestation have provided the ACs with the space to carry out divergent public policies. However, the central government has aimed to direct the ACs towards convergent policies in order to guarantee equal economic and social rights of citizens and the effective coordination and implementation of central policies. Under these circumstances, the outcome of the recent financial crisis has led to a recentralization of the system, reinforcing the trend towards convergence. While ACs are responsible for quite large amounts of spending, framework acts operate as powerful surveillance tools that guarantee all of them comply with similar rules.

Our analysis has shown that there are also some characteristics of the model that haven't been changed during the past decades, not least of which being the distribution of powers and responsibilities between the Central state and the ACs. Today, the constitutional balance between central legislative power and devolved, regional decision-making is quite noticeable in the terrain of education policy. Although many powers were 'decentralized' to the ACs in the eighties and nineties, after 2008, new schemes have pushed towards 'recentralization' through stricter framework legislation despite signs of growing fiscal divergence.

Secondly, since the adhesion of Spain to the EU, all national governments have included EU priorities in their Spanish educational model. The harmonization of the Spanish model with EU standards could be considered as a 'centralising' trend to the extent that ACs have been mostly excluded from the definition of these standards.

As to educational outcomes, the data reflect regional disparities that depend on many factors. It is hard to attribute these patterns to policy variation between autonomous communities. Finally, the existence of a mixed network of public, private and grant-aided private schools is a permanent factor that determines the different levels of spending among ACs.

The decentralization process of the educational system in Spain has shown that collaboration is necessary between different levels of government. The distribution of fiscal resources, the coordination of varying policies and the setting of common targets have become remarkable challenges. However, since 'decentralization' has also opened chances for successful policy change, in this sense the Spanish experience could give important lessons to other multicultural and linguistic countries.

REFERENCES

Branchadell, A. (2012). Language politics and conflicts in Spain. In H. Monteagudo (Ed.), *Languages, societies and politics. A multidisciplinary debate* (pp. 137–168). Santiago de Compostela, Spain: Consello da Cultura Galega.

Calero, J., & Choi, Á. (2013). The financing of the education system in the autonomous communities. In J. Tudela Aranda & M. Kölling (Eds.), *Autonomy and evolution of the Spanish education model* (pp. 57–90). Zaragoza, Spain: Fundación Manuel Giménez Abad.

Centro de Investigación y Documentación Educativa. (1995). *The Spanish Education System.* Madrid, Spain: Ministerio de Educadción y Cultura.

Colino Cámara, C. (2012). Intergovernmental relations in Spain: the state of art and some considerations in a comparative perspective. In C. Colino, S. León, M. Ferri, & M. Salvador (Eds.), *Intergovernmental cooperation in Spain* (pp. 31–44). Madrid, Spain: CEPC.

Consell d'Avaluació del Sistema Educatiu. (2014). *The system of education indicators in Catalunia.* Barcelona, Spain: Generalitat de Catalunya.

Cotino, L. (2013). Constitutional decentralization and distribution of competences in the Spanish education system. In J. Tudela Aranda & M. Kölling (Eds.), *Autonomy and evolution of the Spanish education model* (pp. 13–56). Zaragoza, Spain: Fundación Manuel Giménez Abad.

Cueto, B., & Suárez, B. (2015). The role of active policies: a perspective from the Autonomous Communities. *Ekonomiaz, 87*(1), 283–309.

Egido, I., & Valle, J. (2015). Education and Regional Autonomy. In T. Corner (Ed.), *Education in the European Union: Pre-2003 Member States* (pp. 265–284). London, UK: Colin Brock.

Engel, L. C. (2008). Globalization's strategic union: decentralization, efficiency, and the implications for educational governance in Spain. In R. K. Hopson (et al.) (Eds.) *Power, voice and the public good: Schooling and education in global societies* (pp. 391–417). Emerald Group Publishing Limited.

European Commission. (2013). *Reducing early school leaving: Key messages and policy support. Final report of the thematic working group on early school leaving.* Brussels, Belgium: European Commission.

Ferrer, F., Valiente, O., & Castel, J. L. (2010). The PISA-2006 results from the perspective of educational inequalities: the comparison of the Spanish Autonomous Communities. *In Revista Española de Pedagogía, 25*, 23–48.

Field, S. Kis, V., & Kuczera, M. (2012). *A skills beyond schools commentary on Spain.* Paris, France: OCDE.

Hanso, E. M. (2000). *Democratization and educational decentralization in Spain: A twenty year struggle for reform.* World Bank Country Studies Education Reform and Management Publication Series Vol. I No. 3.

Heywood, P. (1995). *The government and politics of Spain.* London, UK: Macmillan Press.

Holesch, A., & Nagel, K. J. (2012). *Education policy in Spain—A federal illusion?* Political Theory Working Paper, n. 12. Barcelona, Spain: Pompeu Fabra University.

Mancebón, M. J., & Pérez Ximénez-de-Embún. (2010). An assessment of the socio-economic segregation in the Spanish education system. Based on PISA 2006. *Regional and Sectoral Economic Studies, 10*(3), 129–148.

Manzanares, A., & Ulla, S. (2012). An evaluation of the Strengthening, Guidance and Support Plan (PROA). Analysis after six years of continuous evaluation. *Revista de Educación, special issue,* (1), 89–116.

Maravall, J. M. (1996). The pre-history of educational reform in Spain. In Boyd-Barrett & P. O'Malley (Eds.), *Education reform in democratic Spain* (pp. 41–52). New York, NY: Routledge.

Ministerio de Educación. (2006). Organic Law 2/2006, of 3 May, on Education, Madrid, Spain. *Boletín Oficial del Estado*, 17158–17207.

Ministerio de Educación. (2009). *The Spanish education system.* Madrid, Spain: Ministerio de Educación.

Ministerio de Educación. (2011). *General evaluation 2010. Compulsory secondary education.* Madrid, Spain: Ministerio de Educación.

Ministerio de Educación. (2013). Organic Law 8/2013, of 9 December, for the improvement of educational quality. Madrid, Spain. *Boletín Oficial del Estado*, 97858–97921.

Ministerio de Educación. (2014). *Organic law on the improvement of the quality of education (LOMCE).* Madrid, Spain: Ministerio de Educación.

Ministerio de Educación. (2016). *Facts and figures for the school year 2015/2016*. Madrid, Spain: Ministerio de Educación.

Moreno, L., Arriba, A., & Serrano A. (1998). Multiple identities in decentralized Spain: The case of Catalonia. *Regional & Federal Studies*, *8*(3), 65–88.

León, S., & Ferrín Pereira, M. (2011). Intergovernmental Cooperation in a Decentralised System: the Sectoral Conferences in Spain. *South European Society and Politics*, *16*(4), 513–532.

Pérez- Esparrells, C., & Morales, S. (2012). School failure in Spain: An analysis. *Revista de Estudios Regionales, 94*, 39–69.

Rambla X., & Bonal, X. (2007). The limits of compensatory education in Spain: A comparative analysis of some autonomous governments. In *International handbook of urban education* (pp. 505–522). New York, NY: Springer.

Tarabini, A. (Coord.) (2015). *Policies to combat early school leaving in Spain*. Madrid, Spain: Síntesis.

UNESCO. (1987). *Statistical yearbook*. Paris, France: UNESCO.

CHAPTER 9

THE PROS AND CONS OF HORIZONTAL FEDERALISM

Primary and Secondary Education Governance in Switzerland

Béatrice Ziegler, Monika Waldis, Daniel Kübler, Andri Gustin and Andreas Glaser

INTRODUCTION

For Switzerland, the first results from the Programme of International Student Assessment (PISA) published in the year 2000 were devastating, showing scores well below the OECD average, especially in literacy and sciences. The long-standing (and somewhat self-satisfied) conviction of citizens and politicians that Switzerland had a world class public education system was in tatters. In parallel, it became clear that the absence of common standards for awarding teacher certifications and creating school curricula was a major impediment to teacher and student mobility, jeopardizing performance within the education system as a whole.

The 2000 PISA shockwaves caused reform to accelerate in Swiss education policy and governance. Most notably, this reform resulted in reshuffling the partitioning of power and influence of various state levels in the Swiss education

Federalism and Education: Ongoing Challenges and Policy Strategies in Ten Countries, pages 187–209.

system. Traditionally, the institutions of Swiss federalism are designed to enable self-governance and protect the distinctivenesss of various territorial groups, most notably the four cultural-linguistic communities (German, French, Italian, and Romanche). This rationale is particularly prominent in the field of primary and secondary education, with a key role played by the federate states, i.e. the cantons. The decentralized nature of Swiss education policy poses difficulties to overall coordination, most prominently with respect to school curricula and teacher education. Nevertheless, the cantons have been reticent to cede powers to the federation and have managed to resist pressure towards centralization of education policy at the federal level, notably via the strengthening of activities and institutions of intercantonal coordination.

In this chapter, we present the workings of education governance within Swiss federalism, with a particular emphasis on the intercantonal dimension. We posit that Swiss education governance is an emblematic case of *horizontal federalism* that has emerged in an increasing number of policy fields in Switzerland since the new millennium, and we discuss its pros and cons. Empirically, we focus on governance of primary and secondary education. The chapter proceeds in four steps. The first section sets the scene by reporting the results of performance-based accountability measures in the Swiss primary and secondary education sector, and

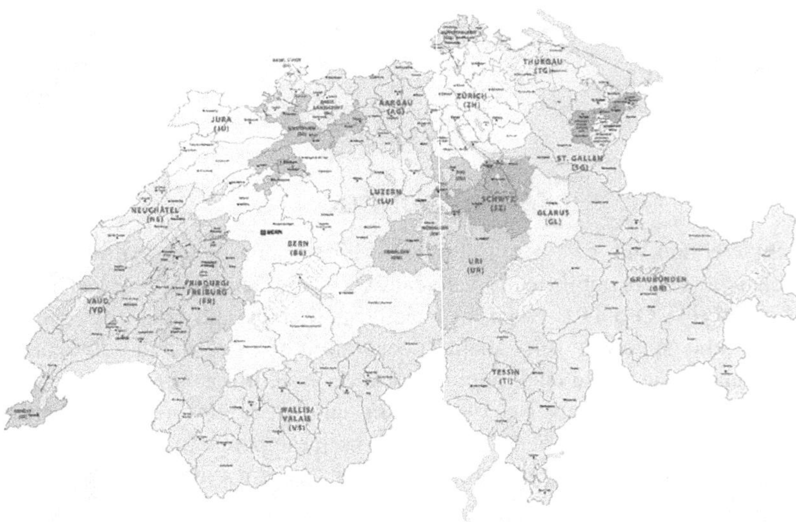

FIGURE 9.1. Map of Switzerland With Administrative Divisions. Source: www.scottshamblottdds.com. Note: German speaking cantons: AG, AI, AR, BL, BS, LU, OW, NW, SG, SH, SZ, TG, UR, ZG, ZH; French speaking cantons: GE, JU, NE, VD; Italian speaking: TI; Cantons with French and German speaking regions: BE, FR, VS; canton with German, Italian and Romanche speaking regions: GR.

presents and discusses cross-cantonal disparities. The next section describes the vertical and horizontal institutions of education governance in Swiss federalism at its current state, and shows the most important trends of change since the 2000s. The third section reiterates how the division of powers and competencies in Swiss education governance is reflected in public expenditure figures by different state levels. The fourth section discusses the political dynamics and conflicts over federalist education governance in Switzerland, by zooming in on the two currently most pressing issues of political debate: the coordination of teacher education and the coordinated development of school curricula. In the conclusion, we wrap up the discussion by emphasizing the limits of horizontal federalism in the field of education governance.

PERFORMANCE OF THE SWISS EDUCATION SYSTEM

PISA 2000 provided the first comprehensive and nationwide overview of educational performance in Switzerland. The results were, however, not encouraging. While the average math performance was significantly higher than the OECD average and thus confirmed results of previous studies such as the Third International Mathematics and Science Study TIMSS (1997), the performance in reading and in science was only midfield in international comparison (Martin et al., 2008; Mullis et al., 2008). The mediocre results in these two areas were noted in the educational community and the broader public with some consternation. One particular cause for concern was the finding that the reading competency of more than one fifth of the young people was assessed as unsatisfactory (OECD, 2001). Further analyses revealed that male adolescents from lower social classes speaking a foreign language at home were particularly at risk (Moser, 2002). These factors compound as pupils from unfavorable sociocultural environments often encounter greater difficulties in attaining higher education levels and foreign language students face greater obstacles in acquiring basic educational skills than native speakers. In response to these results, the Swiss conference of cantonal ministers for education (*EDK—Erziehungsdirektorenkonferenz*) devised an action plan, calling for, among other things, language training on a large scale and specific language training for pupils with adverse learning conditions (EDK, 2003).

Subsequent performance monitoring suggests that, in fact, there was an improvement after reforms (Table 9.1). While the scores in mathematics stayed significantly above the OECD averages in the subsequent PISA studies, the scores in reading and science started to increase from 2003 onwards. The factors causing the improvement cannot be definitively identified and the extent to which the improvement was due to responses by the education system (e.g. better learning support or didactical developments) or to a more favorable composition of the student

TABLE 9.1. Average PISA Performance Score of Switzerland and the OECD-Countries in Three Core Competency Areas.

		Reading	Mathematics	Science
2000	CH	494	529	496
	OECD	500	500	500
2003	CH	499	527	513
	OECD	494	500	500
2006	CH	499	530	512
	OECD	492	498	500
2009	CH	501	534	517
	OECD	493	497	501
2012	CH	509	531	515
	OECD	496	494	501

Source: https://pisa.educa.ch/de/ergebnisse-0. The performance scores published on the official national PISA-website differ partially from the figures published in the national reports

body (e.g. increasing proportions of high-skilled immigrants), or a combination of both remains uncertain.

Cantonal and Regional Differences

These overall measures, however, hide important variations and differential developments between language regions and cantons (see the Appendix). Within the language regions, the average reading performance between PISA 2000 and PISA 2009 remained almost unchanged. In the results of the cantons, a statistically significant improvement in reading performance was found for the cantons Geneva and Jura. These two cantons had the lowest test performance on the PISA 2000 (Angelone & Moser, 2011).

The average mathematics performance in Switzerland has not changed significantly between PISA 2003 and PISA of 2009. In 2003, the average was 537 points, 536 points in 2009. In European comparison, Switzerland is thus one of the countries with the best average student performance score in mathematics. In the language regions, no significant changes were observed. Since 2003, the mathematics performance changed significantly in only two cantons: Jura and Zurich. In the canton of Jura, the average math score rose 16 points to 556 points. In the canton of Zurich, the average score declined 13 points to 523 points.

In science, the performance score differs more between the three language regions than in reading or mathematics. Changes in science performance can be tracked over time only between PISA 2006 and PISA 2009. In Switzerland and in all cantons, the performance scores since PISA 2006 did not alter statistically significantly (Angelone & Moser, 2011).

The fact that the average student performance changed only slightly over time does not speak directly to the effective changes within particular student groups. Indeed, the percentage of pupils with weak reading competency (below competence level 2) declined significantly in Switzerland between PISA 2000 and PISA 2012 from 17.8 to 12.8 percent (Angelone & Keller, 2014). This development is largely due to an improvement in performance of pupils with an immigrant background. In particular, first-generation students with a family language different than the language of instruction in school improved their reading performance. The reading skills of the locals and the second-generation students did not change significantly. Furthermore, the proportion of strong reading pupils remained stable over time.

In mathematics, the percentage of poorly performing pupils (below competence level 2) has changed only marginally. In PISA 2003, the proportion was 9.9 percent and in PISA 2012, 11.2 percent. The slight overall increase of 1.3 percent is not statistically significant. However, when split into groups, a statistically significant increase emerges amongst native-born students and a statistically significant decrease is found in pupils with an immigrant background of the first generation, that figure decreasing from 28.2 to 21.6 percent (Angelone & Keller, 2014).

The national analyses of the PISA 2009 show that the overall results for Switzerland are also valid for the three language regions and the cantons. In all regions and cantons students scored highest in mathematics, followed by a slightly lower performance score in science and a reading score lying near the OECD-average. However, differences between language regions and cantons vary to a considerable amount. The biggest differences were shown in mathematics and in science, partly dependent on the socio-economic background of students' families. These differences in student background represent an important factor explaining cantonal differences. Overachieving cantons are Schaffhausen and the French-speaking part of Fribourg.

Performance scores below average were reported for Ticino, Geneva, Neuchâchtel, Vaud and the french-speaking part of the canton Bern. The national PISA 2009 results show that the plan of action of the EDK (2003) is still a big issue. The percentage of low performing students (below competence level 2) is still quite big. These young people do not acquire the relevant reading and math competencies that are necessary for social and vocational integration (Moser & Angelone, 2011).

CONSTITUTIONAL DISTRIBUTION OF POWER IN PRIMARY AND SECONDARY EDUCATION

In Switzerland, the long term legal trend, accelerated after the 1990s, has been towards an upscaling of decisions in education policy. This has been driven in part by the scientific aspirations of testing and accountability regimes, and in part by ideas about educational adequacy, equal access, and equal opportunity. Over the last 20 years, efforts have been made to standardize curricula, competency requirements, early childhood education, and special education. These efforts have been slowed and sometimes sandbagged by cantonal opposition that often seems to originate in cantonal political and educational bureaucracies. The horizontal and cooperative federalism is, thus, currently in the spotlight of animated debates, due to wide-ranging reforms in the education governance. This section will present the main points of the recent discussion, after describing the vertical and horizontal institutions of education governance in Switzerland at its current state. In particular, we present the institutions and activities of intercantonal coordination, putting particular focus on those relevant for primary and secondary education.

The Constitutional Division of Competencies and Constitutional Instruments of Intercantonal Coordination

Switzerland is a two-layered federal state: 26 cantons and the federal level form the Swiss Confederation. The articles 3, 5a and 42 of the Swiss Constitution attribute the legislative powers between Confederation and cantons. According to the *principle of conferral*, the Swiss Confederation is only competent to legislate insofar as the constitution empowers it. The cantons are sovereign except to the extent that their sovereignty is limited by the Federal Constitution. The Confederation may acquire new competencies only through a constitutional amendment, which must be approved in a referendum both by a majority of the population and the cantons. Furthermore, the *principle of subsidiarity* stipulates that the Confederation should only undertake tasks that the cantons are unable to perform or that require uniform regulation by the Confederation (Art. 43a Cst.). This principle is addressed to the federal legislative body, which therefore should always consider if a task can be achieved at the cantonal level as effectively as at the federal level.

Even if the cantons are competent for a particular matter, the need to solve overarching problems in a collective manner can arise. In this case, the Swiss Constitution offers different instruments for *horizontal cooperative federalism*. Art. 48 Cst. provides for an approach to fulfill common tasks without transferring cantonal competencies to the Confederation. It enables the cantons to create intercantonal agreements in order to coordinate and solve issues amongst themselves. Usually, an intercantonal agreement is not self-executing, but has to be implemented through cantonal laws. The conclusion of an intercantonal agreement is, of course, voluntary; only under strict conditions may an intercantonal agreement be declared generally binding by the Federal Parliament, which obliges all cantons to join it (Biaggini et al., 2015; Haller, 2016).

Competencies of the Swiss Confederation in Primary and Secondary Education

Article 61a to 68 of the Swiss Constitution establishes the general setting for education governance in the country. Art. 61a Cst. is a general provision defining the targets of Swiss education governance, demanding a "high quality and accessibility of the Swiss Education Area" (Art. 61a (1) Cst.). It states that the cantons and the Confederation will cooperate through "joint administrative bodies and other measures" to achieve these goals (Art. 61a (2) Cst.). This provision refers to Art. 48 (2) Cst., which gives cantons the power to implement intercantonal agreements through authorizing intercantonal bodies to enact horizontal legislation. Furthermore, the confederation has several (partial) competencies in the fields of vocational training (Art. 63 Cst.), higher education (Art. 63a Cst.), or continuing education and training (Art. 64a Cst.).

In the sector of primary and secondary education, the Swiss Constitution stipulates that the cantons are responsible for the system of school education (Art. 62 (1) Cst.). This does not only include the right to design the school system or to set the school curricula, but also the burden of funding the schools and organizing teacher education. However, the federal legislator reserves the right to set some rules in advance. Firstly, the Confederation has the power to regulate the beginning of the school year. Secondly, the Constitution obliges the cantonal legislators to provide an adequate, free, mandatory, and state-controlled education that is open to all children (Art. 62 (2) Cst.). The right to an adequate and free basic education is guaranteed as a fundamental right (Art. 19 (I) Cst.). The Federal Supreme Court has specified the content of an "adequate education." It requires an education lasting at least nine years that teaches the abilities necessary for a self-reliant life (Federal Court decision 130 I 352).

A pertinent paragraph concerning primary and secondary education was introduced by a constitutional amendment in 2006. Art. 62 (4) Cst. confers to the federal legislator the right to regulate the issues of school entry age, compulsory school attendance, the duration and objectives of various levels of education, the transition for one level to another, and the recognition of qualifications, only if the cantons are not able to realize a harmonization in these areas themselves by means of coordination. Therefore, this provision holds two meanings: On the one hand, it puts pressure onto the cantons to draft an intercantonal agreement which regulates these issues. On the other hand, it furnishes the federal legislator with a tool to ensure system-wide harmonization if horizontal coordination cannot be realized. Although a nationwide coordination has not yet been achieved, the Swiss Parliament has yet to make use of its competence in this field.

Horizontal Institutions of Education Governance and its Instruments

Given the decentralized division of legislative powers in Swiss education governance, the different state levels—and in particular the cantons—have long had to work together to prevent having 26 completely uncoordinated school systems. To do so, the cantons formed an intercantonal strategic coordination scheme in 1897: The Swiss Conference of the 26 cantonal Ministers of Education (Erziehungsdirektorenkonferenz—EDK). Even today, the EDK remains the most important institution for the cantons to exchange views and coordinate measures in educational issues. Although the EDK has no binding legislative powers, it fulfills important functions for the cantons: Firstly, it works on agenda-setting and lobbies for cantonal interests in the federal decision-making process. Secondly, the EDK can release non-binding recommendations to the cantons, and thirdly, it is the panel where drafts for new intercantonal agreements concerning education are prepared.

The most important issue the EDK had to deal with in the last few years was the implementation of the so-called HarmoS-Concordat (Intercantonal Agreement on Harmonization of Compulsory Education). The agreement has been the main instrument for promoting harmonization of the 26 cantonal education systems through cooperative federalism (and therefore complying with the regulations of Art. 62 (4) Cst.). The modifications that the participating cantons have had to make are related to preschool and primary school starting age, the duration and organization of primary and secondary school, rules on language teaching, and the agreement to implement a standardized school curriculum (Gächter, 2010). Fifteen Cantons have ratified the HarmoS-Concordat, whereas the remaining eleven cantons have, at least partially, orientated their autonomous laws around the concordat.

To fulfill the requirement of a standardized school curriculum, the three main linguistic regions of Switzerland (the French-, German- and Italian-speaking parts) each drafted or are drafting a separate, but coordinated, school curriculum. The German-speaking cantons of the EDK presented their school curriculum in 2014; the so-called Lehrplan 21. The Lehrplan 21 is intercantonal soft-law and therefore must be implemented by the cantons. Seventeen cantons have already adopted it (Glaser & Fuhrer, 2015).

The Development of the Division of Competencies in Primary and Secondary Education, and Current Debates

Education governance is traditionally among the core competencies of the cantons in Switzerland. With the first Swiss Constitution of 1848, the Federation had almost no competencies in the field of education and since then, the cantons have tried to defend their powers. Nevertheless, the 26 cantonal school systems have developed similarities over the last 150 years. This trend comes partially because, over the years, the Confederation gained some competencies and thus ensured a (partial) harmonization. At the same time, the cantons have coordinated some educational issues themselves. The first steps to harmonization were made in 1874 and 1902 with the introduction of two articles into the Swiss Constitution that declared primary school to be mandatory, obligating the cantons to provide a sufficient primary education and establishing that the federal government had to bear its costs. Although a certain degree of harmonization had been achieved through these changes, there were several subsequent attempts to enlarge the competencies of the federal government. In the fields of higher education and vocational training, this goal was accomplished through different amendments of the constitution. In primary and secondary education, the Swiss electorate remained rigorous and impeded a harmonization by voting against proposed legislation in 1882 and in 1973, fearing paternalism by the federal government ("school reeve"). The only draft law that was passed by the voters (1985) was an article harmonizing the beginning of the school year for all cantons. After a longer period of calm, pressure for change increased in the 1990s. An increasingly mobile population combined with the relatively small scale of the cantons demanded more uniformity. And adding further fodder for change, international developments like the PISA-Program (Programme for International Student Assessment) gave strong indication that the Swiss education system was not as good as anticipated, Switzerland ranking just in the mid-field of all participating nations in the first PISA-Program in 2000 (Ehrenzeller & Sahlfeld, 2014).

In the late 1990s, the dissatisfying situation led to new reforms: On the federal level, the Swiss parliament planned—in strong cooperation with the cantons—slight adjustments to constitutional articles concerning education, aiming to create a high quality nationwide Swiss education area. The draft law did better than previous attempts in balancing the federalist interests of the cantons and the interests of centralization. In particular, the draft focused on improving cooperation between the federal government and the cantons. In 2006, Swiss voters adopted the draft with an overwhelming majority of 85.6%. On the cantonal level, the HarmoS-Concordat was drafted in 2007, with the goal not just of harmonizing the formal aspects of the 26 systems of education, but also of unifying their educational goals by means of national education standards, educational monitoring, and unified school curricula. While the concordat was initially well received, resistance formed against it in several cantons. From 2007 to 2016, fifteen cantons ratified the agreement. The voters of seven cantons, however, rejected the HarmoS-Concordat in a referendum. And in the German-speaking cantons, the implementation of the Lehrplan 21 has been (and continues to be) contentious. Both the implementation and the agreement itself have been criticized by the political opposition for being undemocratic, dictatorial, and ponderous. As expressed in the ballot box, the voters of several cantons sided with this argumentation. The strong tradition of self-independent states, the tools of direct democracy, and the delicacy of education as a subject together virtually guarantee that there will be ongoing debates on this issue.

FUNDING RESPONSIBILITIES IN EDUCATION

This section will present the patterns of public expenditures in the Swiss education sector and the changes in these patterns since the 1990s. We will focus on overall expenditures by different state levels in the different education sectors, but also examine disparities of per-capita expenditures across different cantons. We will also explore how resource inequalities between cantons are equalized, reiterating the changing patterns of intergovernmental transfers that reflect the cantons' increasing role in Swiss education policy shown in the previous section.

Education Expenditures in Swiss Federalism

Overall, public expenditures for education have substantially increased within the 1990 to 2010 period (Table 9.2). Nominally, expenditures have more than doubled, and a look at the deflated figures shows that the real increase was still almost fifty percent. In terms of shares of the Gross Domestic Product, overall education expenditures in Switzerland amount to roughly six percent. This share has remained stable since 1990, as the increase in education expenditures in the last 25 years is paralleled by an increase of GDP over the same period.

Most of the public expenditures for education go into the compulsory school sector. Together with the special schools, expenditures for compulsory schools comprise roughly half of the overall expenditures. These two sectors are also the ones with the highest number of pupils: two thirds of all students in Switzerland are found in these two sectors. Higher education comes next, followed by expenditures for vocational training. In this sector, it is important to note that public expenditures only cover about half of the overall expenditures for vocational training. The other half is covered by private businesses who, due to the dual professional training system which is widespread in Switzerland, play an important role in providing educational training for young professionals.

Over the last 20 years, there has been a slight shift in the relative weights of the various education sectors. Most importantly, the sectors of higher education as well as scientific research have gained in importance. Today, roughly 30 percent of overall public expenditures in education are spent on higher education and scientific research.

Regarding the role of the three state levels in the field of education, the expenditure figures are commensurate with the formal division of powers and competencies, and show a quite differentiated picture. With less than 10 percent of the overall share of education expenditures, the federation clearly plays a minor role, except in scientific research where it is clearly dominant, as well as, to some extent, in higher education. The cantons, on the other hand, clearly are the main players

TABLE 9.2. Public Expenditure for Education Categories According to State Levels (Percentages of Overall Expenditures, 1990 and 2010)

	1990				2010			
Education Category	**Overall**	**Fed**	**Cant**	**Munic**	**Overall**	**Fed**	**Cant**	**Munic**
Compulsory schools	48.7	0.3	46.5	53.3	43.3	0.1	42.5	57.4
Special schools	2.9	0	60.0	40.0	5.4	0	75.7	24.3
Vocational training	13.6	2.1	69.8	28.2	11.0	2.1	93.5	4.4
Other schools	7.8	0.1	96.0	3.9	7.2	0.1	98.5	1.4
Continuous education	2.4	1.8	95.5	2.3	0.8	17.3	82.3	0.4
Higher education	19.9	31.2	68.3	0.5	21.4	13.0	86.5	0.4
Research	2.7	100	0	0	9.4	68.5	31.4	0.1
Miscellaneous	1.9	2.6	81.1	16.2	1.6	1.0	92.5	6.5
Overall	100	9.4	58.9	31.7	100	9.7	63.4	26.9
Total in CHF: nominal (deflated to 2010)	**16,610 mio** (21,937 mio)				**32,694 mio.** (32,694 mio.)			

Source: Swiss Statistical Office.

in the rest of the educational landscape, and their weight has increased since the 1990s. More than two thirds of overall education expenditures were made by the cantons in 2010. The cantons have also increased their relative weight compared to the federation, notably in higher education and scientific research. Finally, the municipalities also play an important role in the field of education, even though their role is increasingly confined to the sector of compulsory schooling, where they are almost on a par with the cantons in terms of expenditures.

Cantonal Differences in Education Expenditures

Public expenditures for education vary considerably across cantons (Table 9.3). The expenditures per pupil in compulsory schools ranges from 10,947 CHF in the canton of Valais, to almost double that figure, coming to 19,485 CHF in the canton of Basel-City. When put in the context of overall cantonal expenditures, education spending ranges from roughly 20 to 30 percent, which corresponds roughly to 3 to 6 percent of the cantonal GDP in the various cantons.

While the share of education expenditures out of overall expenditures can be taken as a proxy for the effort to invest in education as compared to other policy fields, the share of education expenditures in the cantonal GDP indicates the cantonal efforts to extract fiscal resources for education purposes. The figures in Table 9.3 suggest that expenditures per pupil are loosely related to the level of economic wealth of cantons, but also to the efforts made by cantons. Different patterns emerge. First, we find poor cantons where spending per pupil is below average, in spite of education claiming high shares of overall expenditures and GDP. This is the case for the cantons of Fribourg, Neuchâtel and Bern, for example. In these cantons, spending per pupil is low in spite of considerable efforts to invest in education, mainly because of scarce resources. Second, there are rich cantons, where spending per pupil is high despite only average efforts to invest in education because of the availability of fiscal resources. This is the case of the cantons of Nidwalden, Schaffhausen, Schwyz and Basel-Landschaft. Third, there are cantons in which efforts to invest in education are relatively weak, and spending per pupil is primarily a function of the availability of fiscal resources. This is the case of the cantons of Zug at the upper end, and Valais, Ticino, Jura, Obwalden, and Graubünden at the lower end. Fourth, there are cantons with average resources, but that deploy considerable efforts in education, resulting in rather high levels of spending per pupil. This is the case for St. Gallen, Aargau, Lucerne, and Thurgau. Finally, there are some cantons that not only benefit from comfortable levels of resources, but also deploy strong efforts to invest in education, resulting in a high or very high spending level per pupil. This is the case for Geneva, Zurich, and Basel-Stadt.

Variations in levels of education spending across cantons are thus not simply determined by disparities in economic and fiscal resources. At least in part, these variations are caused by policy choices that result in different profiles of education policy and spending. These differences are epitomized, for instance,

TABLE 9.3. Differences in Education Expenditures Across the 26 Cantons (2013 Data).

Canton	Expenditures per pupil in compulsory schools (indexed) a	Education expenditures, in percent of total expenditures b	Education expenditures in percent of cantonal GDP c	Percent of pupils with matura exam d
Valais	81	19.5	5.3	16.8
Ticino	81	19.8	3.8	28.9
Fribourg	81	31.7	7.8	22.2
Jura	81	18.2	4.8	22.1
Neuchâtel	84	22.3	5.3	24.3
Appenzell I. Rh.	87	24.3	4.7	20.4
Bern	89	25.3	4.8	18.1
Vaud	93	23.1	5.7	23.7
Obwalden	96	20.4	4.0	19.4
Graubünden	96	16.9	4.6	20.6
Schwyz	97	23.6	4.6	16.9
Appenzell A. Rh.	98	21.8	4.8	18.8
Basel-Landschaft	100	21.7	4.3	20.8
Uri	101	23.6	5.3	19.4
St. Gallen	102	30.2	5.2	12.7
Solothurn	102	23.1	4.3	14.2
Aargau	103	28.5	5.1	16.3
Schaffhausen	104	21.1	3.3	15.0
Glarus	104	24.4	4.4	15.9
Genève	107	22.6	5.2	28.0
Thurgau	108	29.9	5.7	13.4
Luzern	109	26.9	4.9	18.4
Nidwalden	110	23.7	3.9	23.1
Zürich	113	29.9	4.7	19.3
Zug	127	23.0	2.4	20.1
Basel-Stadt	143	28.4	4.2	28.8
National average	100 (13,586 CHF)	25.4	4.8	19.9

Source: Swiss Statistical Office

Note: (a) Defined as personnel costs of all compulsory schools in a given canton divided by the number of pupils in these schools, indexed to the national average (=100); (b) defined as the percentage of education expenditures of a canton and its municipalities with respect to the overall expenditures; (c) defined as the percentage of education expenditures of a canton and its municipalities with respect to the GDP within the cantonal territory; (d) defined as percentage of pupils with a degree that grants free access to Universities throughout Switzerland ('gymnasiale Maturität').

by the varying proportions of pupils holding a degree that gives them free access to University studies. Indeed, the percentage of students holding such a *matura* exam ranges from a very low 12.7 percent in the canton of St. Gallen to 28.9 percent in the canton of Ticino. Seeking to explain these intercantonal differences in education expenditures and policy profiles, previous studies have shown that not only socio-demographic and structural variables have an influence, but also political variables such as the nature of cantonal governmental coalitions (Freitag & Bühlmann, 2003). In addition the proportion of elderly people in the cantonal population has been found to have a negative influence on cantonal politicians' willingness to spend on public education (Grob & Wolter, 2007).

Fiscal Federalism, Equalization and Transfer Payments in Education Finance

Swiss fiscal federalism is strongly decentralized (Braun, 2003a). At its core is the principle of tax autonomy of all three state levels, deeply enshrined in the federal constitution since 1848. Not only the federal government, but also the cantons and the municipalities have the right to raise their own taxes. At the federal and cantonal levels, the principle of tax autonomy includes the power to define the type of tax levied, as well as to set the tax rates. At the municipal level, tax autonomy is limited to setting the tax rate, with a base for municipal tax defined by cantonal legislation.

Subnational tax autonomy has sparked fiscal competition at the subnational level, which has become a characteristic feature of Swiss federalism (Braun, 2003b). Fiscal competition between cantons has led to the emergence of a wide range of different cantonal tax regimes, which differ not only with respect to overall levels of taxes, but also with respect to the progressivity of income tax (Gilardi, Kübler, & Wasserfallen, 2013). Additionally, there is fiscal competition between municipalities within cantons, and the municipal tax rates differ quite substantially across municipalities. Over the 20th century this system has produced horizontal fiscal imbalances, i.e. disparities between cantons resulting from the differences in their abilities to raise revenues from their tax base. High-tax cantons are also often those with fewer wealthy taxpayers, causing them to struggle with budget deficits and to have to limit public service provision. In contrast, low-tax cantons are usually those with wealthy taxpayers and, thus, their public finances are in good shape and they can afford high service levels.

The deepening of such horizontal fiscal imbalances after World War II led to the setting up of systems for horizontal fiscal equalization since the mid-20th century, both at the federal level, as well as within most cantons. They establish transfers of fiscal resources from wealthy low-tax jurisdictions to poor high-tax ones, in order to ensure a decent level of services without excessive differences in tax burdens across jurisdictions. As a result, the share of transfer payments in subnational public finance in Switzerland has substantially increased (higher expenditures for affluent cantons and municipalities and higher revenues for the

TABLE 9.4. Ear-Marked Intergovernmental Transfer Payments in Education (1990—2010).

State levels	1990	2000	2010
From federation to cantons in mio CHF constant prices (1990 = 100)	881 mio 100	1,140 mio 107	2,231 mio 192
From cantons to cantons In mio CHF constant prices (1990=100)	275 mio 100	677 mio 203	2,567 mio 707
From cantons to municipalities in mio CHF constant prices (1990=100)	1,168 mio 100	1,542 mio 109	1,149 mio 74

Source: Swiss Statistical Office.

deprived ones). These transfer payments consist of general purpose grants, which the receiving jurisdictions can use at their own discretion. The aim of these transfer payments is to equalize resource disparities without intervening in specific policy fields. Indeed, the explicit goal of the equalization system is to support economically weak cantons until they reach the minimal level of 85 percent of the average resource potential (Eidgenössisches Finanzdepartement, & Konferenz der Kantonsregierungen, 2007). The overall volume of general-purpose transfer payments is roughly 5 billion CHF per year; they consist of vertical transfers from the federation to the cantons (68 percent of the overall volume), as well as horizontal transfers from rich to poor cantons (32 percent).

In addition to these general purpose transfers, ear-marked transfer payments between state levels exist in many policy fields (Eidgenössische Finanzverwaltung, 2012). This is true for the education sector, where federal-cantonal transfer payments involve contributions for vocational training (where the federal government is obliged by law to cover 25 percent of cantonal expenditures), as well as contributions to the cantonal universities and funding of scientific research conducted in the cantonal universities. There are also horizontal transfers between cantons because of financial obligations resulting from the intercantonal agreements (see section 2 above), most significantly those that institute joint funding of cantonal universities and universities of applied sciences. Finally, there are also transfer payments from cantons to municipalities that are ear-marked for education purposes—these involve mainly contributions to fund expenditures in the compulsory education sector.

Above, Table 9.4 shows the levels of intergovernmental transfer payments in the Swiss education sector since 1990. Overall, these figures show that intergovernmental transfers play a minor role in overall education expenditures (see Table

9.2), i.e. between 13 and 18 percent.[1] Although transfer payments have strongly increased, this increase is counterbalanced by the general increase in overall expenditures.

Notwithstanding the general stability in the share of transfer payments in overall education finance, the figures in Table 9.4 suggest that the patterns of intergovernmental transfers have changed. On the one hand, transfers from cantons to municipalities (concerning compulsory education) have decreased since 2000, probably due to centralization of competencies in compulsory schooling at the cantonal level, away from the municipalities. On the other hand, transfers from the federation to the cantons have strongly increased, mostly as a result of increased engagement of the federation in funding of higher education and research. Finally, the most substantial increase in transfer payments can be observed with respect to intergovernmental transfers between cantons: from 1990 to 2010, the volume of these horizontal transfers has increased by a factor of seven. On the whole, this reflects the strengthening of the role of the cantons in Swiss education policy, a strong role that is supported mainly via an intensification of horizontal intergovernmental cooperation.

CURRENT POLICY ISSUES AND DEBATES

The intensification of horizontal cooperation in education governance also follows an intention of strengthening coordination and harmonization of cantonal education systems. This effort triggered some resistance by the cantons worried for their autonomy, eventually leading to tensions and conflicts. As an illustration, we report on what stand currently as the two most controversial issues: the coordinated development of school curricula and the coordination of teacher education. These areas involve strong collaborations within the federal system, and they are therefore good illustrations for the workings of the institutions of education governance in Switzerland. They also emphasize one of the major limits of institutions of horizontal federalism, namely the lack of democratic legitimacy when issues become politicized (as in the case of school curricula). We discuss the reasons for this politicization and the resistance in the cantons against coordination.

Intercantonal Coordination of School Curricula

With the approval of the education article in the Federal referendum of 2006, the Swiss population obliged the authorities to work towards a harmonization of the education system. As mentioned above, the HarmoS-Concordat was drafted in

[1] Note that sectoral transfers (as in education) cannot be equalled to revenue-sharing, and do not necessarily contribute to equalization of resources between cantons. Indeed, the amounts of sectoral transfers are determined on the basis of criteria other than financial strength and follow a rationale that is different from that of the general equalization system.

2007 with the goal not just of harmonizing the formal aspects of the 26 systems of education, but also of unifying the school curricula. As a result, regional language curricula were created: the *Piano di studio della scuola dell'obbligo* in Ticino, the *Plan d'Etudes Romand* (PER) for the French speaking, and the curriculum *Lehrplan 21* (LP21) involving the 21 German speaking cantons. The driving force was the EDK, whose newly created linguistic regional commissions were assigned the responsibility for the leading the process of curriculum reforms. This process was carried out as an administrative process without substantial involvement of the legislative institutions in the cantons. With the final curriculum soon to be implemented in the cantons, it seems to suffer a lack of democratic legitimacy, encountering resistance that is particularly visible in the German-speaking cantons. In some cantons, popular initiatives have been launched to trigger a direct democratic vote on controversial components of the *Lehrplan 21*. The central focuses of dispute are: foreign language teaching from the second and/or fifth year of primary school, the competence orientation of the curriculum, and domain-specific school subjects in the social sciences (e.g. history and geography) versus an interdisciplinary school subject called "space, time, society" in secondary I education. Behind these contentious issues, profound conflicts can be located: Firstly, regarding whether the people, the elected politicians, or the education bureaucracy should be in charge of the development of curricula. Second, the cantonal educational institutions defend the democratic legitimation of educational decisions on a cantonal level drawing attention to the difference of the non-legitimation of to the inter-cantonal (EDK) or national (federal) consultation on governmental level. Third, teachers respond to the fact that the new curriculum, although developed with great participation of teachers, was administered from educational experts who work for a larger part in universities of teacher education and the educational bureaucracies. Associated with this latter conflict is the worry of a status reduction of teachers in the structure of the education system, a loss of prestige of the teaching profession, and the increased vulnerability of teachers in public discussion.

Issues in Coordinated Teacher Education

For years, teacher education in Switzerland remained relatively settled, organized through teacher seminars at the Secondary II level. The installation of the teacher education at the tertiary level was accompanied by a fierce battle between cantons over the centerpiece of the cantonal sovereignty within the educational system: teacher training for compulsory school. This change came in part from an effort to support the harmonization of compulsory school by standardizing teacher education. To serve that purpose, the curricula of teacher education and its practical implementation became controlled through an accreditation process of the EDK, the major institution of horizontal federalism in Swiss education governance. However, a more extreme move of reducing teacher education to only a few federally-approved universities failed. But pushback against harmonization efforts, fiscal considerations force intercantonal cooperation, and for certain fields (such as special needs education), cooperation is indispensable. One consistent, but by no means uncontroversial, example of cantonal cooperation comes from the teacher education at the University of Applied Sciences FHNW, which is supported by four cantons. In this area, the federalist-centralist line of conflict with the teachers is nurtured by an increasing stratification of the body of experts involved in teacher education. While in former teacher training, the majority of teacher trainers were experienced teachers themselves, they are now increasingly lecturers who underwent a scientific socialization. Additionally, international demands for a Bachelor or Master training must be fulfilled. As a consequence, the science-based teacher training is perceived as somehow alienated from practice. In public, these differences are discussed as a conflict between a traditional, holistically-viewed teacher education versus a science based professionalization of the teaching profession.

Both the federal government and the cantons supported the process of standardizing educational goals in compulsory school so as to define competences and standards that could be subject to educational monitoring. These changes, however, were only implemented for school subjects that were judged to be central to educational and occupational success (first language, first foreign language, mathematics, science). Apart from an assessment of the value of each discipline, which would require further discussion, these definitions created differences between the so called HarmoS subjects and subjects such as geography, history, religion, music, and sports. While the former receive strong attention in the cantons (i.e. assessment of the achievement of learning objectives monitored through the EDK, financial support for further educational research, etc.), the latter experience a very different appreciation. This far-reaching destabilization of the composition of school subjects, a composition long-defended as child-friendly or based on the tradition of humanistic education, has been used as a further argument for opposition against current trends in the development of the educational system.

Other Debates

Another open question concerns the schools of the upper secondary level. The importance of the dual educational path, which is firmly anchored in Switzerland, is a matter of much discussion. In recent years, the secondary school rate in Switzerland (which is rather low compared with other European and International educational systems) has become a focus of debate. Discussion has turned to questions such as how high the high school rate should be, what value a vocational diploma, a college diploma, or a university diploma should have, and how an international competitiveness of Swiss Diplomas can be ensured. Since the schools are conducted with cantonal sovereignty, their control over the requirements for obtaining the federal Matura is comparatively weak. As a consequence, high regional differences can be observed: the ratio of students acquiring the Matura varies between 18% and 30%. These differences sustain heated public debates over educational inequality, particularly in rural and underprivileged areas of Switzerland as well as between cantons and in international comparison.

Early childhood education is another area of discussion, which experienced not only emotionalized public clashes founded in different ideas of family life, gender roles and social structure, but has also created conflicts relating to federalist distribution of power. In their harmonization drafts, the EDK planned mandatory early childhood education in the basic level (2 years of mandatory kindergarten with permeability for enrolment in the first 2 years of school). Political disputes in some cantons led to the relativization of this requirement. The cantons feared the future costs of a nationwide mandatory regulation. They were successful in their opposition because the EDK does not hold competence to impose arrangements to individual cantons against their will. The result of the legal dispute has caused a variance of solutions that could be consulted for equality of educational opportunities.

CONCLUSION

Education governance in Switzerland bears a number of characteristic features that are closely related with the workings of Swiss federalism more generally. In the field of primary and secondary education, the cantons clearly are the main players, and have covetously defended their prerogatives against attempts of centralization of education policy competences at the federal level, even when aimed at the functional necessities of harmonizing cantonal education systems. Such cantonal resistance notwithstanding, the importance of the Confederation has increased since the early 2000s. With the adoption of the new constitutional article in 2006, the Confederation now has considerable powers to intervene in the field of education. However, the Confederation has, as of yet, refrained from using these powers. Indeed, the intensification of inter-cantonal coordination has improved harmonization of policy goals and funding in the field of education. Horizontal federalism has provided the tools for successful self-coordination in the "shadow of hierarchy" (Scharpf, 1997, p. 197), thereby allowing Swiss education governance to have the best of both worlds, i.e. reducing dysfunctional cross-cantonal disparities without resorting to a blunt reduction of cantonal sovereignty via centralization of competencies at the federal level.

However, the recent debates over the HarmoS agreement, over the Lehrplan 21, as well as over teacher education have shown the limits of horizontal federalism. Instruments of horizontal federalism are mainly driven by the cantonal governments and their bureaucracies, and tend to marginalize representative institutions (i.e. the cantonal parliaments) and citizens in the formulation of policy strategies and goals. As a consequence, goals and measures agreed upon in intercantonal coordination schemes tend to be perceived as disconnected from cantonal politics and are easily attacked as technocratic or expertocratic. Indeed, HarmoS, the Lehrplan 21, and the scientification of teacher education are all criticized by their opponents as undemocratic, dictatorial, and ponderous. In the case of HarmoS, fifteen cantons ratified the agreement between 2007 and 2016, while the voters of seven cantons rejected the agreement in cantonal referenda and thereby put a halt to coordinated agreements via direct democratic votes. Opposition in cantons is also growing against the implementation of the Lehrplan 21. The most visible proof of this political movement is, as is typical in the Swiss political system, the launch of people´s initiatives in several cantons, calling for either more direct-democratic participation when the authorities enact the curricula or specific educational approaches, e.g. teaching only one foreign language on the primary school level. However, these initiatives were rejected by the people with vast majoritiy, causing the Lehrplan 21 to be approved. Nevertheless, it is likely that the strong tradition of cantonal autonomy, the tools of direct democracy, and the delicate subject of education will be cause for ongoing debates on this issue in the future. Direct democratic blockades against intercantonal coordination might, in the end, trigger an intervention by the Confederation to settle disputes over educational policy goals. However, as it currently stands, it is uncertain if more federal diversity or more centralism through harmonizing federal laws, e.g. compelling the cantons to teach two foreign languages in primary education, will be the result of this "Swiss educational dispute."

APPENDIX

	Canton	Reading	Mathematics	Science
2009	CH	502	536	517
Significantly above CH average	VS (d)		550	
	VS (f)	522	553	
	SH	522	558	546
	FR (f)	520	558	
	AR		560	533
	JU		556	
	SG		552	
	AG			535
Significantly below CH average	BE (f)	495		497
	NE		524	499
	VD		520	490
	TI	485	518	493
	GE		512	490
	ZH			501
2012	CH	507	531	513
Significantly above CH average	VS (f)	527	539	
	FR (f)	520	550	518
	SG		552	531
Significantly below CH average	GE	501		489
	JU	501		500
	SO	497	524	
	BE (f)	496	516	493
	AG	495	515	
	NE	487	508	485
	TI	485	502	490
	VD			498

Source: Figures Published in Cantonal Analyses Based on Data From PISA 2009 and PISA 2012.

REFERENCES

Angelone, D., & Keller, F. (2014). Leistungsveränderungen in der Schweiz seit PISA 2000 [Changes in performance in Switzerland since PISA 2000]. In Konsortium PISA.ch (Ed.), *PISA 2012: Vertiefende Analysen* [Deeper analyses] (pp. 9–20). Bern, Switzerland: SBFI/EDK and Konsortium PISA. Retrieved from https://pisa.educa.ch/sites/default/files/20140923/pisa2012_vertiefende_analysen_0.pdf

Angelone, D., & Moser, U. (2011). Veränderungen der Leistungen seit PISA 2000 [Changes in performance since PISA 2000]. In Konsortium PISA.ch, *PISA 2009: Regionale und kantonale Ergebnisse* [Regional and cantonal results] (pp. 61–71). Bern, Switzerland: SBFI/EDK and Konsortium PISA. Retrieved from http://pisa.educa.ch/sites/default/files/20111205/pisa_de.pdf

Biaggini, G., Gächter, T., & Kiener, R. (Eds.). (2015). *Staatsrecht* [Constitutional law]. Zürich/St.Gallen, Switzerland: Dike.

Braun, D. (2003a). Dezentraler und unitarischer Föderalismus. Die Schweiz und Deutschland im Vergleich [Decentralised and unitary federalism. Switzerland and Germany compared]. *Schweizerische Zeitschrift für Politikwissenschaft, 9*(1), 57–89 .

Braun, D. (2003b). *Fiscal policies in federal states*. Aldershot, UK: Ashgate.

Ehrenzeller, B., & Sahlfeld, K. (2014). Vorbemerkungen zur Bildungsverfassung [Preliminary remarks to the Educational Constitution]. In B. Ehrenzeller, B. Schindler, R. J. Schweizer, & K. A. Vallender (Eds.), *St.Galler Kommentar: Die Schweizerische Bundesverfassung* [St Gall commentary of the Swiss Federal Constitution]. Zürich/St.Gallen, Switzerland: Dike.

Eidgenössische Finanzverwaltung. (2012). *Finanzstatistik der Schweiz, Jahresbericht 2010* [Swiss Financial Statistics. Annual report 2010]. Neuenburg, Switzerland: Bundesamt für Statistik.

Freitag, M., & M. Bühlmann. (2003). Die Bildungsfinanzen der Schweizer Kantone. Der Einfluss sozioökonoimischer Bedingungen, organisierter Interessen und plitischer Institutionen auf die Bildungsausgaben im kantonalen Vergleich [Education finances of the Swiss Cantons. The influence of socioeconomic conditions, organized interests and political Institutions on expanditure for education in intercantonal comparison]. *Schweizerische Zeitschrift für Politikwissenschaft, 9*(1), 139–168.

Gächter, T. (2010). Welche Gestaltungsspielräume verbleiben den Kantonen im Rahmen des HarmoS-Konkordats? [With which scopes the Cantons remain in the framework of the HarmoS-Treaty?]. In A. Auer (Ed.), *Herausforderungen HarmoS* [Challenges HarmoS]. Zürich, Switzerland: Schulthess.

Gilardi, F., Kübler, D., & Wasserfallen, F. (2013). Cantonal tax autonomy in Switzerland: history, trends and challenges. In *Autonomy in subnational income taxes: Evolving powers, existing practices in seven countries* (V. R. Almendral, & F. Vaillancourt, Eds.). Montréal, Canada: McGill-Queen's University Press.

Glaser, A., & Fuhrer, C. (2015). Der Lehrplan 21: Interkantonales soft law mit Demokratiedefizit [The Curriculum 21: Intercantonal soft law with democratic deficit]. *Zeitschrift für Schwizerisches Recht, 134*, 513–540.

Grob, U., & Wolter, S. C. (2007). Demographic change and public education spending: A conflict between young and old? *Education Economics, 15*(3), 277–292.

Haller, W. (2016). *The Swiss Constitution in a Comparative Context.* Zürich/St.Gallen, Switzerland: Dike.

Martin, M. O., Mullis, I. V. S., & Foy, P. (with Olson, J. F., Erberber, E., Preuschoff, C., & Galia, J.). (2008). Chestnut Hill, MA: TIMSS & PIRLS International Study Center, Boston College.

Moser, U. (2002). Cultural diversity at school: Opportunity and challenge. In Federal office for statistics and Swiss Conference of Cantonal Ministers of Education (Eds.), *Prepared for life? The basic competences of young people—National report of the PISA Survey 2000* (pp. 90–112). Neuchâtel, Switzerland: BFS/EDK. Retrieved from https://edudoc.ch

Moser, U., & Angelone, D. (2011). Zusammenfassung [Summary]. In Konsortium PISA. ch (Ed.), *PISA 2009: Regionale und kantonale Ergebnisse* [Regional and cantonal results] (pp. 72–78). Bern, Switzerland: BBT/EDK and Konsortium PISA.ch. Retrieved from http://pisa.educa.ch/sites/default/files/20111205/pisa_de.pdf

Mullis, I. V. S., Martin, M. O., & Foy, P. (with Olson, J. F., Preuschoff, C., Erberber, E., Arora, A., & Galia, J.). (2008). Chestnut Hill, MA: TIMSS & PIRLS International Study Center, Boston College.

Organisation for Economic Co-operation and Development (OECD). (2001). *Knowledge and skills for life—First results from PISA 2000* [Connaissances et compétences: des atouts pour la vie: Premiers résultats de PISA 2000; Ler-nen für das Leben: Erste Ergebnisse von PISA 2000]. Paris: OECD. Retrieved from www.pisa.oecd.org

Scharpf, F. (1997). *Games real actors play. Actor-centered institutionalism and policy research*. Boulder, CO: Westview.

Swiss Conference of Cantonal Ministers of Education (EDK). (2003). Aktionsplan «PISA 2000»-Folgemassnahmen [Action plan «PISA 2000»—follow-up]. Retrieved from http://www.edudoc.ch/static/web/arbeiten/pisa2000_aktplan_d.pdf.

CHAPTER 10

FEDERALISM AND EDUCATION

The Case of the UK

Deborah Wilson and Llorenc O'Prey

INTRODUCTION

Education policy across the four nations of the UK has a complex, asymmetric history with roots that can be traced back as early as the nineteenth century. In 1999, a series of key devolution settlements for Wales, Scotland and Northern Ireland led to the transfer of both legislative and executive powers from the UK Government to the respective devolved administrations across a range of competencies, including education. These devolution settlements have led to the UK representing what could be considered a quasi-federalist approach (Deacon, 2006).

The aim of this chapter is to consider the effects of devolution on education policy across the four nations of the UK, within the broader context provided by historical, political and wider global influences. We begin by exploring the processes shaping the devolution of legislative and executive powers across the UK administrations. We describe how devolution has influenced education policy across the UK, before considering the implications of these developments across several key themes, including finance, governance, accountability and diversity. We then explore the factors influencing both convergence and divergence of edu-

Federalism and Education: Ongoing Challenges and Policy Strategies in Ten Countries, pages 211–230.

cation policy across the devolved nations, and illustrate some of these using a case study involving school policy in Wales and England. We finish by suggesting some of the broader lessons for federal education systems that may be learnt from the UK experience.

UNDERSTANDING THE UK CONTEXT

As a sovereign state, the UK represents the political and geographical union of four constituent nations: England, Scotland, Wales and Northern Ireland. The last 20 years have delivered significant devolution and decentralization that have redefined the relationships between the four (Moran, 2015). Analysing the nature, extent and implications of these reforms on education policy requires an understanding of some of the broader political and historical trends that have shaped these developments, as the redistribution of executive and legislative powers across the UK forms part of a long and complex process (Scully & Wyn Jones, 2011).

Devolution in the UK followed considerable debate concerning the traditional British constitutional approach. Since the seventeenth century, the UK constitution had developed primarily in accord with a unitary tradition, in which power was centralized around the UK Parliament in Westminster, England (Bradbury, 2006). These arrangements allowed for strong, uniform government from the centre. They were sustained by a broad political consensus, and justified in terms of the supremacy of centralized power in promoting economic and imperial success (Garside & Hebbert, 1989).

Across the UK, the principles of federalism and devolution within the context of constitutional reform began to be discussed as early as the eighteenth century. Even at the time of the negotiations leading to the Union of Scottish and English Parliaments in 1707, there were alternative proposals that included a federal system guaranteeing Scottish legislative and judicial independence (Bradbury, 1988). By the nineteenth century, nationalist and secessionist political movements had emerged in Ireland, Wales and Scotland. With varying degrees of popular support, they opposed the unitary tradition, variously demanding separate parliaments if not explicit self-government (Burrows & Denton, 1980).

The re-emergence of a distinct political consciousness coincided with the re-articulation of national, territorial and cultural identities across the 'Celtic fringe' (Pittock, 1999). The Celtic Revival, for example, was composed of a variety of cultural and linguistic movements and trends that influenced the modern identities of Scotland, Ireland and Wales (Donaldson, 2006). Although the Revival was broad and multifaceted, movements often promoted and celebrated a common ancestry and tradition, as well as a distinct Celtic linguistic and literary heritage. Some sought to counter the perceived dominance of the English language in every day life, which they felt crowded out indigenous Insular Celtic languages, including Welsh, Scots Gaelic, and Irish Gaelige. These perspectives were often critical of an expanding and standardising education system with an English curriculum at its heart, which they felt marginalized and diminished Celtic languages and cultures (McIntyre, 2009). These perspectives and identities continue to inform education debates today, shaping the nature and extent of reforms especially around the role of minority languages within the curriculum (we return to this point below).

Calls for greater legislative and executive independence across the UK ebbed and intensified at various points over the course of the 20th century. At the conclusion of the Irish Wars of Independence, Ireland was granted independence from the UK in 1922. Northern Ireland opted to remain within the Union, and was granted significant devolved powers (Moran, 2015). It wasn't until the late 1960s, however, that pressures for significant change had galvanized around nationalist political movements in Scotland and Wales. By 1997 popular support for greater devolution was impossible to ignore. Referenda in Wales and Scotland both returned significant majorities in favour of greater devolution, leading to considerable restructuring of legislative and executive powers across the four nations. In Northern Ireland, devolution was a key part of the Good Friday Agreement signed in April 1998, which was supported by voters in a referendum held in May 1998 (Flinders, 2008).

Political devolution took effect in the UK when powers were transferred from Westminster to the Scottish Parliament and Welsh Assembly in July 1999; and to the Northern Ireland Assembly on 2 December 1999. Legislative powers across a range of competencies, including education, were accompanied by executive powers that were transferred to the Scottish Government, the Welsh Assembly Government and the Northern Ireland Executive. These institutions were each accountable to their respective Parliament or Assembly. All three nations were still represented in the UK Parliament, enabling Scotland, Wales, and Northern Ireland to have forms of self-government whilst remaining within the UK. A key rationale behind these reforms was the preservation of the UK as a unitary state, whilst responding to the pressures for greater self-determination.

CHARACTERISTICS OF DEVOLUTION IN THE UK

An important distinction to make in the case of the UK is that the distribution of powers across the UK does not reflect a pure form of federalism. Although there are many similarities between federalism and devolution, constitutionally they diverge on an important point. Within a federalist state, the central government is not sovereign but subordinate to the constitution. Under these arrangements, individual provinces or regions possess legislative and executive jurisdiction within their areas of competence. By contrast, devolution preserves the overall sovereignty of central government. Under these arrangements, the UK Parliament can continue to legislate for Scotland, Wales or Northern Ireland even on devolved matters. It can also abolish the devolved bodies, including the Scottish Parliament and the Welsh Assembly Government, by an Act of Parliament as it did with the Northern Ireland Parliament in 1972 (Bogdanor, 2009). In practice, however, devolution has transformed the UK into a parliament for England, a federal parliament for Scotland and Northern Ireland, and a parliament for primary legislation in Wales. In this sense, the case of the UK could be considered to incorporate a quasi-federalist approach (Deacon, 2006).

Another important characteristic to consider is the uneven nature, extent and speed of devolution across the four nations. The highly asymmetrical nature of reforms has created a system with no common framework in which "Scotland, Wales, and indeed, Northern Ireland, have very different devolution arrangements, reflecting different historical traditions and constitutional principles" (Scully & Wyn Jones, 2011, p. 114). In practice there are wide differences in the terms of the devolution settlement, in the change that this represents from previous practice, and in the political and institutional context in which policy is formulated. Asymmetrical devolution has encouraged bilateral, rather than multilateral discussions between governments over policy ideas and objectives (Schmueker & Adams, 2005).

A further source of asymmetry and complexity within the case of the UK is that England sits outside of current devolution arrangements. Whilst Scotland, Northern Ireland and Wales have each developed institutions for directing and managing legislative and executive competencies, no new specifically English institutions have been created in response to devolution. Whilst the institutions of the central UK state remain largely unchanged as a result of devolution, reforms have had a profound impact on what those institutions actually do. The Education Minister of the UK Government is in practice the English Education Minister, with little direct influence over education policy in the other nations. The UK parliament maintains representation from Wales, Scotland and Northern Ireland, however, which in theory enables representatives from other nations to influence English policy (a situation often characterized by the phrase 'the West Lothian question').

While devolution has led to fundamental changes in the political landscape across the UK and the way in which policy is developed and implemented, important questions remain concerning the sustainability of the current political settlement. These have been heightened by the result of the referendum on European Union membership that took place in June 2016, in which Scotland and Northern Ireland voted to remain in the EU, while England and Wales voted to leave. The Supreme Court judgement that the UK Government does not need to consult the devolved administrations on triggering Brexit has led to calls for a second Scottish independence referendum, for example.[1] It will remain to be seen if devolution—post-Brexit—leads to purer forms of federalism, or even the eventual dissolution of the UK.

[1] See http://www.independent.co.uk/news/uk/home-news/brexit-latest-news-nicola-sturgeon-scottish-independence-second-referendum-uk-supreme-court-ruling-a7543941.html, Accessed on 22/02/2017

EDUCATION POLICY ACROSS THE DEVOLVED NATIONS

Education policy across the four nations also has a complex, asymmetric history with roots that predate the political devolution settlements of 1999. Scotland itself has had a role in administering schools since the state acquired its modern role in education with the establishment of the Scottish Education Department in 1872. Education in Northern Ireland has been separately administered ever since its creation under the Stormont Parliament of 1922. Welsh education policy developed largely in tandem with England until 1970, when the Welsh Office assumed responsibility for education. During the 1980s and 1990s, nations were handed greater responsibilities across curriculum, assessment, quality assurance and funding. Therefore, "the main impact of the 1999 settlement was not to create a new tier of government, but to place an existing tier under democratic control" (Raffe, 2005, p. 2). Within this context, all four nations have pursued distinctive education policy paths.

The education systems across the UK are significantly different in terms of size and composition. England is by far the largest, teaching approximately 7.8 million children across 24,345 schools. In Northern Ireland, by contrast, there are just 340,000 children in 1,166 schools (2015 data). There is also considerable variation in the pupil population, both within and across education systems. Scotland and Wales, for example, support a much larger proportion of pupils who are eligible for free school meals, which are provided for school age children whose parents are in receipt of certain welfare benefits and which is a widely used proxy for disadvantage (for more on the use of this measure, see Hobbs & Vignoles, 2010). England has a larger proportion of children for whom English is an additional language, reflecting the diverse range of backgrounds represented in English schools. The variation in size and composition across the education systems

TABLE 10.1. Primary and Secondary Pupil Populations, Size and Baseline Characteristics Across the Four Nations in the State Education Sector.

	Total School Population	Children Eligible for Free School Meals	%	English as an Additional Language*	%
England	7,796,285	1,147,235	14.7	1,185,960	15.2
Northern Ireland	339,854	100,000	29.4	Not collected	
Scotland	680,007	259,139	38.1	35,441	5.2
Wales	465,704	80,668	17.3	Not collected	

Sources: School Census Data, 2015. Sources: England: School Census Data (2015) Office of National Statistics; Northern Ireland: School Census Data (2015) Northern Ireland Department for Education; Scotland: School Census Data (2015) The Scottish Government; Wales: School Census Data (2015) Statistics for Wales.

Note: English as an additional language (EAL) is an administrative term for those pupils whose first language is other than English.

TABLE 10.2. Education Performance Across the Devolved Administrations, National Datasets.

Measure	Source	England	Wales	Scotland	Northern Ireland
Age 7 reading, std score	MCS	50.9	47.3	50.5	47.0
Age 7 maths, std score	MCS	50.0	50.0	49.8	50.4
Age 11 English, % Level 2+	KS2, 2010/11	82	83.4	—	—
Age 11 maths, % Level 2+	KS2, 2010/11	80	84.9	—	—
5+ GCSEs A*– C or equivalent	GCSE exams or equivalent 2009/10	76.1	63.8	78.3	74.3
A*–C GCSE in maths	GCSE exams or equivalent, 2006/07	54.6	50.0	48.3	54.7
A*- C GCSE in English	As above	60.2	58.9	69.8	62.9
% of 16-year-olds participating in post-compulsory education	Staying on rates(ONS website), 2006/07	80	78	70	84
% of 17–24-year-olds with no qualifications	LFS, 2009	7.0	7.8	7.4	12.7
% of 18-year-olds with 2 or more A-levels	A-level results, 2010/11	51.8	27.1	33.2	50.2

Source: Machin et al. (2013), Table 2, p. 145.

presents different policy challenges, and may account for some of the divergence in practice between the four nations (Raffe, 2005).

The types of schools that make up the state sector in each of the four nations also differ considerably. England, Scotland, and Wales all have a comprehensive model of education, in which the majority of schools do not select children by ability (although some academic selection into Grammar schools does still occur in certain regions of England). Northern Ireland maintains a system of academic selection, in which pupils are sorted into different types of school according to ability. More recently, policy reform in England has focused on increasing the diversity of the types of school that make up the comprehensive system, including Academies and so-called 'free schools' which, much like charter schools in the United States of America, seek to give schools greater autonomy in how they are managed while remaining accountable to central government (discussed further below). In Wales and Scotland, there has been no such policy either to create diversity within the comprehensive system or to grant schools greater autonomy (Machin et al., 2013).

TABLE 10.3. Education Performance across the Devolved Administrations, International Datasets

Measure	Source	England	Wales	Scotland	Ireland
Reading score of 10-year-olds (average over sample of 35 countries = 500. SD = 100)	PIRLS, 2001	551	n/a	530	n/a
40 countries	PIRLS, 2006	530	n /a	536	n /a
Maths score of 10-year-olds (average over sample of 49 countries = 500, SD = 100)	TIMSS, 2003	531		490	
59 countries	TIMSS, 2007	541	n/a	494	n/a
Maths score of 14-year-olds (average over sample of 49 countries = 500, SD = 100)	TIMSS, 2003	498	n/a	498	n/a
59 countries	TIMSS, 2007	513	n/a	487	n/a
Maths score of 15-year-olds (average over sample of 47 OECD countries = 500, SD = 100)	PISA, 2006	495	483	506	494
32 OECD countries	PISA, 2009	493	471	499	493
Reading score of 15-year-olds (average over sample of 47 OECD countries = 500, SD = 100)	PISA, 2006	496	480	499	489
32 OECD countries	PISA, 2009	495	475	500	500

PIRLS, Progress in International Reading Literacy Study: TIMSS. Trends in International Mathematics and Science Study ; PISA. Programme for International Student Assessment.
Source: Machin et al. (2013), Table 3, p. 146

There is also diversity in educational performance across the four administrations. Although there are some differences across datasets and through time in Table 10.2, the analysis by Machin et al. (2103) shows that there is variation across the four nations at each age at which performance is measured. This includes literacy and numeracy at ages 7 and 11, and at 16 and 18 when pupils undertake GCSEs and A-level examinations. A widely accepted measure of attainment, five GCSE passes at grades C or above, represents the minimum requirement to go on to study A-levels. There are also differences across the four nations in the number of pupils staying on in education: Northern Ireland, for example, while reporting a significantly higher proportion of young people leaving school without any qualifications, also reports a higher proportion of 16-year olds participating in post-compulsory education.

Variations in pupil performance across the four UK nations have also been reported in various international comparative datasets and rankings, including

PIRLS, PISA and TIMSS.[2] Table 10.3, also taken from Machin et al (2013), illustrates some of these differences. The implications of national performance in international rankings for education policy across the UK will be discussed in more detail later in the chapter.

Neither international comparisons nor national averages, both of which draw on aggregated data, reveal the more complex geographies of spatial variation in outcomes *within* specific education systems across the UK. In England, for example, socioeconomic background remains one of the strongest predictors of educational attainment, with poorer children continuing to underperform relative to their more affluent peers (Shane, 2016). The importance of factors such as family background contribute to significant and relatively high levels of variation in pupil and school performance across different communities and regions. This presents significant challenges, and may contribute, in part, to local mediation and variation of national education policies in practice.

EDUCATION POLICY TRENDS ACROSS THE DEVOLVED NATIONS

In this section we consider the trends across the four UK administrations with respect to different aspects of education policy, focusing on the key themes that are relevant across all the case studies in this volume.

Governance

Through the process of devolution, the administration of education has placed existing agencies and institutions under the control of their respective, democratically elected, devolved national governments. There are now, in effect, no areas of shared responsibility. This has meant a diminished role for the UK Parliament that now essentially holds a legislative role for England only. The role and powers of the current UK Government's Minister for Education, and the Department of Education that she leads, are now correspondingly focused on the governance of England's education sector.

Historically in the UK, local government has played a significant role in education governance. However, they have been subordinate to central government, in the sense of having to administer local education policy within the scope of national legal, governance and financial frameworks. While this is still true post-1999, there is now variation between England and the other nations. In Wales, for example, local authorities maintain strategic leadership over school admissions policy in their region, and there are similar arrangements in Scotland and Northern Ireland. In England, however, the strategic role of local authorities on admissions and the planning of school places has been reduced due to the opening of

[2] For more information on these datasets, see PISA: http://www.oecd.org/pisa/pisaproducts/ and TIMSS and PIRLS http://timssandpirls.bc.edu/timss2011/international-database.html

different types of schools (Academies and so-called 'free schools.' for example) that are their own admissions authorities and are accountable directly to central government.

There has been some continuity in the working relationships between local and national governments post-devolution. McConnell (2004) argues that the pattern of central-local relations in Scotland has not changed significantly since devolution, although the 'centre' has moved from the UK Parliament to the Scottish Parliament. The UK Parliament has become less relevant to the workings of Scottish local government on a day-to-day basis, as most of the responsibilities of local councils are devolved to the Scottish Parliament and Executive (Bennett et al., 2002).

Finance

It is in the area of finance that the UK Government is the most influential across the devolved states, each of which are currently still funded by what is known as a block grant and formula system. Northern Ireland and Wales raise only a small proportion of their own revenue through local taxation and currently have no tax raising powers. Scotland is able to set the rate of income tax, but has so far chosen to keep levels of taxation in line with the rest of the UK. Table 10.4 summarizes HM Treasury data for identifiable expenditure on education across the four devolved states from 2010/11–2014/15.

Under the block grant and formula system, the grant allocated to each devolved state is determined by the annual Comprehensive Spending Reviews undertaken by the UK government, and then by the Barnett formula. The Barnett formula is calculated to provide a proportionate share of public expenditure to be allocated to each of the devolved administrations for spending on 'comparable' public service functions within each state, taking into account their populations compared to England. The formula accounts for a large proportion of each administration's budget—85% of Scotland's budget in 2013/14, for example.[3] Once allocated, the subsequent block grant can be spent freely by the devolved administrations as they see fit. They are not tied to spending it on any particular functions, either within education or between education and other public services.

The Barnett formula is controversial, and there is little consensus on how to address the perceived limitations of such a mechanism (Institute for Fiscal Studies, 2014). The formula ties Scotland, Wales and Northern Ireland to budgetary priorities and spending levels determined by the UK Government. This can, critics have argued, limit the Welsh, Scottish and Northern Irish administrations' ability to address their own priorities, and may therefore serve to promote policy convergence across the four nations as discussed below (Midwinter, 2006).

[3] http://www.gov.scot/Publications/2012/09/7829/22 (accessed 3 March 2016)

TABLE 10.4. Total Identifiable Expenditure on Education in the UK, 2010–11 to 2014–15 (£million)

	Stage of Education	2010–11	2011–12	2012–13	2013–14	2014–15
England	Pre-school and Primary	25,655	25,536	25,755	25,799	26,103
	Secondary Education	31,416	30,566	31,013	31,665	31,124
Northern Ireland	Pre-school and Primary	709	711	715	737	788
	Secondary Education	1,104	1,029	984	974	1,022
Scotland	Pre-school and Primary	2,840	2,813	2,809	2,916	2,996
	Secondary Education	2,768	2,778	2,685	2,575	2,588
Wales	Pre-school and Primary	1,453	1,490	1,531	1,560	1,555
	Secondary Education	1,529	1,680	1,678	1,533	1,780

Source: HM Treasury (2015)

Academic Standards, Quality Assurance and Performance-Based Accountability

There is broad similarity across the four nations regarding the role of inspection as part of a model of quality assurance in education. Inspection regimes, which are independent of government, assess schools' performance in each nation within a common framework. There are some differences regarding the details of what inspections cover and the way in which information is shared across the administrations, but all four nations have maintained a roughly common approach. This is despite ongoing debate concerning the role and limitations of inspection within quality assurance in public services more broadly.

There is less consensus across the four administrations regarding the form and role of performance-based accountability mechanisms within a broader model of quality assurance. Annual school league tables still feature every English and Northern Irish state primary and secondary school, but were scrapped in Scotland in 2003 (Chitty, 2009) and in Wales in 2001 (Burgess et al., 2013). We discuss the policy divergence between England and Wales in this area in more detail below.

International comparative performance measures such as PISA, TIMSS and PIRLS, which have reported aggregate variation in attainment across a range of measures, have been featured in policy debates to varying degrees across the UK. PISA scores have heavily influenced education debates in England, which highlight international examples of high performing 'educational utopias' as providing a rationale for reform (Morris, 2015). Comparatively poor PISA results have had a significant role in driving the rationale behind education policy reform in Wales. The Welsh government faced significant political pressure from relatively poor results in PISA 2012 and, as a result, introduced a 'banding' system to rank schools, a measure that partly reversed the 2001 decision to scrap annual school rankings (discussed further below). By contrast, in Scotland there is less debate about PISA and similar measures, partly because the prevailing narrative is that Scotland performs comparatively well.

There is a lack of consensus regarding the broader accountability mechanisms of which such performance measures and inspection regimes play a part (Bevan & Wilson, 2013). In particular, the emphasis on the role of choice and competition, informed by published rankings and inspection results, differs across the four devolved administrations. There are two distinct models of education emerging in the UK. The first, exemplified by Wales and Scotland, emphasizes the links between schools and communities and the need for common content and standards of provision across all schools. The second, exemplified by England and Northern Ireland, emphasizes choice and institutional diversity. There is both convergence and divergence. Northern Ireland is moving towards England, although this convergence is motivated by different political agendas and overall objectives (Raffe, 2005). Scotland and Wales appear to be continuing a divergent path from England, partly reflecting political differences across national divides. We return to this point below.

Diversity

Here we highlight two issues within education policy between the four nations that seek to accommodate diversity: minority languages and religion. The expansion of Irish, Welsh and Scots Gaelic language medium education has sought to reverse the decline of indigenous languages in common usage. Minority languages have become increasingly popular within provision in Wales, Scotland and Northern Ireland, albeit from a very small base. In Scotland in 2014, for example, 1.7 per cent of the school population received some form of Gaelic medium provision (2014 data). In Wales, where 19.5 per cent of the population speak Welsh, there have been significant discussion and efforts to improve and expand Welsh medium provision.

The role of religion in education provision has also received significant attention within education debates in the UK. This is especially apparent within Northern Ireland, where there are significant historical and violent divides between the Catholic and Protestant communities. It is estimated that 95 per cent of pupils attend a school whose religious affiliation matches their own, which critics argue contributes to the segregation of the two communities. Efforts to address this separation include the expansion of integrated education models of schooling that are non-denominational, and encouraging schools to collaborate in shared education spaces (such efforts have parallels with those aimed at improving integration across schools and neighbourhoods with high proportions of different ethnic groups in England (Burgess et al., 2005)). However, these efforts are again starting from a very small base, in which only an estimated 6.1 per cent of pupils are attending integrated schools (2015 data).

POLICY CONVERGENCE AND DIVERGENCE

There are several factors that influence education policy development across the devolved nations in the UK. These factors can lead to both policy divergence—where different jurisdictions adopt unique policy approaches—as well as policy convergence—the adoption of similar policies across different jurisdictions. Although devolution permitted the administrations to follow different policy paths across a range of competencies, including education, there are also subtle pressures promoting convergence. Within this context, education policy is influenced by a range of local, UK and global trends, pressures and debates. We first consider the factors that have driven both education policy divergence and convergence in the context of a devolved UK, before looking more closely at a comparison of Wales and England that illustrates some of these tensions.

Divergence: Historical/Cultural/Political

The ways in which education policy within and across the four nations has diverged on important issues reflects different historical traditions, constitutional principles and both economic and—increasingly—political realities. A key piece of context is political difference: since 2010 no one party has been in power in more than one UK nation (Paun et al., 2016). There is considerable, and potentially increasing post-Brexit, diversity in both the general political landscape and in attitudes towards education. There is a higher degree of confidence in the state system of education in Scotland, for example, and proportionally fewer Scottish children attend private schools than in England, with an estimated 5 per cent and 7 per cent of pupils respectively (Social Mobility and Child Poverty Commission, 2015). Moreover, politically, there are stronger social democratic tendencies in Wales and Scotland than in either England or Northern Ireland. It has been argued that devolution has allowed Scottish politicians to reinforce their 'welfarist' spirit (McEwen & Parry 2005, p. 43) and that Scotland's tradition of placing priorities on social democracy increased the likelihood that some aspects of education and health policy in Scotland would diverge from England after devolution. In the Welsh context, Reynolds (2008, p. 754) has argued that the change in education policy away from the consumer-driven reforms in England was motivated by "the left wing political history of Wales and the use of government to ensure enhanced social justice for Welsh citizens, [which] created a climate of greater trust in producer determined solutions."

Divergence: Path Dependency

As Tuohy (1999) has argued in her development and application of the concept to analyze the evolution of the systems of health care of the UK, the USA and Canada, the "accidental logics" of history "have shaped national systems at critical moments in time, and in the distinctive 'logics' of the systems thus created" (Tuohy, 1999, p. 6). Her analysis shows how governments respond to "windows of opportunity" to enact major reforms through political settlements and policies. These reforms then tend to develop on paths that follow the underlying logic of those settlements. In a temporal comparative study of the Dutch and English health care systems, Pollitt et al. (2010) go further and suggest 'logics of escalation' may emerge, whereby technical and political forces combine to create endogenous forces of reproduction, leading these systems to evolve in a way that makes it hard to imagine their abandonment (Wilson, 2011). Within the context of education policy across the four nations, therefore, any differences since 1999 may be reflected in the different trajectories that were present prior to political devolution.

Divergence: Responsiveness and Innovation

Devolution has led to divergence both in the different foci of education policy in the four nations and in the preferred policy responses. This has in turn influenced the nature and extent of reforms, often promoting divergence in approaches. For example, the debates about the need for greater cohesion between different communities in Northern Ireland has driven innovation in integrated models of education provision. Together, the different political settlements, path dependencies, and specific policy issues in each of the four nations have spurred policy innovation in education. This is especially true of curriculum and assessment arrangements, where the Scottish and Welsh governments have undertaken significant reviews and have implemented reforms that are a radical departure from what has gone before. An inevitable consequence of increased 'localism.' of policy becoming more responsive to the particular needs of a smaller national or sub-national population, is a divergence of provision across those populations. This may in turn cause tensions akin to the so-called 'postcode lottery' debates in health care, which run counter to public expectations around common standards of service and extent of provision, regardless of where they live (see Cairney et al., 2016, for a broader discussion of some of these issues in the Scottish context).

Convergence: International Comparisons and Metrics

Running counter to factors that encourage divergence, there are also subtle pressures that encourage policy convergence. International education debates have influenced domestic discussions concerning the nature of 'education utopias.' and the policy levers that could deliver them. This is most prevalent in broader debates around PISA scores, which have encouraged Wales to take policy examples from Scotland in developing reforms. This includes the significant reforms proposed to curriculum and assessment arrangements in Wales, which largely mirrored the reforms implemented in Scotland. Moreover, as discussed further below, the poor showing for Wales in PISA led to a re-evaluation of a key element of its education policy. Research by Breakspear (2012) for the OECD shows that there were differing degrees of policy response to PISA 2009 across three of the UK nations (Table 3.1.2; no results reported for Northern Ireland): in a 'breadth of policy impact' index, England scored highest, followed by Wales then Scotland. This was despite Wales scoring below both Scotland and England in PISA 2009. This links to the analysis by Martens and Niemann (2013) who suggest that two conditions need to be met for international rankings have an impact: the focus of the ranking is framed as crucial in policy discourse, and there is a substantial gap between the country's relative performance and its self-perception.

Convergence: Funding Arrangements and Compatibility

It could be argued that the fact that funding is still centrally controlled and allocated across administrations according to a common funding formula continues to promote policy convergence. Whilst devolved governments can implement different priorities within their budgeting arrangements, they cannot radically increase the overall funding for education. At a UK level, there may be additional factors that encourage compatibility across the different education systems, partly related to the degree of cross-border traffic by both students and teachers (linked with broader labour market flexibilities) and the need therefore for some compatibility across different policy areas. In Wales, for example, debates concerning reforms of assessment arrangements were curtailed in order to ensure that Welsh awards remained compatible with English systems (based on personal communication with one of the current authors).

POLICY LEARNING OR POLICY AVOIDANCE?

As discussed above, there are different factors that drive education policy divergence and convergence across the UK nations following devolution. Linked to these arguments is the question of whether opportunities for policy learning and/or transfer that may subsequently arise are taken up; or whether, conversely, there are forces acting towards more of a state of policy avoidance; of being seen to be different. Key to this is the realization of any potential for sharing best practice and evidence across the different systems, which in turn may depend on comparable data and information systems. A recent report by the Alliance for Useful Evidence (Paun et al., 2016) considers the UK as a 'policy laboratory' and concludes that, while devolution has led to increased innovation and policy divergence, significant barriers remain that reduce the potential for the sharing of any resulting evidence on what works.

Before drawing together some of the key lessons from the UK experience to date, we illustrate a number of the tensions that have surfaced around education policy convergence/divergence by way of a case study of school policy in England and Wales.

Case Study: School League Tables in Wales and England

Notoriously, early editions of the *Encyclopedia Britannica* had in the index the entry "For Wales see England" (Robbins, 2001), which was seen as a good descriptor of schools policies in Wales prior to devolution (Bevan & Wilson, 2013). In 1999, when the Welsh Assembly took responsibility for education spending and policy, it sought to create "clear red water" in its schools policies for Wales (Greer, 2009). In July 2001, following a consultation exercise, the Welsh Assembly government announced that it would stop the publication of school league tables with immediate effect. Prior to that point, league tables had been a fixture of both Welsh and English schools' governance since the early 1990s, providing a high-profile, transparent public ranking of schools' comparative performance across a range of measures, predominantly based on test score outcomes. These transparent public rankings (TPR) were used as part of a range of governance structures: they informed parental choice and encouraged schools to compete as part of a quasi-market, while also being used to set targets and identify 'failing' schools, with subsequent sanctions sometimes attached.

This system continued in England. After league tables were abolished in Wales, the data was still collected and used by schools and local authorities. What stopped was the very public, high-stakes nature of that information, with a shift to increased reliance on trusting the schools to use data for improvement purposes without the need for explicit external intervention. Wales essentially shifted from TPR to a governance model based on trust and altruism (T&A). Parental choice remained in both England and Wales, but with recognition of its limited impact in Wales' many rural localities (Reynolds, 2008).

Burgess et al (2013) exploited this 'natural experiment' to evaluate the effect on school performance of the abolition of school league tables in Wales, with students in England providing the control group. Using census data from all non-selective, state schools in England and Wales, the study compared outcomes (based on test scores at age 16) in the two countries before and after the 2001 reform, and found a negative impact on school performance in Wales relative to England by almost two GCSE grades per student per year. This effect was concentrated in the lower 75 per cent of schools (as measured by student prior attainment and by disadvantage (free school meal eligibility)), with the most disadvantaged and lowest average ability schools falling behind the most. The results did not vary by degree of competition across the two countries. The authors therefore argued that the key policy driver for improved performance came from the reputation effects of "naming and shaming" in the TPR model (for more on this, see Burgess et al., 2013 and Bevan & Wilson, 2013).

The evidence was originally published in a working paper in November 2010. The following day, questions were put to the First Minister of Wales in the Welsh Assembly. He responded that they would wait until the latest PISA results were published and was confident that they would show a different story for Welsh educational outcomes. PISA 2009 was published the following month and showed that Wales had fallen further behind since the last tests, and scored worse than before in each of reading, maths and science. Moreover, scores in Wales had fallen relative to England and the other devolved nations. Wales' Education Minister, Leighton Andrews, described the results as reflecting "systemic failure."

The PISA results prompted a re-think of education policy in Wales, set out in a major speech in Cardiff by Leighton Andrews in February 2011. One of the central components of the new policy focussed directly on school accountability:

> We will introduce a national system for the grading of schools which will be operated by all local authorities/consortia … All schools will produce an annual public profile containing performance information to a common format.

The new "banding" system was announced in December 2011, reversing the decade-long policy of not publishing school performance information, but in a different format to the continuing system in England.

So what does this story tell us about the tensions around policy divergence/convergence; around policy avoidance/learning in a newly devolved system? It seems apparent that an initial reaction was one of divergence: to have an education policy that could be seen to be different from that of England was a priority for the Welsh Assembly Government post-devolution, and the abolition of school league tables can be viewed as an innovative response to broader political and cultural concerns regarding consumer-driven education policy. Bevan and Wilson (2013) suggest another reason for the abolition of a system of TPR in Wales. As Hibbard et al. (2003) point out, the TPR model is effective in generating incentives for improved performance by inflecting reputational damage through ranking, but such pressure is unpopular with those who are "named and shamed." Hence governments vulnerable to producer capture (whereby they reflect the interests of public service providers—here, schools—rather than those of the broader citizenry) will seek alternatives. Hood et al. (1999) have argued that the greater scale in England, for example, creates a greater degree of relational distance between governments and providers of public services in Scotland and Wales. If Wales, by virtue of its smaller scale, is vulnerable to producer capture, that may be part of the explanation.

The initial reaction to the evidence on the effects of school league table abolition, and the fact that it was scores in PISA that mattered, is indicative of the broader, global, policy convergence regarding what educational outcomes are important and how a nation's performance with regard to such outcomes 'should' be measured. But when Wales scored badly in PISA, with regard to both temporal and international (particularly UK) comparisons, the Welsh Assembly Government had to be seen to act. And its response was one of convergence—back towards the policy it had previously, publicly, retreated from: the publication of school performance information.

CONCLUSIONS: LESSONS FROM THE UK EXPERIENCE

Innovation and Learning

Devolution has enabled a closer relationship between government and the governed, especially in the smaller polities of Scotland, Wales and Northern Ireland (Raffe, 2006). Across the four nations, devolution has opened up the possibility for more responsive governance of local issues within education, driven by local values and priorities (Paun et al., 2016). Distinctive institutional arrangements, processes, and dynamics of change have emerged, which in turn have promoted policy divergence and innovation across a range of domains, including curriculum and assessment arrangements, and integrated non-denomination school models. Greater autonomy and policy innovation have created new opportunities for learning and policy transfer, especially where there is apparent policy divergence on common policy problems.

Significant barriers still remain, however, both political and institutional. As Paun et al. (2016) point out, transaction costs for evidence exchange have increased since devolution due to multiple factors such as the separation of legislatures and supporting civil service, the resulting decline in the interchange of staff, and increasing cultural differences regarding policy priorities and potential solutions. Crucially, devolution may further inhibit the collection and sharing of comparable data across the four UK nations, data that would enable inter-system evaluation of policy interventions and their effects on a range of educational outcomes using the UK as a 'policy laboratory' (Bevan & Wilson, 2013; Paun et al., 2016; Wilson, 2011). From a policy learning perspective, there is now the opportunity to use the experiences across the UK nations to address the common policy problems faced by the respective administrations. Reducing the barriers that currently inhibit such learning is therefore a necessary, but not sufficient, first step.

Legislative Competencies, Institutional Capacities and the Size of the State

The ability of the new devolved institutions to deliver effective governance over significant education reform has been dependent on broader competencies and capacities. We highlight two points here. First, there is inevitably a period of policy learning following transfer of responsibility over a specific policy area to a devolved administration, which in turn suggests the need for mechanisms by which best practice and policy intelligence may be shared. There is a recognized need for a continued emphasis on raising skills in the civil service across the UK around the use of different kinds of evidence, for example (Paun et al., 2016). Second, the size of the state may have consequences regarding the type of policies that are implementable from a political perspective, given the increased potential for producer capture arising in smaller states (Bevan & Wilson, 2013). Both may have an impact on the extent to which the devolved administrations are able to deliver effective policy solutions.

Finally, devolution in the UK has largely been a politically driven project. The role of subsidiarity in improving educational quality and progress was not a central concern within arguments surrounding devolution. As such, the experiences of individual nations have been very different and have resulted in different outcomes, the roots of which pre-date the 1999 devolution agreements. It is still too early to predict how either these experiences or outcomes will be affected as the UK—and its constituent administrations—embark on a future outside the European Union.

REFERENCES

Bennett, M., Fairley, J., & McAteer, M. (2002). *Devolution in Scotland: The impact on local government.* York: Joseph Rowntree Foundation.

Bevan G., & Wilson, D. (2013). Does "naming and shaming" work for schools and hospitals? Lessons from natural experiments following devolution in England and Wales. *Public Money & Management, 33*(4), 245–52.

Bogdanor, V. (1979). *Devolution.* Oxford, UK: Oxford University Press.

Bogdanor, V. (1999). *Devolution in the United Kingdom*, Oxford, UK: Oxford University Press.

Bogdanor, V. (2009). *The New British Constitution.* Oxford, UK: Hart.

Bradbury, J. (1997). Introduction. In J. Bradbury & J. Mawson (Eds.), *British regionalism and devolution: The challenges of state reform and European intergration* (pp. 1–33). London, PA: Jessica Kingsley.

Bradbury, J. (2006). Territory and power revisited: Theorising territorial politics in the United Kingdom after devolution. *Political Studies, 54*(3), 559–582.

Breakspear, S. (2012). *The policy impact of PISA: An exploration of the normative effects of international benchmarking in school system performance.* OECD Education Working Papers No. 71. OECD Publishing. Retrieved on March 9, 2016 from http://www.oecd-ilibrary.org/education/the-policy-impact-of-pisa_5k9fdfqffr28-en

Burgess, S, Wilson, D., & Lupton, R. (2005). Parallel lives? Ethnic segregation in schools and neighbourhoods, *Urban Studies, 42*(7), 1027–1056.

Burgess, S., Wilson, D., & Worth, J. (2013). A natural experiment in school accountability: The impact of school performance information on pupil progress. *Journal of Public Economics, 106*, 57–67.

Burrows B., & Denton G. (1980). *Devolution or federalism? Options for the United Kingdom.* London: MacMillan.

Cairney, P,, Russell, S., & St Denny, E. (2016). The 'Scottish approach' to policy and policymaking: what issues are territorial and what are universal? *Policy and Politics, 44*(3), 333–350.

Chitty, C. (2009). *Education policy in Britain* (2nd ed.), London: Palgrave Macmillan.

Colley, L. (2014). *Acts of union and disunion.* Prole Books.

Deacon R. (2006). *Devolution in Britain today.* Manchester: Manchester University Press.

Donaldson, A. (2006). Performing regions: Territorial development and cultural politics in a Europe of the Regions. *Environment and Planning A, 38,* 2075–2092.

Fairclough, P. (2009). *Multi-level governance in the UK: A road to nowhere?* In P. Fairclough & E. Magee (Eds.), *UK government & politics annual survey 2009.* London, UK: Philip Allan Updates.

Flinders, M. (2008). *Delegated governance and the British state: Walking without order.* Oxford: Oxford University Press.

Garside, P., & Hebbert, M. (1989). Introduction. In Garside, P. & Hebbert, M. (Eds.), *Bristish Regionalism 1900–2000.* London: Cassell.

Greer, S. L. (2009). *Territorial politics and health policy: UK health policy in comparative perspective.* Manchester, UK: Manchester University Press.

Hibbard, J. H., Stockard, J. & Tusler, M. (2003). Does publicising hospital performance stimulate quality improvement efforts? *Health Affairs, 22*(2), 84–94.

HM Treasury. (2015). *Country and regional analysis: November 2015.* London: HM Treasury.

Hobbs, G. & Vignoles, A. (2010). Is children's free school meal 'eligibility' a good proxy for family income? *British Educational Research Journal, 36*(4), 673–690.

Holtham, G. (2009). *Funding. Devolved government in Wales: Barnett & beyond.* Independent Commission on Funding and Finance for Wales. http://gov.wales/docs/icffw/report/090708barnettfullen.pdf accessed 9 March 2016

Hood, C., Oliver, J., Jones, G., Scott, C., & Travers, T. (1999). *Regulation inside government.* Oxford: Oxford University Press.

House of Lords Select Committee on the Barnett Formula. (2009). *The Barnett formula HL Paper 139.* London: The Stationery Office.

Institute for Fiscal Studies. (2014). *Business as usual? The Barnett Formula, business rates and further tax devolution, IFS Briefing Note BN155.* London: Institute for Fiscal Studies.

Machin, S., McNally, S. & Wyness, G. (2013). Education attainment across the UK nations: Performance, inequality and evidence. *Educational Research, 55*(2),. 139–164.

Mackintosh, J. (1968). *The devolution of Power.* Middlesex: Penguin.

Martens, K., & Niemann, D. (2013). When do numbers count? The differential impact of the PISA rating and ranking on education policy in Germany and the US. *German Politics, 22*(3), 314–322.

McAteer, M., & Bennett, M. (2005). Devolution and local government: Evidence from Scotland. *Local Government Studies, 31*(3), 285–306.

McConnell, A. (2004). *Has devolution transformed Scottish local government?* Refereed paper presented to the Australasian Political Studies Association Conference, University of Adelaide. Retrieved on 9 March 2016 from https://www.adelaide.edu.au/apsa/docs_papers/Others/McConnell_final.pdf

McEwan, N., & Parry, R. (2005). Devolution and the preservation of the UK welfare state. In N. McEwan & L. Moreno (Eds.), *The territorial politics of welfare.* London, UK: Routledge.

McIntyre, M. (2009). *The revival of Scottish Gaelic through education*: New York, NY: Cambria Press.

Midwinter, A. (2006). The Barnett Formula and its critics revisited: Evidence from the post-devolution period. *Scottish Affairs*, 55(First Series, 1), 64–86. Available Online May/Spring doi: http://dx.doi.org/10.3366/scot.2006.0021

Moran, M. (2015). *Politics and governance in the UK* (3rd ed.). London: Palgrave MacMillan.

Morris, P. (2015). Comparative education, PISA, politics and educational reform: A cautionary note. *Compare: A Journal of Comparative and International Education, 45*(3), 470–474.

Paun, A., Rutter, J., & Nicholl, A. (2016). *Devolution as a policy laboratory: Evidence sharing and learning between the UK's four governments*, Alliance for Useful Evidence. Retrieved on 26 February 2016 from http://www.nesta.org.uk/publications/devolution-policy-laboratory-how-uks-four-governments-share-evidence-and-learn-each-other

Pittock, G. (1999). *Celtic identity and the British Image*. Manchester: Manchester University Press.

Pollitt, C., Harrison, S., Dowsell, G., Jerak-Zuiderent, S., & Bal, R. (2010). Performance regimes in health care: Institutions, critical junctures and the logic of escalation in England and the Netherlands. *Evaluation, 16*(1), 13–29.

Raffe, D. (2006). *Devolution and divergence in education policy.* In J. Adams & K. Schmueker (Eds.), *Devolution in practice 2006: Public policy differences within the UK.* Newcastle: IPPR.

Reynolds, D. (2008). New Labour, education and Wales: The devolution decade. *Oxford Review of Education, 34*(6), 753–765.

Robbins, K. (2001). 'More than a footnote? Wales in British history,' *North American Journal of Welsh Studies, 1*(1), 20–24.

Schmuecker, K., & Adams, J. (2005). Divergence in priorities, perceived policy failure and pressure for convergence. In J. Adams & K. Schmueker (Eds.), *Devolution in practice 2006: Public policy differences within the UK.* Newcastle: IPPR.

Scully, R., & Wyn Jones, R. (2011). Territorial politics in post-devolution Britain. In R. Heffernan, P. Cowley, & C. Hay (Eds.), *Developments in British politics* (9th ed.), Palgrave: London.

Shain, F. (2016). Succeeding against the odds: Can schools 'compensate for society'? *Education, 44*(1), 8–18. DOI: 10.1080/03004279.2015.1122318

Social Mobility and Child Poverty Commission. (2015). *State of the nation 2015: Social mobility and poverty in Great Britain.* Retrieved from https://www.gov.uk/government/uploads/system/uploads/attachment_data/file/485928/State_of_the_nation_2015__foreword_and_summary.pdf

Tuohy, C. (1999). *Accidental logics: The dynamics of change in the health care arena in the United States, Britain and Canada.* New York, NY: Oxford University Press.

Wilson, D. (2011). Comparative analysis in public management: Reflections on the experience of a major research programme, *Public Management Review, 13*(2), 293–308.

CHAPTER 11

PUBLIC EDUCATION AS A SHARED STATE-FEDERAL FUNCTION IN THE UNITED STATES

Institutional Changes and Policy Challenges

Kenneth K. Wong

INTRODUCTION: PHASES OF STATE-FEDERAL RELATIONS IN PUBLIC EDUCATION

States assume a leading role in primary and secondary education in the United States. Article I, Section 8 of the U.S. Constitution specifies the "enumerated powers" that the U.S. Congress enjoys, but does not include public education within their realm of authority, thus delegating the matter to the states. The Tenth Amendment to the Constitution further reinforces this setup, granting states autonomy in all domestic affairs not explicitly delegated to the federal government, including education. State sovereignty is not dependent on the federal government but instead comes from the state's citizenry. Indeed, the constitution in each of the

Federalism and Education: Ongoing Challenges and Policy Strategies in Ten Countries, pages 231–255.

50 states affirms state responsibility in this policy domain. Thus, states and their localities have continued to provide about 90% of the funding in public education.

State dominance notwithstanding, public education has become a shared state-federal function in the United States. This paper examines the evolving state-federal arrangement in meeting key policy challenges. As suggested in Table 11.1, since the 1960s, the state-federal relationship has gone through several phases of institutional changes. First, in response to socio-economic challenges, the federal government has become a junior, but active, partner in public education. The U.S. Congress has established a grants-in-aid system to target federal support for students with particular needs, such as low-income students, English Language Learners, Native Americans, and students with learning disabilities. Currently, grants from the federal government account for about 10% of total public school spending.

With growing public concern over school performance since the 1980s and 1990s, the federal government has expanded its attention to student outcomes, a key feature of the second institutional phase. Since the Congressional enactment of the No Child Left Behind Act of 2001 (NCLB), federal involvement has significantly expanded on outcome-based accountability for all children. NCLB

TABLE 11.1 Three Phases of State-Federal Relations in Public Education

	Phase 1: Equity as a National Focus (1960s-)	**Phase 2: Performance-Based Accountability (1990s-)**	**Phase 3: Competing Approaches: Federal Disruption and State Control (2015-)**
Constitutional responsibility of public education	States	States	*States*
Primary funding sources for public schools	States and localities	States and localities	States and localities
Key federal action and legislation	*Elementary and Secondary Education Act of 1965* and related social programs	*No Child Left Behind of 2001*, including annual testing and reports on subgroups; *Race to the Top* and other competitive grants;	*Every Student Succeeds Act of 2015*, including annual testing and reports on subgroups; Trump administration to promote school choice
Federal fiscal and regulatory strategies	Federal Categorical Grants that target on eligible students with specific needs	Federally-defined Corrective Action and Intervention based on Adequate Yearly Progress of schools (standardized tests on school status); Federal promotion of Common Core of Standards	States determine rigorous academic standards, multiple measures on performance (such as growth), identify low performing schools, and decide on intervention; Trump administration to reduce regulation

required annual testing of students at the elementary grades in core subject areas, mandated the hiring of "highly qualified teachers," allowed parents to move their children from failing schools, and granted states and localities authority to take "corrective actions" to turn around low performing schools.

After the U.S. Congress's 2007 failure in reauthorizing NCLB, the federal government began granting waiver approval to over 40 states, signaling the beginning of a more active state role in the third phase of institutional development. Waivers exempted states from meeting the original NCLB target of academic proficiency for 100% of their students and encouraged them to set their own education policy priorities. However, in exchange for these exemptions, the federal government was able to yield significant control over other realms of education policy. States had to demonstrate their efforts toward several federal requirements, including voluntary adoption of the common core state standards, annual testing of students in grades 3 to 8 and one high school grade in core subjects, and holding schools accountable for performance standards.

In late 2015, the U.S. Congress replaced NCLB with the Every Student Succeeds Act (ESSA). ESSA has signaled a return of state dominance in education policy, as suggested in Table 1 on the third institutional phase. ESSA restricts federal prescriptions on intervening in low performing schools. The law no longer requires state adoption of common core standards in exchange for federal funds. Further, it specifies that the federal government cannot use fiscal and regulatory incentives to encourage certain accountability practices, such as test-based teacher evaluation system. Following the 2016 presidential election, the Donald Trump administration has used executive actions to reduce federal regulations and has proposed federal support for school choice programs. These latest presidential initiatives aim at disrupting the long-established federal role by rebalancing not only state-federal relations but also enhancing school choice as a key priority.

In the following sections, we will discuss the institutional design and the implementation lessons in each of the three phases of the state-federal relationship. To be sure, the three phases are not mutually exclusive. The focus on equal educational opportunity during the first phase does not fade away as the second and the third phases arrive. Instead, schooling opportunities continue to be a joint federal-state responsibility up to the present. Similarly, the focus on outcome-based performance that started in the second phase has continued to shape education policy, even when the third phase rebalances federal-state power relationship. The 2015 ESSA also allows states to use multiple measures to assess student performance. Consequently, U.S. federalism accommodates an expanding education agenda that simultaneously addresses equity, accountability, standards, and choice.

PHASE ONE: EDUCATION EQUITY AS A NATIONAL FOCUS SINCE THE 1960S

The 1965 passage of the federal Elementary and Secondary Education Act and other social programs marked the creation of a complex intergovernmental policy system that stands unique in American history. The legislation established a federal role in the American system of education. To avoid centralization of administrative power at the national level, Congress increased its intergovernmental transfers to finance state and local activities. During the Presidency of Lyndon Johnson, the number of categorical (or single purpose) programs, including Title I, increased from 160 to 380. By the end of the Jimmy Carter administration, there were approximately 500 federally funded categorical programs. Particularly important was the redistributive focus of many of these categorical programs that were designed to promote racial desegregation, protect the educational rights of the handicapped, assist English language learners, and provide supplemental resources to children from at-risk backgrounds. Despite several revisions and extensions, ESEA Title I, for example, continues to adhere to its original intent "to provide financial assistance . . . to local educational agencies serving areas with concentrations of children from low-income families to expand and improve their educational programs . . . which contribute particularly to meeting the special educational needs of educationally deprived children."

Federal engagement in redistributive policy has contributed to persistent growth in real-dollar federal spending on programs for special-needs students. Between 1996 and 2005, these programs amounted to over 60 percent of the total federal spending in elementary and secondary schools (Wong, 1999; Wong & Sunderman, 2007). Spending on the Title I program for the education of disadvantaged students increased from $8.9 billion to $14.6 billion in 2005 constant dollars. Federal aid in special education grew by over two times, while the school lunch program increased its funding from $9.8 billion in 1996 to $12.2 billion in 2005. Additionally, funding for Head Start early childhood programs jumped by 50 percent in real dollar terms during this period.

This trend of growing federal involvement in programs for the disadvantaged continued under the Obama Administration. Congress appropriated $98.2 billion dollars to support education in the American Recovery and Reinvestment Act in 2009. ARRA provided additional funds to several major categorical programs for a 2-year period, including $10 billion for Title I, $12.2 billion for IDEA, $650 million for technology, and $100 million for impact aid construction.

Further, federal redistributive grants have taken on several institutional characteristics that resemble a policy framework:

- Grants-in-aid arrangements: the federal government provides funding and sets the programmatic framework, but delivery of services is up to state and local agencies.
- Categorical or single purpose grants: grants of which well-defined eligible students are the sole intended beneficiaries.
- Supplementary and non-supplanting guidelines: designed to guard against any local tendency to shift federal resources away from the disadvantaged.

- Bipartisan support: Special needs programs are often connected to well-entrenched political interests. For example, the free and reduced price lunch program has received political support from the agricultural business.
- Incentives for local government to meet anti-poverty objectives: Federal funds tend to be widely distributed to ensure broad political support. The territorial impact of federal grants has contributed partly to the popularity of Title I in Congress over time. For example, in the 1990s, the federal grant provided supplemental resources to 64 percent of all the schools in the nation, covering virtually every congressional district. Clearly, big city districts were not the only beneficiaries of compensatory education funds. Indeed, over 20 percent of federal aid went to districts with fewer than 2,500 students. Districts with enrollments between 2,500 and 25,000 received almost 45 percent of the funds. Because there are Title I programs in almost every congressional district, partisan conflict has generally been limited during the appropriations process.

PHASE TWO: PERFORMANCE-BASED FEDERALISM GAINS PROMINENCE SINCE 1990S

While redistributive grants-in-aid strategies have gained bi-partisan support overtime, their effectiveness has been increasingly called into question in a broadened climate of outcome-based accountability. The passage of Improving America's Schools Act in 1994 signaled the beginning of federal efforts to address accountability in its anti-poverty programs. This legislation aimed to reduce program isolation of at-risk students from their peers through creating incentives for whole school reform and requiring districts and states to use their system-wide standards to assess the performance of at-risk students.

As the U.S. Congress enacted the No Child Left Behind Act of 2001, federal involvement expanded on educational accountability for all children. The federal law required annual testing of students at the elementary grades in core subject areas, mandated the hiring of "highly qualified teachers" in classrooms, and granted state and local agencies substantial authority in taking "corrective actions" to turn around failing schools. Further, the law provided school choice to parents to take their children out of failing schools. Equally significant in terms of federal intervention was the legislative intent of closing the achievement gaps among racial/ethnic subgroups as well as income, English Language Learners (ELL), and special education subgroups. During the initial phase of NCLB, the federal government increased its Title I allocation by $1.7 billion, reaching a total of almost $11 billion, as well as distributing over $900 million for early childhood reading initiatives.

This expansion of the federal role occurred largely during the post-September 11th climate, an unusual set of political conditions in which the presidency gained broad public support. From a governing perspective, the passage of the 2001 NCLB may be characterized as a "regime change" in which well-entrenched political interests set aside their traditional policy positions to support the new policy (McGuinn, 2006). Proponents of state power were ready to set aside their beliefs in state and local control and to endorse a visibly stronger federal presence in education. Advocates of accountability pushed for a fairly comprehensive set of accountability measures, including annual testing of students in core subject areas with consequences. Political interests across the board were supportive of disaggregated reporting on achievement. As a result, federal expectations on academic proficiency have come to apply to all students, schools, and districts, regardless of whether they receive federal Title I funds. The federal government has elevated education performance to the top of the nation's policy agenda.

The unusual convergence of political interests in 2001 allowed NCLB to craft a new framework for the federal role in education: to promote proficiency across all student groups, including those who come from disadvantaged backgrounds. In terms of academic performance, these changes allowed the federal government to hold states, districts, and schools accountable for a comprehensive set of standards, including annual academic progress, teacher quality, and achievement gaps. To determine whether a school had met Adequate Yearly Progress (AYP) annually in NCLB, student achievement was aggregated by grade and by subject area for each school. All students in grades three through eight and one additional grade in high school were tested annually in mathematics, reading/English language arts, and, in selected grades, science. The school-level report would include the percent of students proficient in each of the core-content areas, student participation in standardized testing, attendance rates, and graduation rates. Many of these accountability measures are included in NCLB's successor, ESSA.

An equally prominent aspect of NCLB was its focus on equity. Depending on community socioeconomic characteristics, NCLB required schools to report the academic proficiency of students in the following subgroups: economically disadvantaged students, students from major racial and ethnic groups, students with disabilities, and Limited English Proficiency (LEP) students. In this regard, NCLB made the achievement gaps within schools more transparent for accountability purposes. Schools that were persistently failing to meet AYP would be subject to various forms of intervention, including school closure and conversion to charter school.

The federal accountability agenda, as articulated in NCLB, has created tension in the intergovernmental policy system. As Manna (2010) puts it, there is a significant gap between the theory of accountability based on the federal intent and the practice of accountability at the state and local level. The literature on the implementation of NCLB has suggested several key challenges in aligning the federal reform agenda with our current intergovernmental system of education governance (see, for example, Cohen & Moffitt, 2009; Hess & Finn, 2007; Hess & Petrilli, 2006).

First, federalism allows for varying degrees of policy specification in meeting the federal expectations. Federalism is not designed to support a uniform set of accountability measures across the 50 states and the District of Columbia. Under NCLB, states defined their own set of proficiency standards and measures in meeting the federal Adequate Yearly Progress (AYP) (Wong & Nicotera, 2007). Broadly speaking, states chose several different methods to ensure that students reach proficiency by the 2014 deadline: equal yearly goals, steady stair-step, and accelerating curve (Wong & Nicotera, 2007). Within each state, the decision-making process allowed for multiple stakeholders to weigh in on the rigor, scope, timing, and cost of student academic assessment. Consequently, state assessments varied (and continue to vary) widely in terms of the level of rigor, as indicated by the substantial gaps between student proficiencies on state tests and differentials in performances on NAEP in many states.

Second, political negotiations among key stakeholders within states tended to slow the pace of initial implementation of NCLB, which came as no surprise to observers of education reform. Four out of five states were not ready to meet the federal requirement on placing highly qualified teachers in the classroom during the initial implementation period. The annual testing requirement, a core concept in the new accountability system, faced major resistance. Virginia, Connecticut, Utah, Michigan, and several other states registered their opposition with legislative and legal actions. In a 2011 study conducted by the Center for American Progress, state education commissioners pointed out that strong accountability and innovative practices were the exceptions in state education agencies (Brown et al., 2011).

Third, the federal agenda encountered significant social constraints. The extent to which districts or a schools met AYP was affected by the number of students in the various subgroups, including low-income students, English Language Learners, students with disabilities, and racial and ethnic minorities. In their analysis of this issue in California, Kim and Sunderman (2005) found that the percentage of schools meeting AYP tended to decline as the number of subgroups in those schools rose. While 78 percent of the schools with only 1 subgroup met the reading AYP in 2003, only 25 percent of the schools with six subgroups were able to do so. When the authors considered the AYP data in Virginia, they found that 85 percent of the schools that met both the state and federal proficiency standards had two or fewer subgroups. Only 15 percent of the schools that met the AYP had three of more subgroups.

Faced with state power and differences in the socioeconomic characteristics of student enrollment across states, the federal government loosened up the standards in meeting the AYP by allowing for a "safe harbor" provision. Under this guideline, a subgroup would be deemed as "meeting" AYP if the percentage of students in the "below basic proficiency" level was reduced by 10 percent from the previous year. In Philadelphia, a large urban school district with 266 schools, for example, 37 percent of the 158 schools that made AYP in 2010 met the proficiency standards by achieving the safe harbor target.

The "safe harbor" flexibility, however, may not have provided sufficient incentives to avert irregularities in student assessment practices at the local level. Reports on test cheating in Atlanta, Philadelphia, and other urban districts called for a stronger state role in monitoring student testing. In Philadelphia, data on 2009 test results were shelved by the state education agency for two years. Until a local news article exposed the problems in about 30 schools, the district was not formally notified by the state of any testing problems. These findings of cheating led to a closer working relationship between the state and the district on test administration and monitoring.

Fourth, the federal agenda on accountability may not have aligned effectively with the federal system of formula-based grant allocation. NCLB did not fundamentally alter the categorical grants-in-aid system, a structure in which federal grants are largely allocated by formula, based on a well-defined group of eligible students (Peterson, Rabe, & Wong, 1986). In NCLB, the federal government was able to take only incremental steps in aligning its formula-based allocation to support its ambitious goal of improving persistently low achieving schools. A key federal strategy became reallocating existing Title I funds such that they were roughly proportional to the problems of student achievement. More specifically, NCLB called for a set of progressively intensive "corrective actions" when districts and schools fail to make AYP for consecutive years. These sanctions required low-performing districts and schools to use their Title I funds differently. The sanctions began with the relatively modest requirement for a school-improvement plan, including options for families in schools not making adequate yearly progress to transfer to another public or charter school, and the implementation of Title I-funded supplemental educational or tutorial services after-school. In other words, sanctions in the first years of academic failure were not designed to change the structure or governance of the low-performing school, but instead to tweak around the edges. Following four consecutive years of failure, however, NCLB allowed for more intensive sanctions. These included state-driven interventions that altered school governance and hiring decisions, such as school or district takeovers and replacement of personnel in poorly performing schools. Only in the most drastic restructurings were federal resources integrated with local and state funding to support the federal objectives.

Finally, as can often happen, federal reform generated new conflicts in terms of management and delivery of educational services. NCLB encouraged a broader set of providers, including for-profit organizations and charter management organizations, to manage low-performing schools. Not surprisingly, local districts were generally protective of their control over Supplemental Education Services (SES) and were slow in supporting parents to transfer their children from low performing schools. In his study of California, for example, Betts (2007) observed that school choice, as stipulated by NCLB, was largely underutilized throughout the state. Reasons for limited local implementation included the delay in making data available to parents, failure of districts to communicate clearly to parents the choice program, an inadequate number of seats in better performing schools, and lack of parental interest in moving their children outside of the neighborhood schools.

As performance-based federalism gained prominence, the federal role began to shift the policy focus from inputs to outcomes, open service delivery to a diverse array of providers, and require local and state agencies to publicly report on student performance. There were, to be sure, intergovernmental conflicts over hot button issues such as annual testing, federal intervention in persistently low performing schools, and the cost of meeting the new federal mandates. However, efforts to manage the federal goals in both accountability and equity continued during the Obama Administration, though their status under the Trump Administration may fall into question.

STATE REFORM WITHIN THE FEDERAL FRAMEWORK: FISCAL INCENTIVES AND NCLB WAIVERS

Fiscal Incentives for State Reform

The Obama Administration broadened NCLB accountability by creating new competitive funding streams to promote institutional innovation at the state and local level. Under federal direction, states and districts competed in the Race to the Top, i3 grants, and other federal funding sources to "transform" their current policy and practices in educator accountability, charter schools, and turning around low-performing schools. These innovative initiatives, defined and promoted by the U.S. Department of Education, sought the support from key state and local actors—including governors, state commissioners, mayors, unions, and networks of diverse providers, among others.

Building on the NCLB framework for "corrective actions," the Obama Administration continued the push for more direct district intervention in persistently low-performing schools. Education Secretary Duncan argued for four strategies to "turnaround" the nation's lowest performing 5 percent of schools (or approximately 5,000 schools) (Wong, 2013, p. 169). The federal government committed $5 billion during 2010–2012 to support these efforts. The four strategies tightened the approaches that were established under NCLB, allowing for fewer district options. More specifically, the Duncan strategies included:

- *Turnaround school* under a new principal who can recruit at least half of the new teachers from the outside, (p. 169);
- *Transformation school* that strengthens professional support, teacher evaluation, and capacity building, (p. 169);
- *Restart school* will reopen as either a charter school or under management by organizations outside of the district, (p. 169); and
- *School closure* that results in moving all the students to other higher-performing schools, (p. 169).

In making its first School Improvement Grants (SIG) to support school turnarounds, the Obama Administration allocated $3 billion in federal fund to over 730 schools in forty-four states in December 2010. Of these schools, an overwhelming number of them (71 percent) had chosen the "transformation" option while very few decided to use either "restart" (5 percent) or "school closure" (3 percent). The remaining 21 percent opted for the "turnaround" option where the principal and a majority of the teaching staff were replaced (Klein, 2011). Equally important, only 16.5 percent of the students in all the SIG schools were white, as compared to 44 percent African American and 34 percent Hispanic. The choices made by the SIG awardees seem to suggest a leaning toward a more incremental approach to school improvement. This tension between the federal push for innovation and consideration of constraints at the local level seems likely to persist. In anticipation of the local inertia toward incremental organizational changes, the Obama Administration created the Office of School Turnaround in late 2011 to monitor and support local efforts to raise school performance.

Equally important was Obama's strong guidance on local and state institutional reform through competitive grants such as the Race to the Top. Departing from formula-based categorical allocations, the Obama Administration invited states to submit their best ideas on system transformation and school innovation to the national competition for the Race to the Top program. Delaware and Tennessee were selected as the first two awardees in the first round of Race to the Top competition in April 2010. The competition resulted in awarding grants to a total of 19 states and Washington D.C.

With financial support from the federal government and grants from several non-profit foundations (such as Gates Foundation), 80% of states voluntarily adopted the common core standards and assessment by early 2010s. These common core standards were not federal mandates, although the federal government used financial and deregulatory incentives to encourage state adoption. These standards and assessments were organized by two independent professional organizations (PARCC and SBAC), similar to the Australian Curriculum, Assessment and Reporting Authority (ACARA). With the common core, states are able to compare themselves to their peers in terms of academic progress, create economies of scale for technical assistance, streamline teacher recruitment and support, and, most importantly, raise academic rigor to meet 21st century expectations. At the same time, as discussed below, the early implementation of the common core was contentious in some states, specifically on topics such as teacher readiness, web-based assessment capability, and perceived "federal" intrusion in state and local academic affairs.

State Differences in Waiver Implementation

In the absence of Congressional action on ESEA reauthorization, the U.S. Secretary of Education began to use waivers granted under Section 9401 in the NCLB Act to engage states in education reform initiatives. Section 9401 gives the

Secretary of Education the authority to "issue waivers of any statutory or regulatory requirement of the ESEA for a state educational agency (SEA), LEA [local educational agency], Indian tribe, or school (through an LEA) that receives funds under an ESEA program and requests a waiver" (U.S. Department of Education, 2009). From the states' perspective, waivers tended to create new opportunities to regain programmatic control, but they also generated a certain sense of uncertainty, as many of the proposed ideas were untested (Bowling & Pickerill, 2013). From the Obama administration's perspective, waivers promised to address some of the key reform concerns at the state and local level (Gamkhar & Pickerill, 2012). In liberating states from the need to demonstrate improved proficiency for all students (as previously stipulated in NCLB's target of 100 percent proficiency by 2014), the federal government solicited political support from states toward adopting more rigorous and uniform standards for college and career readiness, a requirement most easily satisfied by adopting the common core standards and assessment. Waivers also created an incentive for states to implement teacher evaluation systems that used measureable student outcome data. Seeing the need to balance sanctions and support for low performing schools, the Obama administration leveraged waivers to incentivize states to implement a comprehensive system of recognition, accountability, and support for all schools. In other words, the Obama administration saw a policy window in the absence of ESEA reauthorization to advance some of its reform priorities. Indeed, a survey of thirty-eight states conducted in the fall of 2012 suggested a generally favorable view. State respondents believed that the waivers were designed to address problems associated with NCLB accountability; they were also positive about college- and career-ready standards for student learning and recognized the importance of moving toward new teacher evaluation systems (Center on Education Policy, 2013).

ESEA waivers had been issued on a regular basis for several years prior to 2011. The Bush administration, particularly from 2005 to 2008 during Margaret Spellings's tenure as Secretary of Education, issued various waivers from particular aspects of the NCLB Act. During the Obama administration, Secretary Arne Duncan in 2009 granted waivers allowing four states to use "growth models" for measuring annual academic progress, signaling a federal response to state complaints about the inflexibility of using NCLB's Adequate Yearly Progress to report on student proficiency (Congressional Research Service, 2011). The Secretary also granted waivers to three states to implement a more differentiated designation of low-performing schools for accountability purpose. The bulk of the waivers, 196 out of 351 in 2009, were related to local alternative use of federal Title I funds on public school choice and supplemental education services in schools and districts.

The broadening of waiver approval started in 2011 when the Obama administration invited state applications for waivers from meeting the original NCLB goals of attaining 100 percent student proficiency in core subjects by 2014. In the first cycle of applications in November 2011, eleven states formally sought alternative ways to implement their accountability systems in exchange for fulfilling a new set of federal assurances. By early August 2012, thirty-three states and the District of Columbia received federal approval on their NCLB waivers. By the summer of 2014, almost 90 percent of the states received ESEA waiver approval.

Waiver applications were generally in alignment with the priorities of the Obama administration (Riddle, 2011). For example, the post-NCLB Nevada system of accountability, which received federal approval in August 2012, planned to use student achievement growth and other measures to differentiate schools that were in need of particular support and intervention. Nevada's state superintendent of public instruction touted the significance of the waiver approval: "This next generation accountability system is a central lever in statewide efforts to substantially elevate student performance. This system was built through robust collaboration with key partners, together with whom we will re-engineer Nevada's educational system to realize true college and career readiness for all students" (Whaley, 2012). In other words, waiver states expressed their intent to implement the Obama administration's reform agenda, such as adopting the common core standards. However, the extent to which states have actually carried out their proposed reform initiatives remains a key issue.

Given its focus on institutional reform at the state and local levels, the Obama administration used NCLB flexibility waivers as incentive for reform actions. At issue with this tactic was the question of whether waiver states were actually meeting the new federal expectations. We have examined the extent to which waiver states met the key waiver requirements, drawing in part on the state-by-state monitoring reports issued by the U.S. Department of Education. In its report, *ESEA Flexibility Part B Monitoring Plan Summer and Fall 2013*, the U.S. Department of Education provides an assessment of a State Education Agency's (SEA's) implementation of ESEA flexibility in eighteen sets of requirements across four reform areas. First, *SEA Systems and Processes* focuses on SEA's role in supporting monitoring, technical assistance, data collection and use, and family and community engagement. Second, *College- and Career-ready Expectations* aims to ensure that SEAs are adopting standards and assessments that allow all students (including English Language Learners) to be prepared for college and careers. Third, *Differentiated Intervention* enables SEAs to implement their own system of differentiated recognition, accountability, and support for all schools, especially low performing "focus" and "priority" schools. Fourth, *Effective Instruction and Leadership* requires SEAs to develop and implement fair and thorough evaluations and support systems that provide meaningful feedback regarding teacher and principal effectiveness, including a new teacher and principal evaluation system that draws on student achievement.

To understand state variation on waiver implementation, our study focuses on a sample of sixteen waiver states that represent different levels of student performance and varying degrees of political control by the two major parties (Wong & Reilly, 2014). These states are Connecticut, Idaho, Indiana, Kentucky, Louisiana,

Maryland, Massachusetts, Michigan, Minnesota, Missouri, Nevada, New Jersey, New York, Ohio, Oregon, and Utah. Based on our study, we found that these states made greater progress in meeting some of the federal expectations than others. In our sample of sixteen states, every state met the following four requirements: Develop and Administer Alternate Assessments, Develop and Administer English Language Proficiency Assessments, Adopt English Language Proficiency Standards, and Data Collection & Use. The first three requirements pertain to the reform area of implementing college-and-career-ready standards and assessments for all students. The other expectation met by all sixteen states was Data Collection & Use, which falls under the reform area of SEA Systems and Process. This high level of state implementation suggests that the federal requirement is consistent with many states' current practices in compiling and reporting data for accountability purposes. For example, under NCLB, districts and schools were required to report academic proficiency for several subpopulations (Wong, 2013). SEAs and LEAs seemed to have developed the capacity to meet this federal requirement on data reporting.

In contrast, fewer of the sixteen states in the sample met several of the other federal expectations. These included: Principal Evaluations and Student Support Systems (with only eight of the sixteen states meeting the expectation), Monitoring (eight states), Teacher Evaluations and Student Support Systems (seven states), and Priority Schools (seven states). Not surprisingly, these expectations often required legislative and gubernatorial involvement in enacting more fundamental changes in current policies and practices. Teachers' union opposition to some of these reform issues also contributed to the lack of progress in half of the sample states. Further, only eight states in our sample were implementing the monitoring requirement. Under this requirement, states had to provide evidence that a state's monitoring process was on track and was resulting in continuous improvement. SEAs had to proceed incrementally with the monitoring function in order to avoid local perceptions of excessive policy intrusion.

Finally, federal requirements on personnel (teacher and principal evaluations and support systems) were amongst the areas that were met by no more than half of the states in the sample. Personnel decisions are typically controversial and require legislative action. Interestingly, these challenges seemed to affect states with various different characteristics, including Indiana (a Republican-controlled state), Kentucky (a state with divided governance), and Michigan (a state with unified governance). For example, Indiana, a state with strong Republican control, received pushback from its Superintendent of Public Instruction, Glenda Ritz. In Indiana, the Superintendent is an elected office, and Ritz, who is a Democrat, engaged in continued conflicts on education reform and teacher evaluation with then governor Mike Pence, a Republican. In short, our analysis of waiver implementation finds federal success in certain reform areas but political resistance in other areas depending on the context of state politics.

PHASE THREE: COMPETING APPROACHES ON STATE CONTROL IN THE CONTEXT OF FEDERAL DISRUPTION SINCE 2015S

Beginning with the second term of the Obama Administration, the federal government has tried to encourage state-driven education reform. With the Race to the Top competitive grants and the granting of state waivers from major provisions of the NCLB, states were able to implement their own approaches to school improvement. However, these state practices had to align with federal requirements on reform. In contrast, the Every Student Succeeds Act of 2015 dismantled many of these federally directed reform requirements. Under ESSA, states are given the primary responsibility in defining academic standards, adopting multiple measures of academic performance, identifying schools that are the target for intervention, and deciding on the scope and nature of intervention. In other words, the third phase of the institutional change involves a shift from a federally-defined framework of state reform to a state-defined agenda of education reform.

State Control Restored: Every Student Success Act of 2015

In contrast to federally driven competitive grants and NCLB waivers, the 2015 ESSA restores substantial state control over education reform. The legislative battle took several years and involved compromises between the executive and the legislative branches. The No Child Left Behind Act was enacted into law in January 2002 and was scheduled to go through the reauthorization process in 2007. Over the last seven years, several failed attempts were made by the Obama administration as well as both parties in Congress to pass a new federal law in elementary and secondary education. There was bi-partisan agreement that NCLB's original goal of reaching 100 percent proficiency was unrealistic and unattainable. During its fourteen years of legal force, NCLB created tension in the intergovernmental policy system, including unevenness in state content standards and assessment, an absence of student growth measures in the accountability framework, cost concerns regarding the mandate of annual testing, lack of reliable data to track teacher performance, and local resistance to diverse service providers in turning around low performing schools (see for example Cohen & Moffitt, 2009; Hess & Finn, 2007; Manna & McGuinn, 2013). The Obama administration attempted to address these implementation problems on a limited scale through various pilot initiatives in specific states and districts, such as the competitive Race to the Top grants, i3 grants, and other federal funding sources to "transform" policy and practices in educator accountability, charter schools, and turning around low-performing schools. Many of these pilots have produced promising results.

Recognizing the limited scale of its pilot initiatives, the Obama administration launched a comprehensive effort on ESEA reauthorization that coincided with the president's 2012 re-election campaign. The administration's February 2012 proposal aimed to maintain funding for all major federal K–12 programs, such as Title I, and sent a strong signal on its new priority to promote college and career readiness. Title I, Part A of ESEA, for example, would be renamed as the College- and Career-Ready Students program. The proposal also included competitive grants for early learning and for instruction in science, technology, engineering, and mathematics (STEM). The administration's legislative proposal, however, did not receive much support from the Republican-controlled House of Representatives.

Policy disagreements between the House and Senate and between Republicans and Democrats are so strong on education policy (as on other policies) that Congress has not been able to pass a reauthorization statute. Instead of working with the administration, legislative leaders from both parties made their own attempts at ESEA reauthorization in the 113th Congress (2013–14). Political fragmentation, however, precluded enough support for any of these proposals. In the Senate in early June 2013, Democratic Senator Tom Harkin of Iowa introduced a 1,150-page bill (*Senate Bill 1094, Strengthening America's School Act of 2013*) that retained the key accountability requirements from NCLB, such as annual testing and reporting on all student and subgroup performance (Harkin, 2013). The Harkin bill also directed states to implement a teacher evaluation system that used student achievement data and other measures by 2015–16. Low performing schools were targeted for state intervention, including turnaround. The Harkin bill made it to the Committee on Health, Education, Labor, and Pensions where it was marked up, amended, and then placed on the Senate Legislative Calendar in October 2013, where it remained.

The Republican-controlled House of Representatives responded to Senator Harkin's proposal with the introduction of House Resolution 5, Student Success Act, in early June 2013. HR 5, sponsored by Republican Representative John Kline of Minnesota, proposed greater state autonomy over the accountability system, although states were required to report on graduation rate, subgroup performance, and annual proficiency in core subjects (Kline, 2013). HR 5 would allow states to develop their own intervention strategies in improving low performing schools. It also granted states greater flexibility in using federal funds. Representative Kline's bill passed the Republican-controlled House with a vote of 221–207. The bill was received by the Senate and sent to the Committee on Health, Education, Labor, and Pensions on July 21, 2013. However, the committee did not take any further action during 2014.

Not to be overshadowed by the Democratic proposal, Republican Senator Lamar Alexander of Tennessee sponsored Senate Bill 1101, Every Child Ready for College or Career Act of 2013, two days after Senator Harkin's bill was introduced (Alexander, 2013). SB 1101 would reduce federal requirements and allow for great state autonomy on accountability issues. It was referred to the Committee on Health, Education, Labor, and Pensions on the day that it was introduced. The committee did not take any further action during 2014. However, the 2014 midterm election resulted in a Republican majority in the U.S. Senate. Since Senator Alexander became the chair of the committee in January 2015, he played an instrumental role in getting the new bill enacted by the end of 2015.

To be sure, under the newly enacted Every Student Success Act of 2015, states continue several accountability requirements as established in NCLB. These include:

- Annual testing of students in core subjects in grades 3 through 8 as well as a grade in high school
- Annual report cards must include student performance for various subgroups, including low income, English Language Learners, children with learning disabilities, and various minority groups

At the same time, states have gained control over several important aspects of education policy. These include:

- Choice of academic standards, including developing their own standards and multiple measures of academic assessment as long as they are comparable to the common core standards
- Criteria in identifying low performing schools for direct intervention, although ESSA expects that states will focus on the bottom 5%
- Scope and nature of direct intervention
- Evaluation of teachers will be determined by states and does not have to use student test results as the basis for the evaluation
- Engagement in early childhood education, establish school-community support partnerships, and other innovative practices

It is too early to know whether ESSA will create sufficient conditions for states to raise performance for all students. Equally important, the question remains of whether ESSA creates unanticipated consequences. For example, in the absence of federal guidance on accountability, how do state politics shape the readiness of state intervention in low performing schools?

Clearly, states will need to leverage their resources and capacity to address several major challenges. First, there is growing state concern over participating in the two consortia of common core standards (namely, PARCC and SBAC), as encouraged by the Obama Administration through their competitive grant strategy. By 2015, only 28 states remained members of the two consortia. The remaining 22 states opted to work towards developing their own standards that align with the common core standards and assessment. To be sure, implementation of common core assessment was (and continues to be) particularly complicated because the assessment is web-based. A substantial number of teachers had to receive professional development in the new assessment technology and the new standards. Many schools, especially in rural communities, lack the information technology to support blended learning, computer-based testing, and technology-based professional development for teachers.

In anticipation of the need to integrate technology as part of the common core, the Obama administration announced the ConnectED initiative to promote the implementation of digital learning in November 2014. The key components include:

- Expansion of Connectivity: In the next several years, the federal technology plan aims at enabling 99% of the K–12 students to have access to broadband connectivity. The Federal Communication Commission has budgeted $2 Billion, which will be matched by another $2 Billion in pledges from the private sector.
- Teacher Training: Teachers will receive professional development to adopt digital tools, such as real time student assessments, interactive online lessons, and collaboration with professional experts.
- Private Sector Innovation and Private-Public Partnership: Pricing will become competitive (against traditional textbooks) for learning and teaching devices and soft ware. Innovation will drive the global education marketplace of at least $1 Billion.

As part of the ConnectED initiative, the federal government promotes Future Ready Districts across the country. These Future Ready districts, with signed pledges by the superintendent, aim at implementing the key strategies as proposed in ConnectED. The key commitments of the Future Ready Districts include:

- Fostering and leading a culture of digital learning
- Assisting schools and families transition to high-speed connectivity
- Empowering educators through professional learning opportunities
- Accelerating progress toward universal access for all students to quality devices
- Providing access to quality digital content
- Offering digital tools to broaden access to college, career, and citizenship
- Mentoring other districts and supporting their transition to digital learning

As of February 2015, over 1,600 districts had pledged to participate in the Future Ready network across 50 states and territories. These "districts" included not only public school districts but also charter schools and Catholic schools. At the February 2015 mark, California had the largest number of Future Ready Districts (246), followed by Texas (109), Michigan (108), and Illinois (98).

The achievement gap remains another notable challenge within American education. Teacher shortages must be filled to narrow the gap in particular areas. During the 2014–15 school year, 94% of states experienced teacher shortages in special education programs, 88% with teacher shortages in mathematics, 86% in science, and 62% in English as a Second Language (http://www2.ed.gov/about/offices/list/ope/pol/tsa.pdf). By all measures of international comparison, students in the U.S. perform about average in mathematics and science. However, when these statistics are disaggregated, all states continue to show a substantial performance gap for students who come from low income, minority backgrounds.

Finally, there is a new political and policy landscape in American states. In recent years, states experienced a significant growth in executive-directed state education systems. Governors are more keenly interested in education since the domain accounts for at least 25–30% of the state budget and accounts for an important source of state employees. Over two-thirds of governors appoint the state school board and fewer than one-third of state school superintendents are elected. At the same time, state legislatures have tended to become more active in K–12 activities, doubling the average number of education-related bills from 10.2 to 21.6 between 1994–2001 and 2002–2008 (Henig, 2013, p. 196). Among the top education priorities in the state legislature during 1994–2009 were: curriculum and teaching (20%), logistics and facilities (11%), safety (10%), finance (9%), governance (8%), and special populations (7%).

With activism among state elected officials, there is a growing risk of policy gridlock in state capitals. With the state as the locus of power, will ESSA deepen the education policy impasse? For example, the governor and the state legislature in Illinois and Pennsylvania did not agree to a state budget for months. Interestingly, while the Illinois Republican governor wanted to reduce union rules and to reallocate state aid away from urban districts, the Democratic governor in Pennsylvania advocated for more funding for urban schools. Without an approved state budget, school districts in these states ran out of money, experienced a downgrade in their credit ratings, continued to incur debts to run the schools at a high interest rate, and saw growing threat of teachers' strike. These fiscal and political battles clearly hindered the educational leaders' ability to focus their attention on their core agenda of teaching, learning, and the common core.

The Beginning of the Trump "Insurgent" Presidency

On the cover of *The Economist* on February 4, 2017, the bright red headline reads "An insurgent in the White House." The "insurgent" President Donald Trump wasted little time in setting a new policy tone during the first few weeks in office. His executive orders have aimed to ban individuals coming from several countries with Muslim majority population from entering the U.S., empower law enforcement agencies to strictly enforce immigration policy, and foster greater state autonomy on domestic affairs. On January 30, 2017, the President issued an executive order that required federal agencies to eliminate two existing rules for every new one. In his first budget submitted to Congress in mid-March, the President proposed major cuts in discretionary funding for the Department of Education, the Department of Energy, and the Environmental Protection Agency. President Trump's actions clearly aim at disrupting the federal role across all policy areas.

In this context of an insurgent presidency, K–12 education is subject to a critical reassessment in the Trump White House. This critical reassessment comes as no surprise given the electoral realignment that has deeply shaken the two major political parties (Burnham, 1986; Mayhew 2004). Our understanding of Trump's policymaking can be informed by various policy frameworks, including unilateral presidential politics (Howell, 2003), policy streams and windows (Kingdon, 1995), regime change (Manna & McGuinn, 2013), and policy entrepreneurs (Mintrom, 2000), among others. To be sure, the first few month of the Trump administration can only give limited indication of what is to come. Unanticipated political dynamics and policy changes are likely to occur throughout his term. This early review draws on the administration's announcements, Congressional hearings, and preliminary analyses conducted by policy researchers thus far.

The Insurgent Presidency Attempts to Scale Back the Federal Role

In K–12 education, Trump's White House signals its intent to significantly repurpose the federal role. Taken as a whole, the administration aims to dismantle key initiatives that are associated with the Obama Administration, but it remains to be seen whether the Trump administration plans to fundamentally reconstruct the terms of federal engagement in public education, terms that have been in place ever since the Great Society era of the Johnson administration (Peterson, Rabe, & Wong, 1986). The first few months of the Trump Presidency suggest several key education policy initiatives. These initiatives include:

- Scaling back federal direction and shifting substantial decision making power to state and local government
- Proposing substantial budgetary reductions that may result in a reduction of one-fourth of the employees in the U.S. Department of Education, particularly in programs such as college and career access, arts, health, after school, and technology
- Expanding federal support for a broad portfolio of school choice, including charter schools, vouchers for parents to enroll their children in public and private schools, federal tax credit scholarship program, and magnet programs (Heritage Foundation, 2016).
- Easing possible entry of for profit providers in K–12 education, as indicated by the administration's effort to restore for profit providers in correctional facilities
- Placing limits on federal capacity to promote equal education access, such as taking actions against families of illegal immigrants and limiting the scope of Title IX enforcement
- Reducing investment in data and research infrastructure. Currently, less than 1% of the total federal education spending is devoted to research.

President Trump's proposed initiatives constitute a critical reassessment but do not yet amount to an all-out dismantling of the federal role in K–12 as embedded in the long-established "marble cake" federalism (Wong, 2013). As discussed earlier, the federal redistributive focus is clearly supported by major categorical programs that use funding and programmatic rules to provide supplemental services to well-defined eligible populations or high needs communities. In her March 13, 2017 letter to the chief state school officers on a revised consolidated state plan for ESSA, President Trump's Secretary of Education Betsy DeVos highlighted the administration's commitment to "maintaining essential protections for subgroups of students, including economically disadvantaged students, students with disabilities and English learners." In the budget proposal for FY18, the Trump administration maintains the federal funding for several long-established categorical programs for high needs student, such as Title I and IDEA. It remains to be seen how other categorical programs may be dismantled or replaced by block grants with a less redistributive focus. More importantly, policy analysts will need to pay close attention to Trump's efforts to reverse the long established federal involvement in equity, accountability, and research and development.

School Choice as a Federal Priority

The appointment of Betsy DeVos as the U.S. Secretary of Education signals a major departure from decades of federal involvement in public education. Secretary DeVos's reliance on school choice as a primary federal strategy is grounded in her own activism in school choice. She was the chairwoman of the American Federation for Children and provided financial support to a number of school choice initiatives, including vouchers for private schools. In her capacity as U.S. Secretary of Education, DeVos believes that the federal government can play a catalytic role in scaling school choice (Klein & Ujifusa, 2017). In her prepared remarks at the February 23, 2017 Conservative Political Action Conference, Secretary DeVos stated that "the education establishment has been blocking the doorway to reforms, fixes and improvements for a generation." She then announced that, "We have a unique window of opportunity to make school choice a reality for millions of families." In her meeting with leaders of historically black colleges and universities on February 27, 2017, DeVos initially characterized HBCUs as "pioneers of school choice." Further, in his first presidential appearance before a joint session of Congress on February 28, 2017, President Trump asked the Congress to pass an education bill "that funds school choice for disadvantaged youth, including millions of African-American and Latino children." He then went on, "These families should be free to choose the public, private, charter, magnet, religious or home school that is right for them."

To be sure, this is not the first time a U.S. President advocates for school choice. President Ronald Reagan was a strong proponent of school choice but was unable to gain much Congressional support. Further, President Bill Clinton popularized charter schools with federal start up funding, a position endorsed by both Presidents George W. Bush and Barack Obama. Finally, Congress enacted a pilot school voucher program for private schools in Washington DC. Unlike his predecessors, President Trump intends to scale up his school choice initiatives with a campaign pledge of $20 billion in federal funding. It remains to be seen whether the administration will be able to promote choice at a much wider scale and broaden the types of service providers. If successful, the Trump administration will elevate school choice to a new level of prominence.

The new governing landscape seems supportive of school choice expansion. First, the administration's push for school choice generally aligns with ESSA. With broader policy-making authority, states can choose to promote a broader portfolio of school choice programs with federal funding. Second, with two-thirds of the states under one-party Republican control in both houses following the November 2016 election, Trump's proposal to expand school choice is likely to receive favorable attention. Currently, several states are actively considering proposals on school choice expansion. Third, charter school as a key school choice strategy has continued to receive steady, favorable preference among parents in minority communities (Kahlenberg & Potter, 2014). It was a calculated move on President Trump's part to mention that school choice will benefit African Americans in his first address before the joint session of Congress in February 2017. These facilitating conditions are likely to contribute to school choice growth across several states.

Rebalance the Federal Role in Equity and Accountability

Historically, equity has been a key justification for federal involvement in K–12 schooling. As discussed earlier, the federal government has embraced both equity and accountability over the last several decades. The Trump administration, however, is ready to rebalance the federal-state relationship on these issues. The administration can rely on several institutional opportunities. First, the 2015 ESSA constitutes a bipartisan effort to rebalance federal-state relations by granting state control over standards and other policy issues. ESSA has granted states the primary responsibility in defining academic standards, adopting multiple measures of academic performance, identifying schools for improvement, and mapping the scope of turnaround intervention. Thus, ESSA has essentially replaced a federally driven regulatory framework to a state-defined agenda of education reform.

Further, the administration, with support from the Republican leadership in both houses, is in the process of scaling back federal direction on accountability issues in ESSA. For example, to give Secretary DeVos the opportunity to establish her mark on ESSA, the Republican controlled Congress used the *Congressional Review Act* to repeal ESSA regulatory guidance that was completed during the last few months of the Obama Presidency (Goldstein, 2017). The Congressional repeal was comprehensive in scope, including the requirement that schools must include at least 95% of students in annual assessments, as well as many of the accountability measures on teacher preparation programs, and other civil rights regulations. Instead, Secretary DeVos has the opportunity to grant even more power to states in implementing ESSA.

Third, the federal government may choose to withdraw from some of the already existing equity-oriented practices. For example, Secretary DeVos is reviewing whether the Department's Office for Civil Rights (OCR) will continue to collect the biennial data on schooling opportunities and quality in public schools throughout the country. The OCR has been compiling the Civil Rights Data Collection (CRDC) since 1968. This data set has been used by policy researchers and by states and districts for service improvement for all students (Katz, 2017). Likewise, in the negotiated rule-making process prior to Trump's election, federal regulation on "supplement not supplant" had already been loosened for audit compliance. As Secretary DeVos articulated in her letter to the chief state school officers on March 13, 2017, the federal government will now require "only descriptions, information, assurances and other materials that [are] absolutely necessary." Under Trump's leadership, audit regulations on federal categorical programs may be further relaxed. In other words, equity and accountability measures are likely to be revised to align with Trump's prioritization of school choice and state control.

Challenges and Opportunities Ahead

The Trump administration has embarked on an ambitious agenda to critically reassess the federal role in K–12 education. While the new governing landscape may facilitate the President's policy insurgency, the administration's success in systemic changes will depend on several institutional conditions. First, the Trump White House has to reorganize the federal administrative capacity behind a coherent set of policy goals. The administration will need to go beyond its initial focus on school choice and budget cuts. Instead, the President needs to articulate broader federal leadership in key policy areas, such as upgrading the schools' infrastructure to meet global and technological challenges, ensure schooling quality for a growingly diverse population, strengthen teacher quality, promote student-centered learning, and reduce the achievement gap, among others.

Further, the President leads within the framework of separation of powers. The executive branch has to work with Congress to pass the budget and authorize new initiatives. It remains to be seen whether Trump's education initiatives will be hindered by institutional rivalry or aided by bipartisan collaboration. Finally, federalism takes on its own dynamics. While states and districts engage in competition and innovation, the federal government must address disparity and inequity. These policy challenges await the insurgent presidency to demonstrate its governing effectiveness.

CONCLUSION: THE FUTURE OF STATE-FEDERAL RELATIONS IN PUBLIC EDUCATION

ESSA may allow for several overlapping directions, depending on the political economy of each state. First, states may take the newly gained authority to advance innovative practices and turn states into "laboratories of democracies."

States with bi-partisan support for education are well positioned to take on this pathway. The federal government will then, ideally, take the proven new practices to the national scale. Alternatively, a second possibility is that the gap in reform capacity among states may widen as some states accelerate their propensity for reform. States that have constraining fiscal resources and divided governance are less likely to invest in their capacity to act, including data analytic infrastructure. Under these circumstances, the federal government may be forced to return to a more activist role to support those states that lag behind. Third, the state-federal joint responsibility may lead to incremental changes, making steady progress over time. This pathway tends to build on political bargaining between the federal and the state government as well as among stakeholders within the state. Given differences in capacity and culture, states will chart a variety of reform paths that will form the basis for the next phase of state-federal relations.

REFERENCES

Alexander, L. (2013). *Senate Bill 1101: Every Child Ready for College or Career Act of 2013.* Retrieved from https://www.congress.gov/bill/113th-congress/senate-bill/1101/all-actions

Betts, J. (2007). California: Does the Golden State deserve a gold star? In F. Hess & C. Finn, Jr. (Eds.), *No remedy left behind: Lessons from a half-decade of NCLB* (pp. 121–152). Washington DC: AEI Press.

Bowling, C. J., & Pickerill, J. M. (2013). Fragmented federalism: The state of American federalism 2012–13. *Publius: The Journal of Federalism, 43*(3), 315–346.

Brown, C., Hess, F., Lautzenheiser, D., & Owen, I. (2011). *State education agencies as agents of change: What it will take for the states to step up on education reform.* The Center for American Progress.

Burnham, W. D. (1986 Autumn). Periodization schemes and 'party systems: The 'System of 1896' as a case in point. *Social Science History, 10*(3), 263–314.

Center on Education Policy. (2013). *States' perspectives on waivers: Relief from NCLB, concern about long-term solutions.* Washington DC: Center on Education Policy.

Cohen, D., & Moffitt, S. (2009). *The ordeal of equality.* Cambridge, MA: Harvard University Press.

Congressional Research Service. (28 June 2011). *Memorandum (7–5700): Secretary of education's waiver authority with respect to Title I-A provisions included in the Elementary and Secondary Education Act.* Washington, DC: Congressional Research Service.

Delisle, D. (2014). *Oklahoma Principle 1 Letter from the U.S. Department of Education.* Retrieved from http://www2.ed.gov/policy/eseaflex/secretary-letters/ok1p3ltr.html

Gamkhar, S., & Pickerill, M. (2012). The state of American federalism 2011–2012: A Fend for yourself and activist form of bottom-up federalism. *Publius: The Journal of Federalism, 42*(3), 357–386.

Goldstein, D. (2017, March 9). Obama education rules are swept aside by Congress. *The New York Times* 9 March 2017. Retrieved from https://www.nytimes.com/2017/03/09/us/every-student-succeeds-act-essa-congress.html?hpw&rref=education&actio

n=click&pgtype=Homepage&module=well-region&region=bottom-well&WT.nav=bottom-well

Harkin, T. (2013). *Senate Bill 1094: Strengthening America's Schools Act of 2013.* Retrieved from https://www.congress.gov/bill/113th-congress/senate-bill/1094/all-actions

Henig, J. (2013). The rise of education executives in the White House, State House, and Mayor's office. In P. Manna & P. McGuinn (Eds.), *Education governance for the twenty-first century: Overcoming the structural barriers to school reform* (pp. 178–207). Washington, DC: Brookings Institution Press.

Heritage Foundation. (2016). *Blueprint for a new administration: Priorities for the President.* Washington, DC: Heritage Foundation.

Hess, F., & Finn, C., Jr. (2007). *No remedy left behind: Lessons from a half-decade of NCLB.* Washington, DC: American Enterprises Institute Press.

Hess, F., & Petrilli, M. (2006). *No Child Left Behind: A primer.* New York, NY: Peter Lang Publishing.

Howell, W. G. (2003). *Power without persuasion: The politics of direct presidential action.* Princeton, NJ: Princeton University Press.

Kahlenberg, R., & Potter, H. (2014). *A smarter charter: Finding what works in charter schools and public education.* New York, NY: Teachers College Press.

Katz, M. (2017). Letting federal data drive state and local policy under Secretary DeVos. *Urban Wire.* Washington, DC: The Urban Institute.

Kim, J., & Sunderman, G. (2005). Measuring academic proficiency under No Child Left Behind: Implications for educational equity. *Educational Researcher, 34*(8), 3–13.

Kingdon, J. (1995). *Agendas, alternatives, and public policies* (2nd ed.) New York, NY: Harper Collins.

Klein, A. (2011). Turnaround-Program data seen as promising though preliminary. *Education Week,* January 11. Retrieved from www.edweek.org/ew/articles/2011/01/12/15turnaround-2.h30.html?qschoolturnaround.

Klein, A., & Ujifusa, A. (2017). Democrats press Betsy DeVos on privatization, ESSA, and LGBT rights. *Education Week's Blog,* 17 January 2017.

Kline, J. (2013). *House Resolution 5: Student Success Act.* Retrieved from https://www.congress.gov/bill/113th-congress/house-bill/5/all-actions

Manna, P. (2010). *Collision course.* Washington, DC: Congressional Quarterly Press.

Manna, P., & McGuinn, P. (Eds.). (2013). *Education governance for the twenty-first Century.* Washington, DC: Brookings Institution Press.

Mayhew, D. R. (2004). *Electoral realignments: A critique of an American genre.* New Haven, CT: Yale University Press.

McGuinn, P. (2006). *No Child Left Behind and the transformation of federal education policy, 1965–2005.* Lawrence, KS: University of Kansas Press.

Mintrom, M. (2000). *Policy entrepreneurs and school choice.* Washington, DC: Georgetown University Press.

Peterson, P. E., Rabe, G., & Wong, K. (1986). *When federalism works.* Washington, DC: Brookings Institution Press.

Riddle, W. (2011). *Major accountability themes of initial state applications for NCLB waivers.* Washington, DC: Center for Education Policy.

U.S. Department of Education. (2009) *Non-Regulatory guidance on Title I, Part A waivers.* Washington, DC: U.S. Department of Education.

U.S. Department of Education. (2013, 6 August). *Obama administration approves nclb waiver request for California CORE districts.* Retrieved from http://www.ed.gov/news/press-releases/obama-administration-approves-nclb-waiver-request-california-core-districts

Whaley, S. (2012). Feds approve Nevada waiver from No Child Left Behind," *The Record Courier,* 8 August 2012. Retrieved from http://www.recordcourier.com/article/20120808/NEWS/120809916/1062&ParentProfile=1049

Wong, K. K. (1999). *Funding public schools: Politics and policy*. Lawrence, KS: University Press of Kansas.

Wong, K. K. (2013). Education governance in performance-based federalism. P. Manna & P. McGuinn (Eds.), *Education governance for the twenty-first century.* Washington, DC: Brookings Institution Press.

Wong, K., & Nicotera, A. (2007). *Successful schools and educational accountability*. Boston, MA: Pearson Education.

Wong, K., & Reilly, M. (2014). *Education waivers as reform leverage in the Obama Administration: State implementation of ESEA flexibility waiver request.* APSA 2014 Annual Meeting Paper.

Wong, K., & Sunderman, G. (2007). Education accountability as a presidential priority: No Child Left Behind and the Bush Presidency. *Publius: The Journal of Federalism, 37*, 333–350.

www.ingramcontent.com/pod-product-compliance
Lightning Source LLC
LaVergne TN
LVHW052307200926
848481LV00002B/487